TRANSITIONAL JUSTICE AFTER GERMAN REUNIFICATION

How do societies transitioning from oppressive to democratic rule hold accountable those citizens who contributed to maintaining injustice in the ancient regime by secretly denouncing fellow citizens? Is their public identification a way of fulfilling respect for those who suffered harm as a result of their collaboration? And is public identification respectful of denunciators themselves?

This book pursues these questions through a multidisciplinary investigation focusing on the denunciators for the East German secret police and the Ministry of State Security and the way in which they have been publicly unveiled in contemporary German society. The book evaluates the justifications that social actors offer to support or oppose public identifications; how targeted collaborators react to this social practice; and whether it achieves its intended purpose. At every stage, the book asks whether the motivations and the consequences of public identifications honor or undermine the value of respect for people.

Juan Espindola is an assistant professor at the Center for Research and Teaching in Economics in Mexico City. He has held postdoctoral fellowships at the Centre for Advanced Studies Justitia Amplificata in the Goethe-University of Frankfurt and at the Institute for Social Research in the National University of Mexico. He has been a visiting scholar at the Max-Planck Institute for Comparative Public Law and International Law in Heidelberg and at the Institute of Political Studies in Paris. His work has appeared in journals such as *Ethical Theory and Moral Practice*, *Res Publica*, and *German Studies Review*. His primary research areas include transitional justice, historical rectification, and education. He received his PhD in Political Science from the University of Michigan.

Transitional Justice after German Reunification

EXPOSING UNOFFICIAL COLLABORATORS

Juan Espindola

Centro de Investigación y Docencia Económicas, Mexico City

CAMBRIDGE
UNIVERSITY PRESS

CAMBRIDGE
UNIVERSITY PRESS

32 Avenue of the Americas, New York, NY 10013-2473, USA

Cambridge University Press is part of the University of Cambridge.

It furthers the University's mission by disseminating knowledge in the pursuit
of education, learning, and research at the highest international levels of excellence.

www.cambridge.org
Information on this title: www.cambridge.org/9781107083127

First published 2015

A catalog record for this publication is available from the British Library.

Library of Congress Cataloging in Publication Data
Espindola Mata, Juan.
Transitional justice after German reunification : exposing unofficial collaborators / Juan Espindola.
pages cm
Based on author's thesis (doctoral - Univeristy of Michigan, 2011) under title: The Disclosures of Respect : The Public Exposure of Stasi Informers after the German Reunification.
Includes bibliographical references and index.
ISBN 978-1-107-08312-7 (Hardback)
1. Transitional justice–Germany. 2. Germany (East). Ministerium für Staatssicherheit.
3. Informers–Legal status, laws, etc.–Germany. 4. Political crimes and offenses–Germany (East) I. Title.
KK5245.E87 2015
342.43′0418–dc23 2015006477

ISBN 978-1-107-08312-7 Hardback

CONTENTS

ACKNOWLEDGMENTS

This book benefited from audiences at the Department of Political Science at the University of Michigan, the Max-Planck Institute for Public and International Law, Georgetown University, the Goethe-University of Frankfurt, and the Institute for Philosophical Research at the National University of Mexico. It also benefited from generous funding from the Deutscher Akademischer Austauschdienst and the Consejo Nacional de Ciencia y Tecnología.

At Ann Arbor, Michigan, where an earlier version of this book came to light, I received valuable feedback from members of the Political Theory workshop and from the political theory/philosophy community in general, including Arlene Saxonhouse, Lisa Disch, Elizabeth Wingrove, Elizabeth Anderson, and Lars Rensmann. I am particularly grateful to those who were closest to the project and provided constructive insight: Andrei Markovits (whose feedback came along with a great deal of encouragement), Don Herzog, Mika LaVaque-Manty, and Mariah Zeisberg.

Later, in Frankfurt, I continued working on the book manuscript as a Fellow at the Centre for Advanced Studies Justitia Amplificata. For that I owe a debt of gratitude to Stephan Gosepath and Rainer Forst. Forst's generosity and encouragement also allowed me to extend my stay at the Forschungskolleg Humanwissenschaften in Bad Homburg. For making my stay at the Kolleg a wonderful experience, thanks to Ingrid Rudolph, Beate Sutterlüty, Andreas Reichhardt, and Maria Lorch. I received enormously helpful reactions when presenting some sections of this book at a conference on collective responsibility in Bad Homburg, with the participation of Kasper Lippert-Rasmussen, Avia Pasternak, Mark Osiel, Miriam

Ronzoni, Jesse Tomalty, Alex Leveringhaus, and Barbara Buckinx, among others.

For reading drafts of some of the chapters of the book and/or giving me valuable comments, thanks to Julian Culp, Jonathan Devore, Dorothea Gädeke, Eduardo García-Ramírez, Sabine Hake, Helen Ho, Bronwyn Leebaw, Claudio López-Guerra, Itzel Mayans, Mihaela Mihai, Darrel Moellendorf, Andrea Pozas-Loyo, Alberto Puppo, Christian Schemmel, Christine Straehle, Mauricio Tenorio, Mathias Thaler, and, last but not least, Moisés Vaca. The comments of two anonymous reviewers for the Press were extremely helpful in clarifying many arguments in the book. I much appreciate the assistance and suggestions of John Berger, who was extremely helpful and supportive throughout the editorial process.

Finally, I extend special gratitude to my parents Juan M. Espíndola and Rachel Mata, my sister Monica Espíndola, and my wife Miwa Pierre-Audain for their unconditional and unwavering love. To all of them I dedicate this book.

A shorter version of Chapter 6 appeared in *German Studies Review* 36, no. 2 (2013): 327–345.

1 EXPOSING UNOFFICIAL COLLABORATORS

1.1 THE DISCLOSURES OF RESPECT

Joachim Gauck was sworn in as president of the Federal Republic of Germany in 2012, after his forerunner left office prematurely amid allegations of corruption. His only serious but very distant contender was Beate Klarsfeld, who made a reputation for herself by hunting Nazi criminals. Her appointment as the candidate of Die Linke (the descendent of the East German Communist Party) was a political strategy to symbolically counter Gauck's political capital as one of the main architects of Germany's communist *Vergangenheitsbewältigung* (coming to terms with the past). Gauck was the first federal commissioner of the agency in charge of administering the files of the East German secret police. That Klarsfeld and Gauck were running for the presidency was a truly meaningful episode in German history – an outstanding record in promoting *Vergangenheitsbewältigung* (either in its Nazi or communist version) became a crucial political asset. In his first speech after being sworn in as president, Gauck alluded to the generation of 68ers. According to him, it was thanks to this generation that Germans began to raise questions about their responsibility in the crimes of the past and about their obligations toward victims of political violence. In his words: "This fact-based and values-oriented reappraisal (*Aufarbeitung*) of the past was not only a guide for us after 1989 in East Germany. It is also perceived as an example for many societies that have shaken off a totalitarian or despotic yoke and do not know how they should deal with the burden of the past."[1] When it comes to figuring out how a society should go about addressing its problematic past, he said, Germany is a model.

But the model, particularly in the case of the second *Vergangenheitsbewältigung,* is not one that escapes controversies, expressed as acrimonious debates about the use of the secret files of the East German secret police, the infamous Ministry of State Security (Ministerium für Staatssicherheit, henceforth, the MfS) or Stasi. This book focuses precisely on these tensions, specifically on the use of the Stasi archives in reunified Germany to publicly expose individuals who were involved with that Ministry and wish to hide or deny their complicity. Through a multidisciplinary investigation of Germany's second *Vergangenheitsbewältigung* and the intriguing figure of the unofficial collaborator or coworker, or simply "IM," the acronym for the German (*Inoffizieller Mitarbeiter*), the book elucidates the heretofore-unrecognized complex relationships between respect, on the one hand, and victims and low-level perpetrators of past injustice, on the other hand. The book is based on the premise that though oftentimes caricatured, neglected, played down, or subsumed into other analytic categories, the figure of the unofficial collaborators is crucial for getting a handle on phenomena such as complicity in and responsibility for the preservation of oppressive regimes. Understanding the role of IMs in wrongdoing is as relevant as understanding that of leaders and other public officials. Unofficial collaborators are neither bystanders nor dictators or state bureaucrats: They stand somewhere in an ambiguous position between these two sides. Precisely this makes the unofficial collaborator, with an aura of ambiguity, such a challenging and intriguing figure to study.

Some preliminary information about unofficial collaborators, who need to be differentiated from public officials, is in order before going further. Under the German Democratic Republic (GDR), the secret police recruited a large number of citizens, usually on a temporary basis, to report on the activities of fellow citizens under its radar. In the entire course of GDR history, nearly 600,000 citizens were informers. According to some estimates, in 1989 about 170,000

[1] "Unser Land," in *Frankfurter Allgemeine Zeitung*, March 24, 2012. All translations are mine, unless otherwise indicated.

citizens were active as IMs, most of them within East Germany. Between the 1960s and 1989, the total number of unofficial collaborators per year fluctuated between 120,000 and 200,000. This represents roughly 1 to 1.5 percent of the population at any given point during that period.[2] After the collapse of the GDR, the Stasi became the center of public ire, and IMs in particular were targets of public exposure. Dissident groups during communist rule, most notably the New Forum, orchestrated such exposures. At the very beginning, IM exposures were authentic witch hunts. Many of those accused of secretly collaborating with the Stasi as IMs were publicly shamed almost in a spirit of revenge, and not always on the basis of fully reliable information. The evidence for incriminating specific citizens came from selective and disorganized forays into the files left behind by the Stasi after the death of the communist regime. With the creation of the Stasi Records Office (Bundesbeauftragte für die Stasi-Unterlagen, or BStU) in 1990 and the appointment of Gauck, the process became structured and formalized. The government's resolve to facilitate and even encourage the exposure of all individuals previously involved with the Stasi did not falter.

On request, the BStU provides access to Stasi archives for citizens who were under Stasi surveillance, thus allowing them to learn who (if anyone) ever informed on them. It also offers information for the press and the government to carry out the so-called Stasi screening process, whereby public employees are inspected for past complicity.[3] More than 20 years after the establishment of the Stasi Records Office, interest in the files remains strong. A total of 6,793,201 requests and applications were filed before the BStU from 1991 to the end of 2012. They include 2.91 million applications from citizens

[2] See Helmut Müller-Enbergs, "Die inoffiziellen Mitarbeiter," in BStU, ed. *MfS-Handbuch: Anatomie der Staatssicherheit – Geschichte, Struktur, Methoden* (Berlin: 2008), 35–38.

[3] On these issues see Gary Bruce, "Access to Secret Police Files, Justice and Vetting in East Germany since 1989," *German Politics and Society* 25(4), 2008: 82–111; and Christiane Wilke, "The Shield, the Sword, and the Party: Vetting in Post-1989 Germany," in Alexander Mayer-Rieckh and Pablo de Greiff, ed., *Justice as Prevention: Vetting Public Employees in Transitional Societies*. New York: SSRC, 2007, 348–400.

to receive information or inspect their files; 1,754,838 requests for review by members of the public service; 27,730 applications from journalists and scientists; and 488,691 requests on issues of rehabilitation, compensation, and law enforcement.[4] This flow of information is the basis for publicly exposing former Stasi collaborators.

Citizens of all walks of life have been publicly exposed for collaboration with the secret police. It should not come as a surprise, however, that public opinion is particularly receptive to the exposure of prominent figures within the community. Some examples include writers such as Christa Wolf and Sascha Anderson; politicians like Manfred Stolpe, Gregor Gysi (both of whom deny having worked as IMs), and more recently, Kerstin Kaiser (who acknowledges her participation as an IM); and popular sportsmen and women, such as Katarina Witt and Ingo Steuer. There have also been tales of familial betrayal involving Stasi informers – husbands informing on their wives and brothers or sisters spying on their siblings. Two famous cases are those of historian Karlheinz Schädlich, who in 1992 was exposed for having spied on his brother Hans-Joachim Schädlich, an acclaimed German writer; and a more recent case involving Jenny Gröllmann, who was said to have informed on her partner, Ulrich Mühe, the star of the acclaimed film *The Lives of Others*, an accusation that she consistently denied. There is, of course, irony in the fact that in this film, Mühe played the part of a Stasi public official.

Whether or not it is still desirable or useful to expose IMs is a contested issue. A survey conducted in 2006 showed that close to 65 percent of Germans agree or strongly agree that an end should be put to asking whether or not people worked for the Stasi.[5] In a different survey conducted in 2008, in answer to the question of whether the exposure of IMs is justified or whether that policy should

[4] For some statistical information, see www.BStU.bund.de/DE/BundesbeauftragterUndBehoerde/BStUZahlen/_node.html.

[5] Statista, "Halten Sie die Enttarnung von ehemaligen inoffiziellen Stasi-Mitarbeitern weiterhin fuer gerechtfertigt oder sollte ein Schlussstrich gezogen werden?", in http://de.statista.com/statistik/daten/studie/173483/umfrage/nicht-mehr-nach-stasi-vergangenheit-fragen/. 3,421 individuals over 18 years of age were interviewed.

be drawn to a close, 49 percent answered with the former, whereas 46 percent chose the latter; 5 percent did not venture any answer.[6] Put briefly, some people regard IM exposures as a form of victor's justice; others regard it as valuable input in Germany' second *Vergangenheitsbewältigung*.[7]

With this background in mind, which will be expanded on in Chapter 2, consider the following vignettes illustrating a frequent pattern followed in IM public exposures. Two of these vignettes describe the unveiling of two individuals, who before being exposed were unknown to public opinion. The final one refers to a public figure.

Thomas Klippstein was the manager of a luxury hotel in Germany – the Adlon in Berlin. In 2006, the newspaper *Hamburger Abendblatt* publicly exposed him as a past informer for the Stasi under the code name IM "Benjamin." The exposure was based on information coming from the 58-page file that the Stasi Records Office had prepared on Klippstein. It included details about his activity as a collaborator in the GDR, mostly about his reports on other colleagues and guests of the Hotel Neptun, a prestigious hotel for clients such as Willy Brandt and Fidel Castro.

Klippstein's initial reaction to his public exposure was to enlist two lawyers who used all legal means at their disposal to intimidate newspapers and magazines that were disseminating his Stasi past, including the tabloid *Bild-Zeitung,* the newspaper *Die Welt*, and the magazine *Focus*. Among the legal resources put to the service of Klippstein's defense was the very German *Persönlichkeitsrecht* (right to personality), a right that in the United States would come close to the torts of privacy and reputation. Klippstein gained a few temporary injunctions from lower courts prohibiting further dissemination of news about his past collaboration. In the end, however, he suspended

[6] Statista, "Sollte man endlich aufhoeren danach zu fragen, ob jemand in der DDR für die Stasi gearbeitet hat?", in http://de.statista.com/statistik/daten/studie/195/umfrage/enttarnung-von-stasi-mitarbeitern/. The poll had 1,000 respondents.

[7] On these writers and their exposure, see Dolores Agustine, "The Impact of Two Reunification-Era Debates on the East German Sense of Identity," *German Studies Review* 27, no. 3 (2004): 563–578.

his legal dispute and resigned from his position at Hotel Adlon, from which he probably received little if any support. Cornered, he did what he was expected to do all along – he showed public signs of contrition. He admitted that he had been a collaborator for the Stasi but pointed out, as IMs commonly do, that he collaborated only to protect his family, which in the GDR was under the secret police's radar. He further clarified that he had taken the position at the Neptun to gain independence from his parents, as the communist regime did not allow him to finish high school. He did not see any opportunity to oppose the system. "I really lament that at that time I did not resist the pressure, and I apologize.[8] Public reaction toward Klippstein's statements was as predictable as the statements themselves. Characterizing them as excuses, a commentator writes: "To treason most GDR citizens said no. Klippstein said yes."[9]

Consider now the second vignette. As will be seen later, Germany has pursued relatively strict lustration policies as part of its transitional justice measures. The belief driving lustrations is that public service must be purged of former Stasi personnel so that it is possible to reestablish a value that was lost during communist rule: trust, and particularly trust in government. Apart from public service, the media, particularly publicly owned media, is next in importance as a target of destasification policies.[10] Accordingly, in a 2008 broadcast on one of Germany's largest publicly owned television channels, a senior reporter exposed a number of IMs whose identities he found in his own Stasi file. What one of them does and says, though, is particularly worth our attention. He is asked his opinion about the fact that a former unofficial collaborator is currently a fellow journalist at the same local newspaper where he works. He replies that we should not make too much of something that happened more than

[8] Sven Felix Kellerhoff and Uwe Müller, "Indiskreter Hotelier. Wenn Rechtsstaat und Stasi-Aufarbeitung kollidieren: Der Fall Thomas Klippstein," *Deutschland Archiv: Zeitschrift für das vereinigte Deutschland* 6 (2006): 983–990.

[9] "Kein Opfer. Über die Unfähigkeit von IM über ihre Vergangenheit zu sprechen," *Berliner Zeitung*, September 30, 2006.

[10] Hans-Joachim Föller, "Gestern IM, heute Redakteur beim MDR," *Horch und Guck* 9 (2000): 45–46.

20 years ago. He further says that every man should "receive a chance to rehabilitate himself through work." He is also asked whether he had any involvement whatsoever with the secret police, which he rapidly (and somewhat stiffly) denies. The reporter is skeptical about this answer, so the next day he approaches him again and insists. Did he really have no relations to the Stasi? The individual finally admits his complicity. He used to be an IM: he wrote reports about other citizens' activities for the Stasi. Does he consider it a mistake? the reporter asks. He yields: yes, he regrets his involvement with the Stasi; he admits he flagrantly erred.[11] Our beleaguered IM would have probably preferred his past affiliation with the Stasi to be kept secret and to "rehabilitate" himself through work. His personality type was common among IMs according to a recent study (he had no particular misgivings about his IM activity, performed it as "voluntary work," and was even proud of having distorted some of his reports in order to benefit other citizens). He probably had, like another collaborator, "the sincerest hope that his file [would] molder quietly in an archive" and currently fostered "the modest ambition [...] to maintain a quiet life for himself and his family in unified Germany."[12]

To conclude with these preliminary cases, take the public exposure of Christa Wolf, a popular writer and intellectual before and after the GDR. Even before the implosion of the communist regime, she had made it clear that despite her loyalty to the GDR, she was not a blind sympathizer of the regime. In this spirit, along with other intellectuals she strongly protested against the deportation of singer and dissident Wolf Biermann in 1976. In her barely encoded story, *Was bleibt*, written in 1990, she portrayed herself as a victim of the surveillance system. Only about two years after the story came to light, an examination of her file revealed that she had been an unofficial collaborator: IM Margarete. She wrote reports on fellow writers and even ventured evaluations about their fidelity to the official ideology. Of one, she said that in his journalistic work he would

[11] "Verdrängen, verklären, bereuen." The interview is available at http://daserste.ndr.de/panorama/media/stasi104.html.

[12] John Schmeidel, *Stasi. Shield and Sword of the Party* (Routledge: New York, 2008), 49–53.

eventually oppose the GDR. In another case she passed on personal details of another writer, namely that he was going through a "tense marital relationship." This is the sort of personal information that the Stasi could later use to disrupt the life of a nonconformist or dissident citizen. It is difficult not to describe Wolf's behavior as opportunistic, remaining silent over her involvement with the Stasi.[13]

These vignettes capture the features of what I am calling the public exposure of unofficial collaborators. In public discourse, the process is colloquially referred to as the *Enttarnung* (exposure) or *Enthüllung* (unveiling) of *Spitzel* (informers), as IMs are pejoratively called. The process is the following: A coalition of activists/moral entrepreneurs (at best) or a legion of scandal-seeking journalists (at worst) publicly exposes an ordinary citizen like Klippstein or public figures like Wolf as a Stasi collaborator. The justifications for carrying out such exposures vary, but they include giving victims of the Stasi something that is owed to them: the right to know who informed on them; holding informers accountable for their lack of courage in resisting injustice and for keeping their past hidden; and rebuilding trust in German society. Some IMs may then try to avoid wide public exposure by appealing to their alleged "right" not to be publicly shamed for their past conduct, a claim that finds a modest but telling resonance in German legal culture. Despite their efforts, they hardly ever succeed, and ultimately many of them end up succumbing to the demands for repentance and a public apology. In response, some groups in society are willing to engage with them to construct a reconciliatory environment; others are not so enthusiastic.

A generous amount of literature already documents the functioning of the Stasi (as well as that of other communist state securities) and the way in which its informers (and those of other secret police services in Eastern Europe) have been publicly identified, or subject to what Claus Offe calls "civic disqualifications,"[14] in the postcommunist era. However, none of these works systematically examines

[13] "Die ängstliche Margarete," *Der Spiegel*, January 25, 1993, 158–165.

[14] Claus Offe, "Disqualification, Retribution, Restitution: Dilemmas of Justice in Post-communist Countries," *Journal of Political Philosophy* 1, no. 1 (1993): 17–44.

the link between these public unveilings, on the one hand, and the value of respect for and from victims and victimizers, on the other. In most scholarly accounts, and in public discourse of various actors in civil and political society, the exposure of unofficial collaborators may be understood as one or several of the following: truth-telling mechanisms and part of an unhindered debate about the past; shaming interpellations, whose purpose is to consolidate civic ideals; accountability mechanisms with retributive functions, that is, substitutes for criminal punishment for IMs, who, not having committed any crime and therefore not legally liable, are nonetheless subject to public criticism; symbolic reparations for victims of historical injustice in the form of a public apology, which is supposed to be offered by the exposed informers; and necessary, though insufficient, steps toward social and political reconciliation, a process that will restore civic trust and thereby provide the cultural transformation necessary to consolidate German democracy.

Respect and self-respect play an explicit normative role in some of these accounts. For example, John Borneman[15] emphasizes the importance of "restoring" dignity as one of the goals many institutions put in place after the reunification of Germany to address the legacy of communism. Furthermore, commenting on the work of the German equivalent of the so-called truth commissions, one of whose functions has been to facilitate and encourage public exposure of IMs, Meier argues that they carry out forms of "weak retributive justice" and contrasts them to instances of "strong retributive justice" (i.e., legal punishment). In both cases, he claims, the point of this form of retributive justice is "to reequilibrate the perceived power between perpetrator and victim;" to "mobilize belated public opprobrium against the perpetrators;" and to "publicly acknowledg[e] the suffering of the victim."[16] Public identification of informers is

[15] John Borneman, *Settling Accounts. Violence, Justice, and Accountability in Postsocialist Europe* (Princeton, NJ: Princeton University Press, 1997); John Borneman, "Public Apologies as Performative Redress," *SAIS Review* 25, no. 2 (2005): 53–66.

[16] Charles S. Meier, "Doing History, Doing Justice: The Narrative of the Historian and of the Truth Commission," in Robert Rotberg and Dennis

appropriate, in this viewpoint, because it is instrumental in recognizing the wrong inflicted on victims. This conceptualization of public exposures of IMs is partially accurate and reflects a broader trend in literature on transitional justice, particularly the more normative kind, which often includes the public exposure of former perpetrators as a social mechanism to reassert or protect the respect for victims of nondemocratic regimes.[17] Let us call these approaches *the conventional view of respect* in transitional justice scholarship.

I argue that the conventional approach is thematically constraining as to how the notion of respect is relevant for thinking about a political context like the GDR. This approach rivets the attention of transitional justice scholars to respect for victims, and even then, the way in which respect for victims is understood is rather narrow. Respecting, in this register, means only redressing: expressing recognition that harm was done to victims and identifying the possible ways in which victims should be offered moral and political repair.[18] Although this kind of redress is part of the story, and victims indeed have priority from a normative perspective, this need not circumscribe the scope of scholarly research. This book makes the case for drawing on a more

Thompson (eds.), *Truth v. Justice: The Morality of Truth Commissions* (Princeton, NJ: Princeton University Press, 2000), 268.

17 There is nothing new about the idea that respect is at the forefront of many of the institutions and practices associated with the process of coming to terms with the past, in Germany and elsewhere. See for instance some of the essays in Rotberg and Thompson, *Truth v. Justice*: Amy Gutmann and Dennis Thompson, "The Moral Foundations of Truth Commissions," 2000; Elizabeth Kiss, "Moral Ambition within and Beyond Political Constraints: Reflections on Restorative Justice," 2000; and David Crocker, "Truth Commissions, Transitional Justice, and Civil Society," 2000. See also, more recently, Margaret Urban Walker, *Moral Repair: Reconstructing Moral Relations after Wrongdoing* (Cambridge: Cambridge University Press, 2006); Ernesto Verdeja, *Unchopping a Tree* (Philadelphia: Temple University Press, 2009); Jeffrey Blustein, *The Moral Demands of Memory* (Cambridge: Cambridge University Press, 2008).

18 On the current dissatisfaction with the compensation legislation for victims of abuses of human rights during the GDR, see David Clarke, "Compensating the Victims of Human Rights Abuses in the German Democratic Republic: The Struggle for Recognition," *German Politics* 21, no. 1 (2012): 17–33.

comprehensive understanding of respect in transitional justice theories, particularly when it comes to discussing a topic such as the public exposure of citizen collaborators. This wider scope will allow us to reexamine, and think beyond, the kind of treatment that victims receive. It will also allow us to shift the focus from notions like repair or redress as cornerstones of respect, important as they might be, to other equally pivotal notions such as agency and responsibility.

If we think of respect as a central concept for transitional justice, these are some the questions that need to be posed and that this book addresses: Are there competing claims to respect in postreunification Germany with regard to the public identification of collaborators? Which ones are overriding, and why? Could public exposures of unofficial collaborators be justified in the name of important values and yet be done in such a way that is disrespectful of collaborators? Does respect entail a different kind of treatment for repentant and unrepentant informers? Does the self-respect of collaborators (in addition to respect for victims) figure prominently in justifications for public exposures? When is holding collaborators accountable an act of respect, and when is it the opposite? Do public apologies build respect for victims, or do they actually undermine it by displacing more meaningful, and therefore respectful, acts of repentance? Are repentant collaborators owed a specific kind of treatment on account of the value of respect? A general conclusion of the book is that the public exposure of former collaborators promotes or undercuts the respect *and* self-respect of individuals (victims *and* perpetrators) in ways that have not been properly recognized and theorized.

In sum, this book contends that common understandings of IM exposures fail to do justice to the complexity of the notion of respect. Being such a central concept to the field, it should be presented in a richer way. This book tries to apply the concept in this more comprehensive way, and to the extent that it is successful in doing so, makes an original contribution to scholarship, one that hopefully will relate to the problem of collaboration with unjust regimes in other contexts.

In making the case for a richer and more textured view of respect with regard to transitional justice, I do not suggest that this should lead us necessarily to modify existing transitional justice measures in Germany, or to cast moral doubt on *Vergangenheitsbewältigung*.

This book's intention is not to challenge the way in which the process has been carried out in Germany. The German model of transitional justice is, as was mentioned earlier, exemplary in many regards. But transitional justice settings are beset with moral and political dilemmas. Measures like the public exposure of unofficial collaborators might build respect in one way and for one group but affect that respect in another way for other groups. This book simply tries to chart a map of respectful interactions, as it were.

To conclude, the aim of this book is to offer a richer conceptualization of how exposing unofficial collaborators to the public eye might be understood as a practice of respect *or* disrespect, even when the political actors involved might not articulate their actions in those terms. If one is to take seriously the idea that exposing collaborators has something to do with respecting individuals, then one needs to explore all avenues of respect. As this cursory account shows, and as I will explain in depth in the book, at every stage of the practice of outing, important questions about respect and self-respect may be posed. The practice holds, as it were, many layers of respect. Robin Dillon argues that respect may be seen as a "presumed disclosure," in which "what is disclosed is the worth or worthiness of the object."[19] This book is an exploration of the multiple disclosures of respect in the specific context of "post-Stasi" Germany.

1.2 COLLABORATION AND RESPECT: A FRAMEWORK

The main actors in civil and political society involved in public exposures frequently frame public discourse about IMs in terms of the notion of respect, or alternatively, in terms of notions that, as I will show in the book, are substantively connected to it, such as reputation, degradation, civic courage, responsibility, apologies, forgiveness, and reconciliation. In this section I shall step back from the concrete setting of post-Stasi Germany to offer a brief conceptual framework on the notion of respect, as well as the relationship

[19] Robin Dillon (ed.), *Dignity, Character, and Self-Respect* (New York: Routledge, 1995) 18.

between respect and the terms just mentioned. This section offers a sketch of what subsequent chapters will later undertake in some detail. The following paragraphs will pay particular attention to those aspects of the idea of respect that are more relevant for this book, leaving other aspects relatively neglected.[20]

This book focuses on *respect for persons*, as opposed to respect for nature, laws, institutions, viewpoints, and so on. Respect for persons is the relation between persons (the adjective *mutual* usually accompanies the noun) or between an institution like the state and persons. We respect someone when, first, we give proper attention to her or acknowledge her claim to our attention. Furthermore, in virtue of some feature she possesses, we judge that she deserves or can rightfully demand a specific response from us. Our responses to her can vary and are wide-ranging. They include, among others, awe; reverence; recognition of a status, excellence, or power; or attribution of intrinsic value. All these responses are contrary to degrading; discounting; regarding a person as worthless or insignificant; or having contempt for her. Finally, respect entails a behavioral component; we usually believe that respect makes a legitimate claim on our conduct, not just on what we feel or think. Respectful behavior can be expressed through self-restraint, by refraining from expressions of contempt and arrogance toward others, or by not shaming or humiliating them; or more actively by behaving toward persons in a way that is deemed to be appropriate, deserved, or owed to them; by praising, emulating, or giving them tokens of honor; by accepting their orders or advice; or by talking about persons in ways that reflect their worth, dignity, or status. This is not an exhaustive list.

Respect for a person can be thought out in terms of the notion of agency. In general, we respect persons when we acknowledge that they are agents, fully or to some extent depending on the circumstances,

[20] A more thorough examination of the concept in Robin Dillon, "Respect," *The Stanford Encyclopedia of Philosophy* (Spring 2014 Edition), Edward N. Zalta (ed.), at http://plato.stanford.edu/archives/spr2014/entries/respect/. See also Thomas Hill Jr. "Respect for Persons," *Encyclopedia of Philosophy*, vol. 8, ed. Edward Craig, (New York and London: Routledge), 1998, 283–287, on which the following paragraphs are based.

and we do not unjustifiably obstruct the exercise of their agency, or behave toward them as if they could not exercise it. We respect an agent when we regard her as someone with interests that are worth pursuing and defending; as someone who can be counted on to justify her actions if they unduly affect others, but who can also expect a justification from others for actions that unduly affect her.

The philosophical literature on respect has achieved a high degree of sophistication. This literature distinguishes between different kinds of respect, many of which I have grouped together in the foregoing paragraphs. For my purposes, I need not offer an extensive account of these distinctions, but I will highlight one of them because it is useful in fleshing out the dimensions of respect that matter the most in grappling with public exposures. I will *not* be harking back to it constantly throughout the book, but it should be helpful to keep it in mind.

Many scholars distinguish between *recognition* and *appraisal* respect. Recognition respect is the sense of respect as a regard or attitude that all individuals may command from others simply by virtue of their humanity. Appraisal respect is the sense of respect we accord to people who display or possess a trait (some type of conduct or character) because they do so; this kind of respect comes in degrees, depending on how much the persons exemplifies the trait we respect.[21] In the first sense, what is at stake is *recognizing* the importance of a person as such, valuing her intrinsically, in and for herself; in the second, *evaluating* the quality of her conduct and character. In either case, to respect someone is to perceive and value her as having worth, but worth might be attached to mere personhood *or* to merit, value, status, skill, and so on. In the case of recognition respect, we could go even further and say that recognition respect means not only according worth to a person but also giving her standing or authority to demand respect from others.[22] In other

[21] Stephen Darwall, "Two Kinds of Respect," *Ethics* 88, no. 1 (1977): 36–49

[22] As Darwall himself adds, recognition respect is what he calls *second-personal*. This means that we respect someone when we give her authority in our relations with her. We have earned recognition respect when we "have the competence and standing to address demands as persons to other persons,

words, there is a duty to respect others (in the recognition sense) because of their worth, but respect also means having the standing to require from others that they respect us. For Stephen Darwall, although we may not all be entitled to the same degree of appraisal respect, we must all receive recognition respect.[23]

Consider an example of this distinction. We might disapprove of a bad neighbor or citizen because she never greets fellow neighbors or citizens, she is inconsiderate toward them, and she does nothing for the well-being of the neighborhood or polity; in negatively evaluating her actions, we withhold appraisal respect from her. At the same time, however, we can (and should) still offer recognition respect to her, which simply means, for instance, that we should not humiliate her, regardless of her lack of courtesy.[24]

Although keeping appraisal and recognition respect separate may sometimes be warranted and is useful in analytical terms, it should be noted that in some cases, and the public identification of informers

and to be addressed by them, within a community of mutually accountable equals." *The Second-Person Standpoint: Morality, Respect, and Accountability* (Cambridge: Harvard University Press, 2006), 126.

23 This is how Darwall interprets Kant's idea of respect. Darwall quotes some passages from Kant's *The Metaphysics of Morals*: "Every human being has a legitimate claim to respect from his fellow human beings and is in turn bound to respect every other." Thus "recognition (*Anerkennung*) of a dignity (*dignitas*) in other human beings, that is, of a worth that has no price," is something that "others can require from me." For Darwall, these passages show that "[i]n holding that the dignity of persons is that by which we can 'demand', 'exact,' or 'require' respect from others, that each thereby has a 'legitimate claim' to respect, Kant is committed to the idea that the dignity of persons includes [an] authority to address demands for compliance with the first-order duties of respect." (Darwall, *The Second-Person Standpoint*, 137)

24 Or take another example: We should respect (in the recognition sense) the *capacity* of voters to make a judgment about political issues; this does not mean that we respect (in the appraisal sense) their particular judgments about specific issues, as these might reflect the opinions of an uninformed, unreflective and intolerant person. But, again, while withholding appraisal respect for them we should all the same refrain from expressing our (recognition) disrespect for them, for example by attempting to disenfranchise them.

is one such case, the distinction sometimes collapses. In fact, a tangential purpose of this book is to illustrate how it does collapse.

Let me elaborate on this point about the porous boundary between recognition and appraisal respect by briefly examining Kant's views on respect for persons. An orthodox and oft-rehearsed interpretation of Kant's *Groundwork for the Metaphysics of Morals* suggests that individuals are entitled to respectful (in the recognition sense) treatment no matter what, and under any circumstances. According to this interpretation, in the Kantian argument all rational[25] beings capable of moral agency have dignity and are therefore entitled to respect.[26] From this perspective, dignity cannot be diminished or lost through morally bad behavior. Individuals cannot forfeit dignity and therefore have the right to respect, no matter what they do or refrain from doing. Kant's view is actually much more nuanced than this standard view suggests.[27] Even by Kantian standards, recognition respect is not completely independent of the appraisal of one's standing and merits. Whether or not an individual may command respect is dependent on whether she possesses a valid standing to do so. According to Colin Bird's[28] interpretation of Kantian theories of punishment, the act of punishing involves treatment toward others that would normally be deemed impermissible. Punishment in Kantian theoretical frameworks, he claims, becomes

25 The Kantian account of respect has been criticized for grounding respect on the capacity for rational autonomy; this excludes people with mental disabilities. For an argument that Kantianism cannot offer solid ground for contemporary conceptions of respect for persons see Michael Neumann, "Did Kant Respect Persons?" *Res Publica* 6, no. 1 (2000): 1–15.

26 The capacity to set goals, or value things through rational judgment, and the capacity to be autonomous are the necessary and sufficient conditions for dignity, which among other things means not being treated merely as means toward some other end, but rather being treated as ends in themselves.

27 Elizabeth Anderson, "Emotions in Kant's Later Moral Philosophy: Honour and the Phenomenology of Moral Value," in Monika Betzler (ed.), *Kant's Ethics of Virtues* (Berlin: Walter De Gruyter, 2008); Mika LaVaque-Manty, *The Playing Fields of Eton. Equality and Excellence in Modern Meritocracy* (Ann Arbor: University of Michigan Press, 2009).

28 Colin Bird, "Status, Identity, and Respect," *Political Theory* 32, no. 2 (2004): 227–228.

acceptable because there has been a change in the reprobates' moral status, and therefore the restrictions that would normally govern relations between agents are lifted. Put in slightly different terms, to recognize a person as a criminal or malefactor is to understand that restrictions that would normally prohibit certain forms of treatment are removed. But the weight and number of the prohibitions a person commands are the appropriate indices of the (recognition) respect she is owed. Therefore, the removal of those prohibitions amounts to a sort of moral demotion. It is true that malefactors retain some "residual dignity" that disallows barbaric punishment or abject humiliation, but they have still been deprived of some moral standing. Bird concludes by arguing that moral status, at least to a certain extent, is contingent on existing social forms and practices, an artifact of a particular public culture. In other words, the claim to recognition respect cannot be absolute.[29] Thus, the distinction between recognition and appraisal respect might be somewhat overstated.[30] Nonetheless, it is useful for understanding some of the dimensions of the value of respect for persons.

To illustrate the fluidity between recognition and appraisal respect, consider the following examples based on the theme of this book: When citizens and authorities of the German polity make determinations about how to confront former collaborators and subsequently act on those determinations, an evaluative component

[29] Aristotle, for example, would be willing to accept a proportional theory of respect for persons. For Aristotle, "the degree of respect which one ought to have for each person is in proportion to the character of the relationship which one has to that person." Thus, one might have reasons to respect the interests and claims of members of one's family, one's fellow citizens, even for those with whom one shares an intellectual community. One has fewer reasons (but not none) to respect the interests and claims of foreigners and slaves, barbarians. Anthony Preus, "Aristotle and Respect for Persons," in J. P. Anton (ed.), *Essays in Ancient Greek Philosophy* IV (Albany: State University of New York Press, 1991), 223.

[30] As Mika LaVaque-Manty argues, the appraisal/recognition distinction is historically unwarranted because "we take someone's being a doer to be perhaps the key aspect of what makes her a person." See his *The Playing Fields of Eton*, 2009, 8.

inevitably comes into play, and the negative judgment about the collaborator's past behavior (appraisal disrespect) is factored into the assessment about the regard and treatment they are able to command (recognition respect). Among some circles at least, IMs are not recognized as citizens *with full standing* because the appraisal of their actions, which lacked civic value, is very negative. The belief underlying these public debates seems to be that because IMs behaved in morally and politically problematic ways, this should influence the way we treat them today. Furthermore, in the eyes of many people, informers deserve recognition *dis*respect because of, say, their dishonesty (a moral quality), and they can only be offered respect (again, in the recognition sense) when their past behavior has been exposed and atoned for.[31] In any case, in this book I will be looking at instances of both appraisal and recognition respect. Both matter morally, even if Darwall is right that the latter but not the former is the foundation of morality.

More briefly, let us now turn to self-respect. Although respect is a recurrent theme in transitional justice literature, self-respect plays a minor role. This is striking, given that repressive rule and civil war tend to shatter respect for persons just as much as they undermine self-respect. Having self-respect is appreciating that one has worth, which, as was discussed before, can derive from one's status as a person, as a member to a group, or as a bearer of a social role; or it can be acquired on account of merit or quality of character or conduct. Our sense of having worth can also come from the fact that we regard ourselves as agents, as someone who acts autonomously. The bottom line is that self-respect is fundamental for everyday life because it is deeply tied to the identity of an individual and the

[31] Or take a more familiar case. Hardly anyone would argue that breaking a minor law (running a red light) should strip a citizen of her moral status and right to free expression. Appraisal of your poor qualities as a law-abiding citizen should not translate into a loss of civil liberties. But beyond those clear-cut cases lies a vast penumbral area where it is not entirely clear how the distinction could be helpful. In these cases, what one might call (at the cost of piling up adjectives) civic or political recognition respect (respect I am owed as a political agent, the recognition of my political status) depends on political or civic appraisal respect (my qualities as an upright citizen).

configuration of her life and allows her to lead a flourishing life. Importantly, self-respect includes a desire to defend and maintain it. Many authors even believe that it is morally required.

Philosophers distinguish among several kinds of self-respect, but as in the case of respect for persons, I cannot discuss all of them here.[32] The aforementioned distinction between appraisal and recognition respect applies to self-respect as well. However, the distinction I wish to draw our attention to, because it will be more relevant for this book, is between *entitlement* and *standard* self-respect.[33] Entitlement self-respect is the conviction that one is entitled to due treatment from others. People who are aware of the treatment to which they are entitled from others are prepared to stand up for themselves and protest against deviations from the kind of treatment they believe they are owed. A deferential wife, who accepts anything that her autocratic husband dictates to her, is an example of someone who lacks entitlement self-respect; she has internalized an impaired understanding of her own worth and of what she is entitled to demand from others. A submissive group of citizens who tolerates arbitrary rule is another example; they discount their worth as autonomous political agents and do not act on their entitlement to be regarded as free citizens. Standard self-respect is the commitment not to compromise personal standards or ideals. A fellow who is ready to shamelessly abandon deeply held commitments to just get by has no self-respect. The same is true for a group of citizens who compromise civic ideals that they deeply value to live a life without much complication.[34]

[32] David Middleton, "Three Kinds of Self-respect," *Res Publica* 12, no. 1 (2006): 59–76.

[33] Colin Bird, Self-Respect and Respect for Others, *European Journal of Philosophy* 18, no. 1 (2010): 20.

[34] For a conception of self-respect as the ability to appreciate, and act on the appreciation of, one's worth, which include the willingness to engage in acts of protest and resistance, see Bernard Boxil, "Self-Respect and Protest," 1976; Laurence Thomas, "Self-Respect: Theory and Practice," 1983; Michele Moody-Adams, "Race, Class, and the Social Construction of Self-Respect," 1992. For a notion of self-respect, understood as living without falling below a standard of conduct that one has imposed on oneself, see Thomas Hill Jr.,

This is a rough understanding of respect and self-respect. It does not address head-on some philosophical puzzles around those notions, such as issues regarding the grounds for respect (What quality of a person makes her worthy of respect; what makes that quality so relevant, and do all human beings possess it to an equal degree?), its scope (Must persons always be respected?), or its obligatory character (Even if we establish that persons deserve respectful treatment, why is it a moral obligation to respect them?). Other issues I cannot address here are the relationship between respect and self-respect,[35] or whether self-respect is merely a by-product of political participation and therefore cannot serve as a public justification of political practices and institutions.[36] Carefully addressing these

"Servility and Self-Respect," 1973; Thomas Hill Jr., "Self-Respect Reconsidered," 1985. All of these articles are reprinted in Robin Dillon (ed.), *Dignity, Character, and Self-Respect*, 1995.

35 Usually that relationship is established as one of dependency – to a great extent, the ability of an individual to have self-respect depends on whether other individuals in society respect her. When individuals are treated as if they were invisible, as if they were less valuable, this will have immense repercussions on how much they value/respect themselves. This is the sense in which John Rawls talks about the social bases of self-respect as being one of what he calls "primary goods." John Rawls, *Justice as Fairness: A Restatement* (Cambridge: Harvard University Press, 2001), 60. See also Axel Honneth, *The Struggle for Recognition. The Moral Grammar of Social Conflict* (Cambridge: Polity, 1995).

36 There are opposing views on this issue. According to Jon Elster, engaging in politics as a means to achieve self-respect is a recipe for failure. He argues that it is one thing to act out of self-respect and quite another to use political actions as a means to achieve self-respect. Self-respect is, in Elster's view, essentially a by-product: "There is no such activity or kinesis as 'acquiring self-respect' in the sense in which one may speak of the activity of 'learning French,' although other activities such as that of uniting in the struggle for a common goal may have self-respect as a side-effect." Jon Elster, *Sour Grapes: Studies in the Subversion of Rationality* (Cambridge: Cambridge University Press, 1983), 100. Some outcomes, Elster concludes, cannot be achieved by directly aiming at producing them; they can only be achieved in the course of trying to attain some other objective, and this, for him, is the case of self-respect. In light of this, justifying political institutions and practices by reference to their side effects is both incoherent and self-defeating. Joseph

questions would take us too far afield. With regard to the last point, I simply stipulate that respect and self-respect confer moral standing on persons, and this gives us a reason to care about both notions. To put it more strongly, it gives us a duty to respect others and ourselves. I rely on, rather than establish, the moral importance of respect and self-respect.[37]

To recapitulate the discussion so far: Respect and self-respect can refer to a regard that is owed to all individuals by virtue of their humanity and to a regard that is owed on account of an evaluation of a property that individuals display to different degrees, or may not display at all. Furthermore, self-respect refers to the kind of regards or treatment people should be entitled to command on account of their worth and their standing as moral and political agents;[38] it also refers to the standards of conduct that people should maintain in their behavior to themselves and to others.

There is one final layer of complexity with regard to the notion of respect that deserves mention. As was explained earlier, respect is a matter of actions and attitudes that someone offers, and others interpret as being offered. This means that the world of respect is, unavoidably, a symbolic one.[39] Signs of respect, just as any other sign, are contingent on the context and the situation, and they are neither certain nor stable. This was Hobbes's view. It led him to conclude that demands for respect are a source of conflict. He writes that "[e]very man looketh that his companion should value him, at the same rate he sets upon himself." But this expectation can easily be

Chen and David Miller offer a rebuttal of Elster's views. They claim that when institutions pass an effectiveness threshold, or when there are rival institutions with similar effectiveness, their "educational" value is then an important and additional value to consider. Joseph Chen and David Miller, "Elster on Self-Realization in Politics: A Critical Note," *Ethics* 102, no. 1(1991): 96–102.

37 Michael Neumann, "Can't We All Just Respect One Another a Little Less?" *Canadian Journal of Philosophy* 34, no. 4 (2005): 463–484.

38 Whether they should be equal agents is a matter that cannot be addressed here. See Ian Carter, "Respect and the Basis of Equality," *Ethics* 121, no. 3 (2011): 538–571.

39 Leslie Green, "Two Worries About Respect for Persons," *Ethics* 120, no. 2 (2010), 214–215, 228–229.

contradicted by "a word, a smile, a different opinion, and any other sign of undervalue, either direct in their Person, or by reflexion in the Kindred, their Friends, their National, their Profession or their Name."[40] Incidences of disrespect, perceived or real, are the stuff of everyday life. People can become so emotionally invested in certain practices and institutions, that, as Leslie Green writes, "these investments can be competitive and conflicting, so that acknowledging the value of one may require disavowing another, with the result that we cannot avoid acting in a way that disrespects someone or other."[41]

In some contexts, hegemonic attitudes produce clear social meanings that help us detect unequivocal signs of disrespect. Thus racism and sexism today are unambiguous displays of disrespect. But quite often, social meanings are open to dispute. When this is the case, as it commonly is in transitional justice settings, a practice such as, for example, constructing or removing a memorial can be interpreted as an act of respect, or its opposite. In 2014 Japan's Prime Minister Shinzo Abe visited the Yasukuni shrine, a memorial that honors the death of 2.5 million people during the Second World War. The problem is that among those enshrined are convicted war criminals. Chinese and Korean authorities thus see the shrine as a glorification of Japanese atrocities and the Prime Minister's visit as disrespectful. Abe's perhaps disingenuous response did not reassure Japan's neighbors: "It is not my intention at all to hurt the feelings of the Chinese and Korean people," he said, and added that his intention had been to pay respect to those who died during the War.[42] In similar fashion, in this book IM exposures are interpreted as practices of respect or disrespect depending on the perspective people take on the subject. Whereas in Germany social meanings have converged toward the idea that the Stasi was the repressive arm of an objectionable regime, it is a further question how some of its collaborators should be regarded as a consequence of this, and whether exposures are indeed the ideal

[40] Quoted by Green, "Two Worries About Respect for Persons," 214.

[41] Green, "Two Worries About Respect for Persons," 214–215.

[42] "Japan PM Shinzo Abe visits Yasukuni WW2 shrine," *BBC News Asia*, December 26, 2013, available on www.bbc.com/news/world-asia-25517205

practice for addressing their deeds. In sum, then, what counts as respect can be a contested issue. With regard to some issues there might be a shared understanding of what institutions and practices count as being respectful or its opposite, but in a context of plural social meanings, this is not likely to be the case.

1.3 RESPECT AND ITS RELATIVES

With this succinct conceptual framework on the background, it should be easier to grasp the relationship between respect, on the one hand, and terms such as *reputation*, *civic courage*, *responsibility*, *apology*, *forgiveness*, and *reconciliation* on the other. In this section, I will sketch these relationships with regard to the case of public exposures of collaborators, but also, more generally, with an eye on broader transitional justice cases. I should emphasize, though, that when I speak of collaborators in these pages, what I have in mind are low-level perpetrators (the small fry) rather than leaders (the big fish).[43]

Reputation refers to the estimation that someone possesses in the eyes of others on account of this or that quality. One's reputation conditions how others regard and treat us, and this in turn affects our ability to interact in society. Thus, it comes as no surprise that people want to control access to their personal information to avoid its public dissemination if, for example, they deem it to be somehow shameful. To do this they seek the protection of the law. To the extent that such protection is an acknowledgment that they ought not to be treated in a certain way, and to the extent that it allows them to direct their lives as they wish, such protection can be seen as an instance of respect. This does not mean, of course, that people have an absolute right to control every piece of information that might cast them in a poor light. There might be reasons for lifting the safeguards against reputational harm, for example when another interest is thereby served.

[43] Different moral standards should be applied in each case. See Juan Espindola, "The Case for the Moral Permissibility of Amnesties: An Argument from Social Moral Epistemology," *Ethical Theory and Moral Practice* (issue not assigned), 2014.

In transitional justice contexts, the ideas of reputation and public shame emerge in connection with the dissemination of information contained in archives of the *ancien régime* and the impact that it can have on the lives of victims and collaborators. Questions arise about whether collaborators should be publicly exposed or if veiling their past under a cloak of secrecy is a better course of action because this will prevent their stigmatization and/or facilitate their reintegration into society. The reasons for public exposure can themselves be respect based (respecting victims by fulfilling their right to know who harmed them) or justified on the basis of society's need to use that information for the purposes of historical clarification.

The idea of civic courage commonly arises in discussions about collaboration and resistance in oppressive regimes, but it need not be circumscribed to it. Civic courage is a virtue that can also be put into practice in democratic settings, as when an employee for a government agency brings the corrupt practices of that agency to the public light, thereby putting his job security at risk. In the case that interests us here, however, civic courage is about the kind of attitudes and actions that need to be expressed and deployed whenever citizens believe that public officials or fellow citizens behave in ways that arbitrarily affect them and that therefore they are not being treated according to their due. Civic courage can take many forms. It can be achieved through collective action (e.g., organizing protests). It can also be accomplished through individual acts of resistance. A prime example is civil disobedience, which is the act of disobeying a particular law that one deems to be unjust, bearing the consequences of breaking that rule, while at the same time following the law in other domains. Yet another way a citizen can behave courageously is by refusing to collaborate with an oppressive regime whenever its officials seek assistance for political reasons, something like conscientious refusal. In all of these cases – and this is the crucial point – civic courage embodies a view of moral and political agency that has self-respect at its root. Specifically, it reflects the awareness that one's worth or standing as an equal agent is not duly taken into account, a situation that should not be tolerated and deserves a specific response, namely some form of political resistance. Anything short of this fails to meet a standard of self-respect, for nobody who respects herself accepts being subservient to others or behaving in ways that one considers to be demeaning. Thus, one who lacks civic courage disrespects herself. This retrospective assessment on the civic degradation of collaborators is relevant in transitional justice settings.

Turning now to responsibility. Treating someone with respect means treating her like a fully fledged agent who is answerable for her acts. Provided that she has some degree of autonomy (and this is of course a crucial conditional), she should be considered as someone who can give reasons for her actions and take responsibility for them – she is a justificatory being and a bearer of the consequences of her actions. When others do not maintain this attitude toward her, they do not treat her as an agent but, patronizingly, as a child or a beast, and therefore do not respect her. In transitional justice contexts, the expectation is that collaborators offer reasons for their decision to assist public officials for an oppressive regime. Implicit in this expectation is that collaborators are accountable agents, not passive preys of destiny. One ought to be careful, though. A respect-based principle of accountability can be perverted if holding collaborators responsible is merely a ruse to assign blame to specific individuals to exculpate other individuals (e.g., bystanders, grudge informers, occasional collaborators as opposed to systematic ones) from their contribution in sustaining an oppressive regime.

Apologies are deeply connected to the idea of respect. When a wrongdoer apologizes to her victim, the former thereby recognizes that her actions did not accord the latter the treatment that she was owed as a moral and political agent. Apologies are a way of retroactively recognizing the worth of victims. Put differently, apologies are an acknowledgment that victim and perpetrator have an equal status; they promote a reciprocal recognition of each other as agents who owe one another respect. Furthermore, from the perspective of the wrongdoers, apologizing is one way of taking responsibility for actions; it is also a petition to reacquire the standing the person had prior to (and which was lost through) wrongdoing, or at the very least one that comes close to it. All of this is particularly relevant in transitional justice contexts, where victims do not only expect financial compensation, if appropriate, for their material losses, but also recognition of the harm they suffered. This recognition is a form of respect. It can be expressed through private or public apologies of collaborators to victimized individuals or groups (ethnic or religious groups). Not all kinds of apologies, however, build respect in roughly the same way. Besides apologizing to victims to pay them respect, collaborators apologize to demonstrate their allegiance to the new regime and to find a place in it as ordinary citizens, not tainted by their past behavior.

Forgiving is the obverse of apologizing. Wrongdoers owe victims an apology as a matter of respect for them. By contrast, victims do not owe forgiveness to wrongdoers as a matter of respect for them. There are many reasons why victims should not be forced to forgive perpetrators; for one, forgiving perpetrators can be psychologically exacting on victims; for another, victims have a privileged epistemic access to the harm they suffered and are thus in the best position to judge whether an apology, and of what kind, can repair, to the extent that is possible, the harm done. Forgiveness and apologies, then, are asymmetrical from the perspective of respect; apologizing is a perfect duty; forgiving an imperfect one. But forgiveness is not all that matters in transitional justice settings. Although victims do not have an obligation to forgive unrepentant collaborators, or even repentant ones, they do have a less demanding, but politically very significant, prima facie obligation to display a reconciliatory attitude toward them once the *ancien régime* has collapsed and a new one, with guarantees of nonrepetition of politically motivated wrongdoing, is in place. By reconciliation what is meant is that those perpetrators whose wrongdoings were not egregious should be given an opportunity to reacquire their moral and political standing, which in turn will allow them to exercise their moral and political agency to its fullest extent. When repentant collaborators, or some of them at least, are denied reconciliation, they are not given the opportunity of making progress in moral terms; when, furthermore, they are presumed to be incapable of honoring basic norms for social interaction and discharging their responsibilities as citizens or public officials, their political agency is unjustifiably restricted. These are unjustified encroachments on a person's agency and are therefore not appropriate from the point of view of respect.

This is a rough framework of the relationship between respect and some of the terms that are central to this book. The relationship will be further clarified in each chapter of the book. The point to underscore is that the value of respect is at the heart of debates about the public identifications of IMs. It is invoked when the concern is the stigmatizing potential of public identifications, but it is also at the forefront when public exposures are heralded as tools of civic accountability; the value of respect underlies the view of moral and political agency that serves as a model to justify them, and it sets up expectations about the proper way in which to "resolve" public exposures – through an apology of perpetrators and the construction of a reconciliatory environment that makes it possible for them to have a "second chance."

1.4 THE METHOD AND THE SOURCES

This book is an exercise in empirically oriented political theory. By this I mean that the theoretical puzzles and themes addressed in it have emerged from a rather close observation of a concrete social practice, in particular as it is embodied in public discourses and political and legal institutions. In other words, this is not a book on the history of the Stasi and its informers, but historical and sociological data do figure prominently in the argumentation. Likewise, this is not a book on the most recent refinement of a particular concept in the more abstract and philosophically bent literature on transitional justice. Instead, the book is pitched at a level that tries to bring together the empirical and the theoretical levels of analysis.

The book seeks to understand how the value of respect guides (promotes, structures, limits) the practice of publicly exposing unofficial collaborators. The point is *not* simply to elucidate how participants in the practice of IM exposures understand the idea of respect. At the same time, the goal is not to craft, from a set of abstract principles, an idea of respect, alien to those involved in the practice, and then argue that this idea should regulate the practice. The aim of the book falls somewhere between mere elucidation and mere stipulation – it is to theorize on and evaluate the practice based on the ideas that participants have about it.[44] If respect is as relevant as they claim that it is, then how does that enable and constrain the way in which the practice should be carried out? What are the considerations that actors should bear in mind while publicly exposing collaborators if respect is a value to be honored? Thus, the book teases out a social "grammar" of respect as it is reflected in political practice and public discourse related to the public identification of unofficial collaborators. Having fleshed out these practical and discursive patterns, I turn to a rich scholarly literature on reputation, shame, forgiveness, responsibility, and some others – terms that are linked to respect as shown in the previous sections – to grapple with these patterns. This juxtaposition between the discourse and practice of outings, on the one hand, and respect scholarship, on the other, will allow me to approach the public exposure of unofficial collaborators in a novel fashion, one that hopefully contributes to transitional justice scholarship.

Because I have already said enough about the theoretical/normative motivations behind this book in the previous section, next I shall add a few clarifications on its empirical component. The motivation for focusing on concrete instantiations of outings is to avoid inferential fallacies of the following type: If some actors in civil society publicly expose IMs, it must mean they are doing it for X reasons (they must be interested in unveiling the truth about the past, or they must be interested in retribution, and so on). In most cases, such quick ascriptions of meaning do in fact capture part of what is going on. But the ascriptions also obscure dimensions of outing that are related to respect. Avoiding this inferential fallacy will give me a greater opportunity to grasp how respect may be at work in the public exposure of IMs.

I follow Lisa Wedeen's work to avoid the inferential pitfall just described. According to Wedeen, one needs to look closely at social

[44] I follow an approach similar to what Pablo Gilabert calls "deliberative interpretive approach." See his "Human Rights, Human Dignity, and Power," in Rowan Cruft, Matthew Liao, and Massimo Renzo, eds. *The Philosophical Foundations of Human Rights* (Oxford: Oxford University Press, 2015).

practices to see how and why actors invest political phenomena with meaning, instead of simply making extrinsic ascriptions about what they mean. Inferences about social practices not based on what one might call "native intelligibility" – what actors themselves believe they are doing – run the risk of misrepresenting what is happening on the ground. Consider a fairly standard political practice such as voting. I can observe that a person uses "a pen and checks off a box with a name beside it on a piece of paper, deposits that paper in a box, and later they tally the number of times each name is checked off and the one with the most votes makes political decisions for the next four years." Yet it is an open question what people mean to be doing when they are doing this: "It may be a game, a religious ceremony, a farce, a political event, or something else, or it may be a combination of these things." Wedeen argues that social scientists and, I would add, political theorists, must be able to know and to show that their interpretation is based on a grasp of "native intelligibility, that in checking off a ballot the citizen is affirming the community's norms, or voting, or both, or neither."[45]

Let me now add a word about the criteria I used for selecting the cases, as well as some details on the sources used. Pursuing a thematic approach, the book inevitably relies on a selective reading of numerous events and episodes regarding the Stasi and its informers. These are brought into consideration to construct and illustrate a larger theoretical argument about respect. The most important criterion in selecting cases was whether actors involved in them explicitly invoked the notions of respect and/or related ones; alternatively, I selected cases in which the issues pertinent to a discussion on respect emerged more clearly. For instance, I discuss legal cases related to the right of personality, with its intrinsic reputational concerns because this right clearly reflects a concern about the value of respect. Likewise, I examined the views (and actions) of prominent civil rights activists and public officials such as Joachim Gauck, Hubertus Knabe, Friedrich Schorlemmer, and Marianne Birthler,

[45] The previous quotes come from Lisa Wedeen, "Conceptualizing Culture: Possibilities for Political Science," *American Political Science Review* 96, no. 4. (2002): 721.

just to name a very few, whom I take to be representative of some widely spread views about Stasi collaborators. I also considered opinions of major figures in political parties. Again, what caught my attention analyzing their statements was whether they alluded directly to the idea of respect.

The time frame of the study is broad, covering the entire period from the opening of the files to present day (1990–2012). I chose a combination of *recent* cases that received substantive attention from newspapers, on the one hand, and *earlier*, "classic" cases, such as Manfred Stolpe's, on the other. By doing this I do not intend to suggest that the processes or arguments related to the public identification of collaborators have remained unaltered. There are continuities and changes, and I will try to address both of them.

Earlier cases of IM exposures are the subject of work by scholars such as Anne Sa'adah, James McAdams, and Barbara Miller (who are duly referenced throughout the book). Recent cases were reconstructed from primary and secondary sources. As to the former, I examined a large sample of articles and editorials from relatively recent mainstream newspapers, such as *Die Welt, Die Zeit, Frankfurter Allgemeine Zeitung*, or *Süddeutsche Zeitung*, among others, as well as popular magazines such as *Der Spiegel* or *Cicero*. I relied overwhelmingly on newspapers of national circulation. Reliance on newspapers of national circulation alone, as opposed to local ones, is admittedly a limitation of the study. I tried to compensate for this shortcoming by offering in-depth examination of some cases; local newspapers were consulted in such instances. As to secondary sources, I consulted academic works in German and in English, as well as in-depth case studies prepared by independent journalists or by the body of researchers of the Stasi Records Office. I also examined journals and magazines that frequently cover issues relating to coming to terms with the Stasi past, some of which are semiacademic and some more geared toward political activism (*Gerbergasse 18, Deutschland Archiv, Horch und Guck*, *Freiheit und Recht*, etc.). I would like to recall, however, that the contribution I intend to make to scholarly literature is not a novel description of the practice (the public identification of collaborators), but a way of relating a fairly transparent practice to a set of philosophical puzzles.

1.5 AN OUTLINE OF THE CHAPTERS

Following a background chapter on the GDR, the Stasi, and unofficial collaborators, the structure of the book is organized to reflect the stages of typical IM exposure: the forceful defense by political activists, moral entrepreneurs and victims of the values and goals animating Stasi *Aufarbeitung*, which are said to justify that exposure; the resistance of collaborators (and of some sympathetic groups) to the public disclosure and dissemination of their identity; and finally, the uneasy resolution of these tensions through the establishment and sustenance of a culture of public apology, as well as through the construction of a fragile reconciliatory arrangement. The last stage does not imply that all unofficial collaborators do in fact repent and publicly apologize; some do not. But the expectation is that they do. In each stage there are moral and political implications in terms honoring or undermining the value of respect for persons as moral and political agents. The goal of each chapter is to draw out those implications as clearly as possible.

Chapter 3 explores the "collision" between, as a commentator put it, Stasi *Aufarbeitung* and *Rechtsstaat* (roughly, government by law), that is, between the ideals motivating the public exposure of collaborators and the principles embedded in the law in the form of reputational and privacy guarantees that presumably discourage such exposure. Chapter 4 examines one of the justifications offered in support of publicly exposing collaborators – the belief that such exposure is instrumental in affirming the ideal of civic courage. Chapter 5 discusses the advantages and the limits of ascribing individual moral responsibility in contexts such as that of East Germany. Chapter 6 argues that although public apologies are commonly taken to be an appropriate form of symbolic redress/respect for victims, there is a risk that they depart from that goal. Finally, Chapter 7 considers how Stasi *Aufarbeitung* can create political dynamics and expectations that hinder reconciliation. In all these cases, the point is to examine the ways in which the public exposure of unofficial collaborators promotes (or does not promote) respect for victims and collaborators alike. Let me turn to a detailed account of the arguments of each of the chapters.

Chapter 3, which unlike subsequent ones relies heavily on legal and jurisprudential materials, explains the reasons for the modest, and usually temporary, success that some unofficial collaborators have had in thwarting attempts to expose their past to public opinion. The main reason why some collaborators have temporarily prevented, or at least hindered, exposure of their past is that they have "activated" resources in German law that limit the dissemination of information about an individual's past when such information is deemed to be stigmatizing and harmful to the individual's reputation. Probably the most important of such resources is the right of personality or *Persönlichkeitsrecht*. This right in particular reflects the concern of German legal culture for protecting individuals from shaming exposures. Quite commonly, public identifications are defended as a tool for accountability (more on this later). Although this might be an acceptable justification for the practice, the chapter makes the case for appreciating its potential for disrespecting informers, even if this consideration can and should be outweighed by other considerations. Like subsequent chapters, this one will draw attention to the fine lines that need to be noticed when trying to understand how a social practice such as public identifications might or might not promote respect. This chapter uses the United States as a contrast category. This might seem like an odd comparison because unlike Germany, this nation does not have a precedent of engaging in transitional justice processes. What the United States does have, however, is a legacy of ideas and practices addressing the issue of balancing freedom of expression and reputational claims. The chapter compares American and German legal cultures not only on the assumption that readers in the United States might appreciate the reference to American legal culture, but most important, because the contrast brings to light the importance of reputation in German legal culture, reputation being above all a juridified notion of respect.

Chapter 4 teases out some of the strains of public discourse that conceive of public exposures as shaming interpellations that contribute to upholding an ideal of upright citizenship. Such discursive patterns rest on an understanding of self-respect, which the chapter examines. I draw attention to the argument, present in such discourse, that collaboration with the Stasi as an unofficial informer was degrading, that is, an act of self-disrespect. Even noncollaborators degraded themselves by keeping silent, according to that standard. But the degradation of IMs was, in this view, particularly troublesome, because, unlike noncollaborators, collaborators were approached by the secret police, asked to collaborate, and acquiesced. Such acquiescence is a particularly strong token of degradation. This view, ensconced in public discussions, reflects a view of self-respect along the lines suggested by scholars who argue that self-respect means not falling below a standard of conduct, particularly a civic one, as well as defending one's entitlement to being treated in a nonoppressive way. Having degraded themselves in these terms (having become "barbarians," as Joachim Gauck put it), unofficial collaborators become the legitimate target of public discredit. Now, shaming interpellations are sometimes contested by unofficial collaborators, at whom they are targeted, as well as by citizens who are sympathetic toward them. This is because both groups experience these interpellations not as justified criticism of their past actions or omissions, but as an expression of contempt and arrogance toward them. This shows how attitudes of respect or disrespect can be equivocal and produce social tension.

Chapter 5 explores the theme of moral responsibility in public discussions about IM exposures. The chapter acknowledges that public debates about the degrees and kinds of moral responsibility that must be ascribed to IMs are in and of themselves a deliberative practice that promotes respect. Under ideal circumstances, these debates can serve to exculpate those IMs who were coerced into collaboration, while holding accountable those who were not and carried out their service to the Stasi through interpersonal and civic deceit. Making these distinctions serves the forward-looking goal of building relationships of respect among the citizenry, but the chapter insists that the difficulties involved in accurately determining who was responsible, and to what degree, for joining the Stasi as an informer should not be underestimated. Furthermore, the chapter advances the idea that public identifications can undermine the value of respect if they become a justification for precluding discussion about other kinds of political actions (or absence thereof) that contributed to perpetuating the status quo in the GDR. If IM exposures are aimed at producing scapegoats to exculpate citizens who, even if they never became informers themselves, nonetheless bear *some* responsibility for the injustices committed under the communist regime, then those exposures are very far from honoring the value of respect. In light of this problem and although unpalatable at first sight, the chapter retrieves the notion of collective responsibility and argues that despite its shortcomings it could be conducive to building respect.

Chapter 6 tackles a theme that has garnered a substantial amount of attention from transitional justice scholarship in recent years – public apologies. The chapter distinguishes between the different levels of apologies (personal, interpersonal, public) that are commonly present in transitional justice scenarios. It argues that public apologies allow unofficial collaborators to reacquire their standing as citizens worthy of respect, a standing that, as Chapter 4 shows, they had lost through their actions. The chapter also acknowledges the *potential* of public apologies for fostering respect for victims by accomplishing what some authors call "performative redress" or "retroactive recognition of dignity." However, it also underscores the idea that in another sense, public apologies may undermine respect for victims. Public apologies have been heavily criticized for their insincerity. But they can also be disrespectful. To the extent that they are not always a request from victims, who ideally should get to decide the kind of the apology (public or private) that they would like to receive, and to the extent that they are not always addressed directly to victims, but to what I call apology brokers, public apologies become a ritual rather than a dialogue that contemplates and incorporates victims. In other words, victims are relegated to the background and do not seem to be the central motivation of public apologies. This robs this kind of apology of part of its respect-building features.

Chapter 7 addresses the issue of reconciliation. Appeals to political reconciliation are common in public debates in many societies in transition from authoritarian or totalitarian rule to democracy. Reconciliation in public discourse in Germany is often framed as the potential reward given IMs for the open acknowledgment of their repentance and their public apologies. Public apologies, in this view, can bring about the restoration of political relationships at least for the sake of coexisting in a collective enterprise. However, based on the examination of the case of Kerstin Kaiser, a member of the political party Die Linke and formerly an IM, this chapter argues that as it actually turns out, in contemporary Germany, the prospects of reconciliation following a public apology are uncertain. If the point of reconciling with a former unofficial collaborator is conferring to her full status as a political agent, it follows that she should not be barred from holding elected positions in government. In the German context, militating against this reconciliatory praxis is a strongly ingrained distrust of IMs, one that some political elites have carefully cultivated for strategic purposes, and that the public atonement of IMs often cannot counter. Here IM exposures breed distrust: They create a political environment in which some citizens cannot be fully "rehabilitated." In this sense they may be practices of disrespect.

1.6 IDEOLOGICAL AND PARTISAN REDUCTIONS

In studying IM outings and examining their theoretical relevance, this book will try to avoid an approach that reduces the phenomenon merely to the outcome of current struggles for power between the main parties in the German political system or to ideological disputes around the legacy of the communist past, where, depending on whether the latter is cast in a positive or a negative light, the exposure of citizens for public verbal lynching is regarded as illegitimate or receives a seal of approval. Although ideological and partisan struggles undoubtedly stand in the background of outings, there is more to be said about outings once their ideological motivations or the partisan interests behind them have been uncovered. Beneath the crust of ideological convictions and party interests lie repositories of arguments whose theoretical significance I explore in this book.

Bearing in mind that the ideological and partisan reductions regarding the public exposure of IMs are, by themselves, theoretically impoverishing, let me nonetheless offer a brief account of how ideological and partisan variables are relevant to the topic to be developed here.

Of the five larger political parties in contemporary Germany, four have defined their institutional positions vis-à-vis IM outings.[46] In general terms, Die Linke is the fiercest detractor of the persistent exposure of IMs, whereas parties such as the Alliance '90/Greens or the Christian Democratic Union (CDU) are usually among their most enthusiastic promoters. Although initially sympathetic to outings, in recent years the Socialist Democratic Party (SPD) has maintained an ambiguous position. Some of its representatives share the views of Die Linke regarding the benefits of outings; others are more likely to support pro-outing activists in the other parties.

It is not difficult to fathom the reasons for the existence of such contrasting views vis-à-vis the public exposure of Stasi collaborators. As the inheritor of the communist party of the GDR – the Socialist Unity Party of Germany or SED (*Sozialistische Einheitspartei Deutschlands*) – Die Linke, has an obvious interest in discouraging outings. Among its cadres are prominent as well as not so conspicuous politicians who were deeply involved with the SED. Some of them were even IMs themselves. Obviously, Die Linke disavows the GDR's undemocratic nature and its systematic violations of human rights. Nonetheless, a recurring strategy in Die Linke's political discourse is to "retrieve" the "positive" elements of the communist regime. Thus, although its political program is "sanitized" from many of the positions formerly advocated by the SED, it endorses what it regards as the social agenda of the former regime. More controversially, Die Linke has been criticized for its alleged efforts to "embellish" or trivialize the crimes of the GDR.[47] By contrast, many of the former

[46] The other major national party, the Free Democratic Party, has had a marginal participation in public debates on outings.

[47] Die Linke's role in instigating relatively favorable attitudes toward the communist regime, critics say, is part of a broader phenomenon (sometimes called *Schönrede*) that consists of "softening" the harshness of the now extinct regime. For example, the film *12 heißt: Ich liebe Dich* caused a stir in public opinion for no other reason. The movie narrates the romance of a Stasi victim and her captor at a Stasi prison. The movie did not air without a group of demonstrators requesting that the film be banned. The time spent in a secret service jail was extremely harsh, critics argued in publicly criticizing the film, not an opportunity to begin a love affair. A positive portrayal of the GDR

civil rights activists and dissidents during the GDR – and today administrators of Stasi-*Aufarbeitung* – belong to parties such as Alliance '90/Greens and the CDU/CSU. Their opposition to Die Linke and the set of views it espouses in relation to *Aufarbeitung* are generally based on ideological as well as experiential grounds. From a more cynical perspective, of course, their criticism of Die Linke is not divorced from electoral profit.

A site of contention illustrating the irreducible conflict between these two ideological and partisan positions is the debate around whether the GDR was an *Unrechtsstaat*, a regime that disregarded the rule of law. It is quite common for representatives from Die Linke to deny the claim that the GDR was an *Unrechtsstaat*. They contend, like the coleader of the party, Gesine Lötzsch, that the notion of *Unrechtsstaat* in the context of German reunification is a "propaganda battle cry" (*"propagandistischer Kampfbegriff"*) that does not clarify anything "but is intended to stigmatize."[48] Slightly more complex criticisms point out that the notion of *Unrechtsstaat*, as applied to the GDR, is unduly overreaching. The state, one critic says, is not an entity independent of society but the "political constitution of society."[49] Therefore, the designation of the GDR as an *Unrechtsstaat* applies to society too. In this way, *Unrechtsstaat* puts all GDR citizens

cannot be executed, critics further argue, without throwing the mantle of oblivion over facts. Once that is done, the nature of the "ancient regime" is up for grabs; it becomes a matter of opinion. In view of this distortion of the past, it becomes a public interest to spell out a clear and detailed account of past events, including the precise identity of perpetrators, so the argument goes.

48 "Unrechtsstaat," *Neues Deutschland*, December 6, 2008. The text is available at http://linksfraktion.de/im-wortlaut/unrechtsstaat/. Lötzsch notes that incumbent authorities in Germany shy away from designating autocratic political regimes such as China, Zimbabwe, and Iran as *Unrechtsstaate*, while being unhesitant about classifying the German communist regime as such. For Lötzsch, this double standard goes to show the partisan motivation of the *Unrechtsstaat* label.

49 Gesine Schwan, "In der Falle des Totalitarismus," *Die Zeit*, June 25, 2009. Schwan is a member of the SPD, not of Die Linke, but her arguments in this respect are strikingly similar to those of many representatives of the latter.

"under moral suspicion" and casts them as second-class citizens in unified Germany.[50]

On the other side of the controversy are political actors such as the former president of the Federal Republic of Germany Roman Herzog, a CDU member who in 1996 designated the GDR as an *Unrechtsstaat*, using straightforward and simple criteria: The regime denied democratic rights to its citizens, violated basic human rights, censored the press, and intimidated dissidents.[51] Along the same lines, Chancellor Angela Merkel, CDU leader, noted in applying the controversial term to the GDR that the "SED-System" was an *Unrechtsstaat* system because it required that many lives be lived with lies, because it was based on a structure that operated on fear (*Grundstruktur der Verängstigung*), because it prevented and punished public expression of political views that were contrary to those of the regime, because it produced its own "truth," and because it engineered electoral fraud.[52] The chancellor also warned against presenting distorted views of the *ancient régime*. She argued that even though many citizens had been able to live "normal" lives under the GDR, which to some proved that the term *Unrechtsstaat* should not apply, the system was still profoundly unjust. Surveillance and spying, she contended, were ever-present companions in daily life. Thus, Merkel urged politicians and citizens to reject SPD leader Franz Müntefering's opinion that Die Linke should not continue to be evaluated based on its ideological ties with the GDR.

These ideological/partisan dynamics stand in the background of many of the cases I examine in the book.

[50] Schwan, "In der Falle des Totalitarismus."

[51] "Rede von Bundespräsident Roman Herzog vor der Enquete-Kommission "SED-Diktatur", March 26, 1996. Available at: www.bundespraesident.de/SharedDocs/Reden/DE/Roman-Herzog/Reden/1996/03/19960326_Rede.html

[52] "Kanzlerin Merkel rechnet mit DDR als 'Unrechtsstaat' ab," *Die Welt*, May 9, 2009.

2 THE REGIME, THE SECRET POLICE, AND COMING TO TERMS WITH THE PAST

The main goals of this chapter are to situate readers within the relevant historical and political context and to explain why the infamous German secret police emerged in that context; to offer some details about the informers of the Stasi; and finally to give a brief overview about the transitional justice measures that have been enforced in Germany to come to terms with the past. The chapter has three sections that mirror these goals. Section one offers some historical background on the German Democratic Republic (GDR) and on the emergence of its secret police. Section two deals in greater depth with the main features of the informer network in East Germany – its degree of penetration into society, its methods of recruitment, its mode of operation, and the kinds of IMs it produced. Section three discusses Germany's *Vergangenheitsbewältigung*; after briefly describing some of the mechanisms used to address the legacy of Nazi crimes, the chapter turns to some of the measures put in place to confront the communist past.

2.1 A WEB OF SURVEILLANCE

The communist political regimes that emerged in East Germany and most Eastern European countries after the Second World War were very similar. There were, of course, some differences between these countries, for example in terms of the degree of sheer violence state authorities deployed in each country, their independence in relation to the Soviet Union, or their styles of leadership. But the similarities are far more numerous and relevant than the differences.

The Communist parties in all of these nations had discretionary control over appointments to state positions and public office, as well as over policy making in most spheres of social life; they had pre- and anticommunist leaders imprisoned, tortured, and murdered; they had little if any tolerance for criticism of official ideology or policy; they exercised iron-handed control over mass media as well as artists and their work; they curtailed basic rights such as freedom of travel, expression, association, and religion; and they made career advancement contingent on loyalty to the communist policy and leadership.[1]

More important for this book is the fact that the Communist parties of the region relied on secret political polices. The most infamous of all were perhaps the Soviet KGB (in some way the mother of all communist secret services), the Romanian Securitate, and of course, the Stasi. The methods of social control of secret service organizations throughout Eastern Europe varied but, again, resemblances are significant. The main task of bodies like the Stasi or the Securitate, which were completely subordinated to the Communist party, was to root out dissent and discourage opposition to the government. They were comprised of full-time public officers as well as part-time citizen informers, the German variant of which is the focus of this book. Those who collaborated as informers in Eastern European countries had very diverse motivations in doing so: opportunism, revenge, fear for one's well-being or that of family members, political conviction, and blackmail.[2]

In the case of the GDR, scholars remain divided about how to characterize the regime, more or less in the same way that politicians differ, as we saw in the previous chapter, on whether or not the GDR was an *Unrechtsstaat*. Some scholars stress its *totalitarian* grip on society; totalitarian, it should be noted, not in the sense that the regime terrorized the population, but in the sense that it *aspired* to

[1] Lavinia Stan, "Introduction: Post-communist Transition, Justice, and Transitional Justice," in Lavinia Stan, ed. *Transitional Justice in Eastern Europe and the Former Soviet Union: Reckoning with the Communist Past* (London: Routledge, 2008), 1–14.

[2] Lavinia Stan, "Introduction," 1–14.

control the life opportunities of East German citizens.[3] In contrast to this characterization, other scholars believe that despite its controlling vocation (which they intimate is oftentimes overstated), the regime had some degree of flexibility and commanded some loyalty from East Germans, allowing them to lead ordinary lives. This disagreement is reflected in the profusion of terms used to describe the GDR. They go from "welfare dictatorship," "posttotalitarian bureaucratic dictatorship," and "thoroughly ruled society" to "forced through society," "participatory dictatorship," and some others.[4]

For the purposes of this book, we do not need to settle this debate. I prefer to adopt a different approach, one that starts by underscoring the nature of the GDR's socialist project. In Andreas Glaeser's account, East German socialism was working with a Hegelian rather than a Marxian model of social transformation. This means that in contrast to Marx's base-superstructure model, which analyzes consciousness as an epiphenomenon, the GDR's socialist project revolved around the idea that building and sustaining a socialist consciousness was of the utmost importance for its success. Glaeser calls this the "consciousness-driven model of social transformation."[5] The model had a positive as well as a negative dimension. In the positive dimension, it relied on socialist propaganda. This explains the GDR's heavy investment in a robust ideological apparatus.

But public authorities knew that socialist propaganda could fail. More important, it was vulnerable to "attacks" from the West.

[3] Bruce, *The Firm*, 8, 76. In insisting on the regime's aspiration to totalitarian control, Bruce is drawing on Martin Malia, "To the Stalin Mausoleum," *Daedalus* 119, no. 1 (1990): 295–344.

[4] Bruce, *The Firm*, 7.

[5] Andreas Glaeser, "Power/Knowledge Failure: Epistemic Practices and Ideologies in the Secret Police of Former East Germany," *Social Analysis* 47 (1), 2003: 11. See also Andreas Glaeser, *Political Epistemics: The Secret Police, The Opposition and the End of East German Socialism*. (Chicago: University of Chicago Press, 2011). It is worth stressing that the "consciousness-driven model of social transformation" entails the subordination of individual intentions to collective ones. In other words, it treats individuals not as ends-in-themselves, but merely as means to achieving the socialist project. Hence, it treats them disrespectfully.

The system therefore demanded "tokens of allegiance" from its citizens, to make sure that they remained loyal. This is where the Stasi comes in. Its task was *ideological policing*, which was part and parcel of the Soviet socialist project, not a deviation from it. The Stasi thoroughly monitored the citizenry and "encouraged" those citizens who gave signs of deviance to "realign." In this it was no different, as was mentioned earlier, from other secret police bodies in the region. But the latter paled next to the Stasi in terms of their penetration into society. Sheer numbers speak for themselves: The ratio of secret police officers for every citizen in the Soviet Union was one for 595; in Czechoslovakia, one for every 867; and in Poland, one for every 1,574. None of these figures comes close to the ratio in East Germany of one full-time secret police officer for every 180 East German citizens.[6] The Stasi might not have been the most ruthless secret police in the region, but it was definitely and by far the most pervasive of all.

The Stasi did not become this insidious and powerful institution overnight. Creating a political security police force was deemed to be an imperative right from the beginning of the GDR. From 1945 to 1950, burgeoning intelligence and internal security services were scattered throughout different entities operating independently, among them the *Volkspolizei* (People's Police). The *Cheka*, the first incarnation of the KGB, began to train the earlier cadres of the Stasi. The MfS assumed its modern form in 1950. It operated in an environment in which, according to the official news organs of the state, terrorism was around the corner, and espionage on the GDR was unrelenting. Although American and British intelligence groups were indeed present in East Germany, this diagnosis was an exaggeration. After its creation in 1950, the Stasi progressively consolidated and increased its power. It went through difficult times in 1953, when the SED punished it for failing to anticipate a rebellion of workers that almost got out of control, but it reacquired its prominent role within

[6] Jens Gieseke, *The History of the Stasi: East Germany's Secret Police, 1945–1990*, trans. David Burnett (New York: Berghahn, 2014), 49. This is an English Translation of Jens Gieseke, *Mielke–Konzern, Die Geschichte der Stasi 1945–1990* (München: Deutsche Verlags-Anstalt, 2001), 69.

East German society, always within the aegis of the party. The Stasi budget was augmented rapidly until the mid-1980s, when it stagnated. Not even the National People's Army, or *National Volksarmee*, rivaled the Stasi, which guarded the Party and even had an armed division at its disposal for paramilitary purposes.

The heyday of the Stasi came during the seventies, when its budget and its professional staff increased notably. The two areas that benefited most from this expansion were the foreign branch and, more important for the purposes of this book, its massive internal security department, which was in charge of monitoring and infiltrating dissidents in the underground church and human rights movements. Every time there was a political upheaval in the region, like the reformist Prague Spring of 1968, or after tensions with the West eased up, availability of resources reached new heights.

From the early days, in the 1950s, to 1989, when the regime was about to collapse, the Stasi's goals morphed. The focus shifted from defense against exterior threats (e.g., Western espionage) to a concern for internal enemies. The entire population, aside from SED members, became legitimate targets of Stasi surveillance. As the GDR increasingly came into greater contact with the outside world, greater vigilance was put into place, because, in the minds of leaders, the West had greater opportunities for subverting the regime and for "contaminating" GDR citizens. In light of this, the Stasi had to be preemptive and not wait until the damage was done.[7]

Let me be more specific about the goals and, particularly, the methods that the Stasi used to pursue those goals. According to a disingenuous interpretation, the Stasi was like any other secret service agency – the Central Intelligence Agency (CIA), for instance, or the National Security Agency (NSA). As will become clear in this section, the comparison is absurd, recent revelations about the NSA methods notwithstanding. Certainly the Stasi accomplished unobjectionable goals, such as preventing economic sabotage or even bringing Nazi criminals to justice. But these activities did not constitute the backbone of the Stasi. The key term to explain the Stasi's function within

[7] John Schmeidel, Stasi. *Shield and Sword of the Party* (New York: Routledge, 2008), 32.

the GDR's regime is *Verbeugung* (prevention or hindering), a noun that the Stasi used tirelessly in its documentation.[8] The Stasi sought to prevent any disruptions to the socialist order, be they unofficial propaganda; antistate graffiti; the establishment of groups that did not conform to the SED's worldview, particularly within the nonaligned churches or intellectual circles (almost all of them); defections; and even attempts to flee the GDR.

Perhaps more striking than the goals it pursued (aligning the individual intentions to those of the party) are the methods the Stasi used to accomplish those goals. Here the central concept is *flächendeckende Überwachung*, comprehensive or blanket, as opposed to targeted, surveillance. The Stasi did not merely monitor isolated groups that were suspected of having "subversive" intent. They did that, of course. But the surveillance extended to society in its entirety. In his study of the districts of Perleberg and Gransee, northwest of Berlin, Gary Bruce shows how the Stasi's surveillance penetrated ordinary and clearly harmless domains of East Germany. Those two cities were very far from constituting hubs of subversive activities. Nonetheless, the Stasi deployed an ambitious surveillance apparatus to monitor them. Regardless of the fact that these cities did not pose a threat to the regime, the Stasi placed IMs in pubs, restaurants, and other places of social gathering and assigned them the task of reporting on the mood of the citizenry. Some apologists of the regime dispute whether the GDR used blanket surveillance, which would indicate a totalitarian intent, or a targeted one, which would cast the Stasi in a gentler, albeit nonetheless negative, light. The evidence seems to suggest the former. Comprehensive surveillance was without a doubt the Stasi's aspiration. And in fact, "open" surveillance could give rise to targeted surveillance.[9]

The main point of targeted surveillance was to discourage opposition to the GDR by having informers convince the target to abandon whatever plan he or she had (an attempt to escape from the GDR, antiregime graffiti, and so on). When this failed, the secret police increased pressure by recourse to mild threats, such as blackmail

[8] Bruce, *The Firm*, 140. [9] Bruce, *The Firm*, 11.

(threatening with criminal prosecution, uncovering a dark episode in someone's history, thwarting professional careers). When this also failed, harsher measures were employed, such as imprisonment or expulsion from the GDR and some others that will be mentioned at greater length later. For now I will just mention that only occasionally did the Stasi order the assassination of opponents, especially after the fifties. The GDR did not want to squander its international reputation by brutally repressing domestic opposition, particularly after East Germany signed the Helsinki Accords in 1975, by which it made a public commitment to protecting basic rights.

Before turning to a more detailed discussion about unofficial collaborators, it should be pointed out that, ironically, despite its vast and far-reaching surveillance system, the Stasi remained ignorant about some of the aspirations and goals of GDR society, and this was due to its own dogmatism. As Glaeser points out, a striking fact about the Stasi's investigative abilities is that it mustered an incredible amount of circumstantial information about society (in his example, East Berlin dissident groups) but failed to grasp their motives and their political agenda, some of which in fact were not entirely inimical to socialism. The reasons why the MfS was unable to "understand" dissidents, despite the amount of surveillance besetting their doors, is that the Stasi was riveted to what Glaeser calls the theory of ever-intensifying class warfare, which predefined the motives of dissidents and was resilient to examination. Glaeser defines part of this theory as follows: "Western secret services aimed to establish subversive agencies within socialist countries. They recruited their helpers among those ideologically unstable individuals who were – due to wanting insight into the laws of history and against their best interest – silly enough to let themselves be seduced into collaboration. [Subversive agencies within socialist countries] were to stylize themselves as internal opposition, aiming to undermine socialism from within by driving a wedge between the basic trust between party and people."[10] Put simply, the Stasi (wrongly) believed it fully

[10] Glaeser, "Power/Knowledge Failure," 19.

understood the motives behind oppositional activities. The question was how to control them effectively.

2.2 THE IM NETWORK

The Stasi knit a seamless web of surveillance and control of daily life in the GDR. IMs were a crucial component of this web. In fact, as a highly ranked public officer put it, they were the "respiratory organs" of the system.[11] This section provides an overview of some characteristics of the IM network, a resource that was not a German invention, but a tradition that emerged in Russia; it is no wonder that in the 1950s, before the German regime coined the bureaucratic euphemism of "unofficial coworker," IMs were simply called "secret informers" or "secret collaborators," which were direct translations of Russian terms. But the German disciple did not simply receive Russia's legacy; it improved on it and refined it. In the following paragraphs I will provide some data about IMs; describe their kinds and functions; as well as the motivations they could have had for becoming involved with the secret police.

I have already mentioned some striking figures regarding IMs in the GDR. Following is a chart describing the number of informers active per year from the Stasi's founding to its dissolution. The numbers describe interesting tendencies. Every time public officials deemed that political circumstances were critical, and therefore closer surveillance of society was called for, an expansion occurred in the IM network. This was the case inter alia in the crisis of 1953, where a strike of construction workers turned into a political uprising against the SED; during the construction of the Wall in 1961; during the détente of East and West Germany in the seventies; or when dissident groups grew stronger in the eighties.

Roughly speaking, by 1989 there was about one IM per 80 to 160 inhabitants in East Germany.[12] Some districts were more rigorously observed than others, as can be seen in the following table.

[11] Quoted in Müller-Enbergs, "Die inoffiziellen Mitarbeiter," 5.

[12] Gieseke, *The History of the Stasi*, 82.

Number of IMs per year

Year	IMs	Year	IMs	Year	IMs	Year	IMs
1950	5,200	1960	95,500	1970	122,400	1980	175,400
1951	13,900	1961	103,500	1971	127,500	1981	176,800
1952	14,400	1962	108,400	1972	136,500	1982	178,700
1953	16,100	1963	103,700	1973	145,500	1983	176,362
1954	27,100	1964	93,100	1974	165,000	1984	174,165
1955	38,200	1965	92,400	1975	200,100	1985	175,374
1956	40,900	1966	95,800	1976	202,700	1986	176,400
1957	52,300	1967	102,600	1977	203,000	1987	172,700
1958	58,000	1968	106,900	1978	194,700	1988	173,081
1959	77,800	1969	112,600	1979	186,700	1989	173,000

Source: Müller-Enbergs, "Die inoffiziellen Mitarbeiter," 36.

Distribution of IMs per inhabitant in Stasi administrative districts as of 1988

District	IMs	Population	Ratio	District	IMs	Inhabitants	Ratio
Cottbus	10,546	884,744	1:84	Gera	5,854	742,023	1:127
Schwerin	6,512	595,176	1:91	Dresden	13,654	1,757,363	1:130
Magdeburg	12,684	1,249,518	1:99	K. Marx. St.	13,599	1,859,525	1:137
Suhl	5,293	549,442	1:104	Erfurt	8,351	1,240,394	1:149
Frankfurt/ O.	6,857	713,764	1:104	Halle	11,063	1,776,458	1:161
Rostock	8,749	916,541	1:105	Leipzig	9,984	1,360,923	1:163
Neubr.	5,310	620,467	1:117	Berlin	7,779	1,284,535	1:165
Potsdam	9,287	1,123,759	1:121				

Source: Müller-Enbergs, "Die inoffiziellen Mitarbeiter," 38

The gender and age breakdown are unsurprising. Most IMs were mature men. In the GDR, only about 10 percent of them were under 25 years old, and 17 percent of informers were women.[13] On this last point, it is interesting to note the reasons why the Stasi preferred to recruit men over women, reflecting patriarchal norms and gender stereotypes that were impervious even to the egalitarian ethics that presumably permeated socialist life. For instance, Stasi directives

[13] Müller-Enbergs, "Die inoffiziellen Mitarbeiter," 39.

clearly state that women were unfit for the job description of an IM, among other reasons because they talked too much and were utterly incapable of keeping secrets. Associated with gendered viewpoints, a further consideration was that their work as informers could raise the suspicion that they were involved in an extramarital affair; after all, informers were supposed to meet regularly with Stasi officials, most of whom were male, and it was not uncommon that this happened late at night at locations such as the house of a regular citizen habilitated for holding these clandestine meetings. Finally, the Stasi deemed that because women already had two professional and domestic shifts, adding an extra one for collaborationist purposes would be overwhelming.[14]

The Stasi's views on, and its use of, its informers evolved over time, depending among other things on the perception that political elites had of external threats (real or imaginary) to the GDR; the growing disenchantment of East German citizenry; or the bureaucratization of the Stasi. These transformations are reflected in the training materials on the recruitment and treatment of IMs, particularly in the so-called Richtlinien (guidelines or directives), five of which the Stasi prepared over its lifetime (1950, 1952, 1958, 1968, and 1979). Among these transformations was the ever-increasing aspiration to plant more and more IMs in every domain of civil society. There was also the sophistication in the work of IMs; throughout the years the job description of each kind of IM gained in specificity; clear norms were written down to regulate the relationship between informer and the Führungsoffizier or a guidance officer (a Stasi full-time employee who presided over his or her actions and had, in fact, recruited the informer). Likewise, rules for recruiting IMs were laid down. Last, in the final stages of the regime, some IMs even began to attend Stasi colleges to be trained, in stark contrast to what had happened earlier, when unofficial coworkers were amateurs.

One additional transformation in the Stasi administrative doctrine of IMs was their growing rhetorical glorification. In 1968, not fortuitously after the Prague Spring, the phrase Inoffizieller Mitarbeiter was

[14] Angela Schmole, "Frauen und MfS," *Deutschland Archive* 29, no. 4 (1996): 512–525.

used for the first time, with a characterization bordering on veneration.[15] Ironically, however, whereas on the one hand informers "were lionized as guarantors of security," they were also on the other hand "admired as prize livestock."[16] Schmeidel aptly captures this objectification of IMs when he writes that Stasi officials "doled out to their agents overlapping assignments to check their product, planned for attrition and mischance, and generally husbanded the IM pool as a renewable source to be passed on to future generations of handlers."[17]

How IMs were recruited is a contentious topic in literature. This point will be particularly relevant for the discussion of the notion of responsibility in Chapter 5. The first question that arises is whether IMs were recruited on a voluntary basis, coerced into collaboration, or motivated by other incentives.[18] The answer is not as simple as one might wish. Of course there are clear examples of each of these cases: devout socialists who believed they were contributing to the consolidation of socialism through denunciation, citizens who were blackmailed into collaboration, or opportunists who were willing to denounce fellow citizens for a few coins, or a vacation trip to Finland. But many cases are hard to adjudicate. Blackmail, for instance, could be, and usually tended to be, very subtle, so subtle that in retrospect reasonable people can disagree about whether or not it would have been easy (or morally obligatory) to resist it. Likewise, distinguishing between convinced socialists and reward-seeking opportunists might prove difficult, as one can do things out of conviction but also expect to be compensated for a job well done. In the beginning, Stasi officers had no qualms about resorting to coercive methods to recruit an IM. At some point, however, it became evident to Stasi officers that coerced collaboration did not always render reliable information, as IMs serving under pressure could drag their feet (e.g., turning sloppy, giving misleading reports to their superior) or were simply unfit for the job. In light of this, the Stasi produced a directive indicating that

[15] Schmeidel, *Shield and Sword of the Party*, 30.
[16] Schmeidel, *Shield and Sword of the Party*, 27.
[17] Schmeidel, *Shield and Sword of the Party*, 26.
[18] Gieseke, *The History of the Stasi*, 89–92.

IMs should be taken on board on a voluntary basis. Despite the fact that, as we just saw, voluntary collaboration was the regime's preference, toward the end of the regime, and perhaps even earlier, it became harder to recruit IMs on a voluntary basis as the regime started to lose its social base, signaling civic dissatisfaction with the regime.[19] At the same time, however, the regime was adamant about increasing the number of informers in society. There was tension between the insistence on recruiting voluntary informers only, and the insistence on recruiting ever more informers, which under the circumstance implied recruiting by means of subtle coercion. Last, mention should be made of the fact that, on recruitment, IMs were asked to sign a letter of commitment and to give themselves an alias.

There were many types of IMs at work.[20] The most salient distinction is between IMs who worked for the very selective foreign secret service agency and those who worked domestically. The former tended to be a selected cadre of well-educated and well-prepared individuals. Put simply, they were professional international spies. In this book I focus on domestic IMs. They usually were not highly trained spies but ordinary people, for example factory workers, students, teachers, writers, or hotel receptionists. These citizens were the eyes, the ears (and sometimes the hands) of the Stasi. They matter the most for the purposes of grappling with the notion of respect in domestic transitional justice settings.

Within the domestic branch, there were many types of unofficial collaborators. As comprehensive surveillance became more sophisticated, the Stasi made efforts, sometimes bordering on the ridiculous, to enrich the number and the quality of categories of IMs. Stasi directives are teeming with ever-growing subcategories labeled with bureaucratic names, but three main types of informers had existed since 1950 and remained in Stasi manuals. These categories were the informer proper, the secret coworker, and the person who provided logistic support.[21] In this book I will use, generically, the terms

[19] Gieseke, *The History of the Stasi*, 85–89.

[20] Schmeidel, *Shield and Sword of the Party*, 33–38.

[21] Müller-Enbergs, "Die inoffiziellen Mitarbeiter," 15–35; Schmeidel, *Shield and Sword of the Party*, 34.

informers, *IMs* or even *collaborators* to refer to all of them, making the appropriate distinctions in due case. Nonetheless, it is worth briefly explaining the functions of each of them, with the caveat that one sort of IM could mutate into another, and that informers themselves did not always know which category they fell into.

In the GDR, the most ubiquitous IMs, comprising 70 to 85 percent of the total, were the informers proper, whose most lasting bureaucratic denomination was Inoffizieller Mitarbeiter-Sicherheit, unofficial coworkers-security. Their job was to "infiltrate" and "safeguard" certain areas of society. This meant "securing" important institutions, evaluating suspicious citizens, and hindering attempts to escape from the GDR. They also had to familiarize themselves with the sentiments and opinions of the citizenry in general. In the early days, they were supposed to conduct investigations on their own. Later, however, their job was limited to writing reports of their observations to their guidance officer. The guidance officer used Inoffizieller Mitarbeiter-Sicherheit to obtain information while at the same time making sure that his real interest remained unknown to unofficial collaborators of this kind. In the eyes of the Stasi, the latter were deemed to be suitable for no more than this extremely simple kind of work. They were often colleagues, friends, relatives, or even the spouses of the target, if there was a specific individual target.

Next come IMs who provided logistic support. They were in charge of the conspiratorial infrastructure. For example, they could offer their houses to the Stasi so that conspiratorial meetings could take place between guidance officers and their informers. In return they could receive a small monetary compensation. As a further example, an IM-Expert was an enabler – a doctor who prescribed vacations to a patient, in order to clear the way for the Stasi to wire his apartment, or a personnel administrator who gave access to the company files. They often knew enough about the details of the case.[22]

Finally, some IMs were in charge of confronting most directly the foes of the regime: IM-Blickfeld, more cumbersomely referred to as

[22] Müller-Enbergs, "Die inoffiziellen Mitarbeiter," 26–31; Schmeidel, *Shield and Sword of the Party*, 34.

Inoffiziellen Mitarbeiter mit Feindberührung, or IM in contact with the enemy. Only 3 percent of all IMs belonged to this category. They would be intelligent, highly trained veterans with a background and education similar to those of the "enemy" of the GDR. They were assigned the task of infiltrating "subversive groups," carrying out investigations, producing evidence to be used later to prosecute and imprison individuals, and participating in operations to intimidate individuals or disintegrate dissident activities. In short, they were the most invested and participative of all IMs. They knew about the operations in which they were involved because the guidance officers had confidence in their abilities and their commitment and because the nature of their operatives was such that decisions had to be made in situ.[23] In general the other kinds of IMs had limited discretion, but this kind was encouraged to become participants instead of mere order takers and to go beyond passive reporting into taking preemptive action against so-called enemies of the state.

Let me now say something about the specific actions that the Stasi enforced with the help of IMs.[24]

The Stasi itself classified its activities in the domestic front into three kinds. In ascending order of urgency and costs, they were the following. The first level of investigation was the security check. Inquiries were made into almost anyone who applied for a qualified job, into people living in sensitive places (e.g., the border), and into East Germans living, or receiving visits from, abroad. Scrutiny of public figures was particularly important, as their defections were a public embarrassment for the regime. Security checks did not always involve IMs. Matters were different at the next two tiers of investigation – the Operational Personal Check (Operative Personenkontrolle) and the more involved Operational Case (Operativer Vorgang). Operational Personal Checks were proactive measures against a person or group that had raised suspicion in the eyes of the Stasi. House searches or mail surveillance were the standard procedures. IMs could be deployed here, with the mandate to have the target incriminate him or herself. Things could end there or progress on to

[23] Müller-Enbergs, "Die inoffiziellen Mitarbeiter," 32–35; Schmeidel, 35.

[24] Schmeidel, *Shield and Sword of the Party*, 41–47.

the next level. The Operational Personal Check could result in the targeted individual's career being stalemated. He could be the subject of civil or criminal charges, and this was good ammunition for putting pressure on him or her (usually him) to serve as an IM. In the Stasi's internal usage, the word for blackmail evolved from the bureaucratic "use of compromising materials" in the 1950s to euphemisms such as the awakening of "positive conscience" or "positive convictions," and to acts of "justified repentance" for past misdeeds.[25] The highest level for a Stasi operation was the Operational Case. In contrast to the other two, it knew no budgetary and no manpower constraints. It required the deployment of IMs, usually more than one. If no IM was already associated with the targeted individual, one was "inserted" into the individual's environment. The purpose of the Operational Case was to pull the dissident back into line. Ideally this could be done through mild pressure. When this failed, as was often the case with dissidents associated with churches or artistic and intellectual groups, there was no hesitation in using harsher methods. This is when the Stasi's ruthlessness was unleashed in full force. This did not mean, as might have been the case in other countries in the communist bloc, planning for the assassination of regime opponents (although the SED regime did imprison and torture prisoners).[26] Such a measure would have been the exception rather than the rule. Instead of brute force, the Stasi employed more incisive methods of control, such as the so-called *Zersetzung* (disruption), a psychological method to disrupt the life of an individual or a group. *Zersetzung* was a toolkit for harassment. It made the life of an individual intolerable through "soft" psychological terror. The repertoire included anonymous letters, constant phone calls in the middle of the night, cutting off electricity or water, destroying reputations by spreading false rumors, sabotaging professional careers, and even arranging for an attractive

[25] Schmeidel, *Shield and Sword of the Party*, 43.

[26] In this regard, other secret police bodies in the region seemed to be more brutal than the Stasi. For instance, Bulgaria's secret police, the Committee for State Security, became famous for killing prominent Bulgarian intellectuals living in the West. See Momchil Metodiev, "Bulgaria," in Lavinia Stan, *Transitional Justice in Eastern Europe*, 159.

IM to seduce the target or his or her partner.[27] Individuals or families not connected to a larger group, for instance a church, were the easiest targets.

The Stasi also sought to disrupt entire groups. It had managed to place at least one IM inside every important dissident movement, and it instructed its IMs to sow discord within them, for example, by sabotaging discussions with theoretical subtleties. Matters were arranged so that loyal members were suspected of Stasi collaboration; thus, they were set up so that they appeared to be having clandestine meetings, or their bank accounts were showered with money.

2.3 THE TRIALS AND ERRORS OF *VERGANGENHEITSBEWÄLTIGUNG*

How did unified Germany come to terms with the legacy of its communist past, a very small portion of which was described earlier? Before dealing with the "second" *Vergangenheitsbewältigung*, a word about the first one is in order, in particular because the Nazi-*Aufarbeitung* precedent has, on many occasions, influenced the tenor and the thematic axes of public discussion on Stasi-*Aufarbeitung*. Many critics have found both processes – denazification and decommunization – wanting, especially the former. In a sense, both have been processes of trial and error because they have muddled through conflicting and oftentimes irreconcilable demands and interests and improvised along the way to achieving the best possible outcome. That said, in both cases the results have been very few court trails and too many errors, according to many scholars and political actors, who have gone as far as to say that transitional justice in Germany has been a miscarriage of justice.

In the opinion of numerous critics, Nazi-*Vergangenheitsbewältigung* left an immense deficit and reflected the failure of German private

[27] Hubertus Knabe, "Zersetzungmaßnahmen," in Karsten Dümmel and Christian Schmitz, eds., *Was war die Stasi? Einblicke in das Ministerium für Staatssicherheit der DDR (MfS)* (Konrad Adenauer Stiftung: Sankt August, 2002), 26–27.

citizens and the two German states to assume responsibility for the Final Solution. An early proponent of this view was Hannah Arendt. She criticized the inability of Germans to grapple with the consequences of the war, their "deep-rooted, stubborn, and at times brutal refusal to face what really happened." Arendt further argued that such an escape from reality is also an "escape from responsibility." The average citizen in Germany, she added with sarcasm, "looks for the causes of the lost war not in the acts of the Nazi regime, but in the events that led to the expulsion of Adam and Eve from paradise," and she criticizes the bad habit of Western Europeans, especially Germans, of blaming their misfortunes on some force out of their reach.[28] Arendt also railed against those who blame "all deeds or events on historical trends and dialectical movements" and who hold "a deep-seated [...] fear of passing judgment, of naming names, and of fixing names."[29]

After the fall of the wall in 1989, the precedent of the responsibility deficit of Nazi-*Aufarbeitung* was invoked to persuade those who were reluctant to carry out an immediate and comprehensive collective scrutiny of the communist past. For political activists looking to unveil the Stasi past in reunified Germany, Nazi-*Aufarbeitung,* with its compound of amnesia and amnesty, was a road not to be taken again. In view of the importance of the assessment of the progress of Nazi-*Aufarbeitung* for the trajectory of Stasi-*Aufarbeitung*, let me offer a swift overview of some of the features that inform the belief that the first *Aufarbeitung* offered insufficient mechanisms to deal with the Nazi past.

In East Germany, Nazi-*Vergangenheitsbewältigung* was the victim of one of the communist regime's foundational myths and of its ideological commitments. Even though the GDR did not actually exist in the Third Reich, East German public officials portrayed the regime as the inheritor of the victims of Nazism. The Reich's persecution of communists was "claimed" for itself, as it were, by the communist regime. Part of the legitimacy of the GDR, in fact, rested

[28] The quotes come from Hannah Arendt, "The Aftermath of Nazi Rule. Report from Germany," *Commentary* 10, no. 4 (1950): 342.

[29] Hannah Arendt, "Personal Responsibility Under Dictatorship," 2003, 21.

on its previous Nazi "occupation." By virtue of this official doctrine of covictimhood, the East German government saw itself relieved of any responsibility for the annihilation of Jews or, for that matter, any of the crimes committed by Nazis. Moreover, Marxist ideology was projected onto the past to simplify German history. Pinning blame on "fascist" and "capitalist" forces absolved the majority of the population from confronting its complicity. Although the GDR claimed the German past for its own progressive and socialist tradition, the twelve years of the Nazi regime "were reduced in antifascist rhetoric to 'state monopoly capitalism' and dissociated from the GDR."[30]

This government's conception with regard to the Holocaust was radically transformed only after the fall of the wall. Early in 1990, speaking on behalf of the newly reorganized East German government, its prime minister announced the latter's recognition of "the responsibility of the entire German people for the past" and its readiness to offer material compensation to those who had been persecuted. Shortly afterward, the first democratically elected East German Parliament offered an unprecedented statement: "We ask the Jews of the world to forgive us. We ask the people of Israel to forgive us for the hypocrisy and hostility of official East German policies toward Israel and for the persecution and degradation of Jewish citizens also after 1945 in our country."[31]

The West German process of coming to terms with the past was, according to numerous scholars, as lacking as the East German one, a fact that was attributed to factors as diverse as the Cold War in the international context or the persistent anti-Semitism within the nation. According to Norbert Frei, West German Nazi-*Aufarbeitung* went through four stages.[32] The first stage, a phase of *politischen Säuberung* or political cleansing, as he calls it, lasted from 1945 to

[30] Jeffrey Peck, "East Germany," in David Wyman (ed.), *The World Reacts to the Holocaust* (Baltimore: Johns Hopkins University Press, 1996), 452.

[31] Both statements quoted by Peck, "East Germany," 1996, 447.

[32] Norbert Frei, "From Policy to Memory: How the Federal Republic of Germany Dealt with the Nazi Legacy," in Jerzy Borejsza and Klaus Ziemer (eds.), *Totalitarian and Authoritarian Regimes in Europe. Legacies and Lessons from the Twentieth Century* (New York: Berghahn Books, 2006), 481–489.

1949. This period was defined by the inability of Allies and new German authorities to fully disavow Nazi ideology and anti-Semitic views. During this stage, surviving victims of the Holocaust began to be gradually reabsorbed into society, although many still endured precarious conditions and were not compensated in monetary terms. The second period, called *Vergangenheitspolitik* or Politics of the Past, started with the founding of the Federal Republic and took full swing under the aegis of Chancellor Konrad Adenauer; it extended throughout the 1950s. This period was characterized by important, though insufficient, attempts to both reckon with and draw a line under the Nazi past. According to Frei, these policies show the tendency of Germans to downplay the unjust character of the Nazi regime in the collective consciousness. The third period (the 1960s and most of the 1970s), which Frei calls *Vergangenheitsbewältigung* (Overcoming the Past) proper, is defined by the emerging sense of an unresolved past and the public demand for a more critical analysis of the Nazi legacy. Finally, Frei calls the fourth stage, which began in the late 1970s and continues into the present, *Vergangenheitsbewahrung* (Preserving of the Past). This process has been one of maintaining the efforts started in the previous stage.

The measures adopted in the second and third stages of Frei's chronology are particularly revealing of the way in which postwar German authorities and civil society failed to take full responsibility for Nazi crimes. The general sense of their results is one of disillusionment. Many voices in public opinion agree that Nazi-*Aufarbeitung* advanced with considerable delay and without an appropriate degree of thoroughness. In aspects as diverse as the purge of Nazi officials from the new government, the financial compensation for Jews (*Wiedergutmachung*), and the treatment of the Holocaust by artists and historians, the notion of deficit sums up the state of progress of Nazi *Aufarbeitung.*[33]

[33] To say that the literature on Nazi *Vergangenheitsbewältigung* is extensive is an understatement. This section is based on a limited number of sources that have summarized such literature. Andrei Markovits and Beth Simone Noveck, "West Germany," in Wyman (ed.), *The World Reacts to the Holocaust*; and Jeffrey Peck, "East Germany." For a succinct characterization of the changing

For instance, according to Andrei Markovits and Beth Simone Noveck, the denazification policies of the 1950s in West Germany were poorly designed and enforced. The Trials of Nuremberg, to mention the most important legal process against Nazi perpetrators, were highly selective and had a very restrictive scope, as they sentenced only upper-level officials. Moreover, denazification efforts at the regional level were futile because they relied on voluntary action: A system was put in place so that Nazis would confess to their crimes of their own accord, which they almost never did. Furthermore, denazification in West Germany did not contribute to the creation of local structures for rendering justice, as most trials against Nazi criminals were administered by the Allies in what was perceived by many citizens as an external imposition of justice. There were no instances of German citizens' turning against fellow citizens for their involvement in the Nazi regime. Instead of achieving some measure of success in the "cleansing of Nazis from public life," denazification "guaranteed the alleviation of any collective or individual responsibility via the efficient legal reintegration."[34] In West Germany, in fact, denazification was quite unpopular, a trend that persisted in the years to come. Thus, opinion polls consistently showed that the Auschwitz trials, held between 1963 and 1968, were widely regarded as an unnecessary witch hunt. From the point of view of those directly responsible for the commission of crimes, the notion of *Befehlsnotstand* ("just following orders") emerged as quite a popular defense strategy to eschew individual moral and political responsibility.[35]

approaches to the legacy of the past see Norbert Frei, *Adenauer's Germany and the Nazi Past: The Politics of Amnesty and Integration*, trans. Joel Golb (New York: Columbia University Press, 2002). [The German Version is *Vergangenheitspolitik. Die Anfänge der Bundesrepublik und die NS-Vergangenheit* (Beck: München, 1996)]. On the very distinct approaches to dealing with the Nazi past of Konrad Adenhauer, Kurt Schumacher, and Theodor Heuss, see also Jeffrey Herf, "The Emergence and Legacies of Divided Memory," in Jan-Werner Müller (ed.), *Memory and Power in Post-War Europe. Studies in the Presence of the Past* (Cambridge: Cambridge University Press, 2002), 184–205.

34 Markovits and Noveck, "West Germany," 405.

35 Markovits and Noveck, "West Germany," 423.

Other legal measures were as ineffective in helping post–Nazi Germany come to terms with the legacy of the Third Reich as denazification was. Amnesty laws were granted during the second stage. They exempted Nazi officials and SS members from legal prosecution, or in the case of the so-called 131er law, they enabled the reintegration of a substantial number of previously displaced civil servants, as well as compensation for former professional soldiers who lost their jobs in 1945. Many convicted war criminals were released under the auspices of these laws.

One of the most important pieces of Konrad Adenhauer's *Vergangenheitspolitik* was his policy of monetary reparation for victims of the Holocaust, for which Israel became West Germany's foremost interlocutor. Adenauer's *Wiedergutmachung* took the timid reparation measures implemented by the Allies shortly after the war to a higher level. *Wiedergutmachung* was preceded by Adenauer's attempt to address Israel's complaint that Germany had failed to denounce Hitler's war against Jews. As Adenauer put it:

> The Federal Government and with it the great majority of the German people are aware of the immeasurable suffering that was brought upon the Jews in Germany and the occupied territories during the time of National Socialism [. . .] Unspeakable crimes had been committed in the name of the German people, calling for moral and material indemnity [. . .] The Federal Government is prepared, jointly with representatives of Jewry and the State of Israel [. . .] to bring about a solution of the material indemnity problem, thus easing the way to the spiritual settlement of infinite suffering.[36]

These lines suggest that *Wiedergutmachung* was partly driven by moral considerations, but its timing and its addressee suggest that it was also an attempt to restore West Germany's legitimacy within the international community. The administration, in turn, considered that a good relationship with Israel was a crucial step in this direction. For this reason, monetary compensation was a mechanism to circumvent confrontation with the past rather than a way to engage with it.

[36] Markovits and Noveck, "West Germany," 407.

It entailed recognizing German responsibility on an instrumental level, but it did not represent an act of collective contrition.[37]

The absence of public policies focused on raising awareness of the Final Solution also reflects the poverty of Nazi-*Vergangenheitsbewältigung.* The treatment of the Holocaust in history books and its mandatory incorporation into the curricula of West German schools at all levels happened only in 1961. Even then, the subject did not receive uniform treatment in German schools. Holocaust education was treated more thoroughly in the elite gymnasia than in the less academically oriented *Hauptschulen* (lower secondary schools).

German writers and artists did not make up for these deficiencies in confronting the magnitude of the Holocaust, as is illustrated by the fact that even those writers who did cover the Nazi past and display a philo-Semitic attitude, "omitted the specific plight of the Jews, thus rendering their accounts of Nazi brutality *judenrein.*"[38] Neither public authorities nor civil society initiated a process of responsibility-taking through cultural or educational initiatives. There were, of course, remarkable exceptions. One of the greatest influences on the intellectual debate around the *Aufarbeitung* of the Nazi past is Karl Jaspers's 1946 *Die Schuldfrage* (*The Question of German Guilt*). The book exerted substantial influence on the discourse of German responsibility.

The Cold War created the political climate that mostly accounts for the poverty of Nazi-*Aufarbeitung.* In West Germany, for instance, the United States and its European Allies encouraged a premature abandonment of denazification. Allied powers were pressed to establish the Bundesrepublik (West Germany) as an ally and a counterpoising force to East Germany, and the Soviet bloc more generally. The sooner the remembrance of the *Shoa* was left behind, the better.

Several decades had elapsed before one single event – the broadcasting on public television, with record viewings, of the American film *Holocaust* in 1979 – managed to raise awareness about the magnitude of the Final Solution among the West German public. Among its concrete effects, *Holocaust* changed social perceptions about the

[37] Markovits and Noveck, "West Germany," 410.
[38] Markovits and Noveck, "West Germany," 406.

desirability of Nazi trials. For instance, an unusual display of public outrage followed the acquittal of several of the defendants in the Majdanek trials (1975–1981), one of the country's last trials of Nazi camp guards. Furthermore, prior to *Holocaust*, the Bundestag, the German Parliament, had succeeded in extending the term of permissible prosecution of war criminals only amid controversy. After *Holocaust*, the Bundestag succeeded in abolishing the statute of limitations altogether.

The belief that German government and society did not confront the Nazi past appropriately has become an incentive and a justification for actors in political and civil society in reunified Germany to confront the communist past in a thorough, sometimes painstaking, manner, especially with regard to the Stasi and its informers.[39] Obviously the difference in nature and modality of operation of the two "dictatorships" would warrant a different kind of confrontation with the past for each case. The nature and the acts of the Nazi and Communist regimes are different on a number of fronts. The Communist regime, as one critic put it, did not produce as many corpses as did the Nazis. At the same time, the latter lasted about twelve years, whereas the former was in place for decades. The Nazi regime collapsed purely as a result of external interventions, whereas in the communist case endogenous political change was critical. Furthermore, Nazism was regarded as a domestic phenomenon, whereas communism came to be regarded as a foreign "product," for which the blame could always be assigned to the Soviet Union.[40] Despite all the differences, the Nazi-*Aufarbeitung* deficit has a symbolic weight whose imprint in Stasi-*Aufarbeitung* is beyond question. Let us now turn to the latter. The following paragraphs will give an overview of some of

[39] Andrew Beattie, *Playing Politics with History: The Bundestag Inquiries into East Germany* (New York: Berghahn, 2008), 2.

[40] Eckhard Jesse, "'Entnazifizierung' und 'Entstasifizierung' als politisches Problem. Die doppelte Vergangenheitsbewältigung," in Jesse, Diktaturen in Deutschland. Diagnosen und Analysen (Baden-Baden: Nomos, 2008), 297–311; Rainer Eckert, "'Entnazifizierung' und 'Entstasifizierung,'" in Eckhard Jesse and Steffan Kailitz (eds.), *Prägekräfte des 20. Jahrhundertes. Demokratie, Extremismus, Totalitarismus* (Baden-Baden: Nomos, 1997), 305–325.

the transitional justice measures that were implemented in unified Germany, including criminal prosecutions, lustration, file access, the formation of a truth commission, and compensation.

That the denazification experience had an impact on the perception of many political actors about how to address the legacy of communism is reflected in the response that Foreign Minister Klaus Kinkel gave to a number of journalist and politicians who pleaded for a general amnesty for GDR leaders. In a speech before the parliament in 2000, Kinkel said,

> Violence and vengeance are incompatible with the law in any case. At the same time, we cannot tolerate that the problems are swept under the rug as a way of dealing with a horrible past, because the results will later be disastrous for society. We Germans know from our own experience where this leads. Jewish philosophy formulates it in this way: "The secret of redemption is called remembering."[41]

Many critics of Stasi-*Vergangenheitsbewältigung* complain that the process did not live up to the spirit of those words. For example, focusing on the issue of legal punishment for perpetrators of the SED regime, Bärbel Bohley, a civil rights activist, famously said that, paraphrasing her, after reunification East Germans wanted justice but got the rule of law instead.[42] This statement reflects the frustration of many political and social actors, who expected to see high-ranking SED and Stasi officers prosecuted and behind bars. The expectations were not fulfilled. Erich Honecker, the SED's general secretary, escaped to the Soviet Union, but when that country collapsed, he returned to Germany, where he was arrested. Shortly afterward he was diagnosed with liver cancer, and for this reasons a court decided not to put him through a trial. He went into exile in Chile, where he died in 1994. Egon Kreuze, who succeeded Honecker as general secretary, was sentenced to six and a half years in prison, of which he served only

[41] Quoted by John Koehler, *Stasi: The Untold Story of the East German Secret Police* (New York: Basic Book, 1999), 14.

[42] Bärbel Bohley, "Wir wollten Gerechtigkeit und bekamen den Rechtstaat. Bilanz zwölf Jahre danach," in *Recht und Gerechtigkeit XIII. Bautzen-Forum der Friedrich-Ebert-Stiftung*, Leipzig, 2002, 29.

four years, spending the rest of his sentence on parole. Beyond these cases, three other Politburo members were convicted. A number of border guards who had shot several people trying to escape from East Germany were also convicted, in the famous *Mauerschützenprozesse*, or border guard trials. But most of the accused were either left free or given suspended sentences of between six months and two years; in a few cases, some of the leaders of the border troops received more severe sentences.[43]

As to the Stasi, Erich Mielke, its head, was tried, found guilty, and sentenced to six years for the murder of two police officers. Other charges were dismissed because of his advanced age and failing health. He served less than three of the six years and was 88 when he left prison. By the year 2000, the year in which he died, only thirty-three sentences for full-time Stasi officers had been issued. Twenty-eight of them were suspended, and four of them were settled financially. Only one officer of the Stasi was imprisoned, sentenced to ten years in jail. Intoxicated with alcohol, he had shot two people dead.[44] As for IMs, most did not face criminal prosecution, as in the vast majority of the cases they did not commit crimes in the strict sense of the word. An exception was Peter Haack (IM "Alfons"), who was sentenced to six and a half years in prison. In the context of "Operation Scorpion," and at the behest of Stasi officers, he tried to murder Wolfgang Welsch, a GDR dissident who had helped about 200 people escape to the West.[45]

With this information alone, the accomplishments of Stasi-*Vergangenheitsbewältigung* are far from impressive and would thus seem to confirm the dissatisfaction of critics like Bohley. The criticisms might be unfair, however. For one thing, meting out punishment on perpetrators of egregious crimes or high-ranking leaders is not the only criteria for evaluating transitional justice measures. For another, when compared to other transitional justice efforts in other postcommunist nations, the German attempts stand out. To gauge

[43] Hansgeorg Bräutigam, "Die Toten an der Berliner Mauer und an der innerdeutschen Grenze und die bundesdeutsches Justiz. Versuch einer Bilanz," *Deutschland Archive* 6 (2004): 969–976.

[44] Koehler, "Stasi," 2. [45] Koehler, "Stasi," 12.

the success of transitional justice measures in the region, three indicators are typically considered in scholarly literature: screening and lustration policies, prosecution of communist officials and secret police members, and degree of public access to the archives of the secret police. Lavinia Stan, who has provided the most comprehensive analysis of Eastern European transitional justice, uses this tripartite framework to appraise the situation in the region. She argues that on the continuum stretching from no transitional justice to vigorous transitional justice, Germany falls within the latter category. It is in fact the first place on the scale because it employed all three methods at the beginning of the postcommunist period. The Czech Republic comes second because although it implemented early radical lustration, by which a wide category of representatives of the *ancien régime* were removed from office, it provided delayed access to secret archives, and court proceeding there were not robust enough. After the Czech Republic come, some of the former Soviet Republics (Estonia, Latvia, and Lithuania), which supported lustration through citizenship, electoral, and screening laws; gave access to a rather parse archive of secret intelligence documents; and most notably, pursued former agents who had been involved in massive deportations during the 1940s. Next come Poland, Hungary, and Romania. On the other end of the spectrum come those nations that have not been interested in confronting their past through lustration, file access, or trials: Albania, Slovakia, the former Yugoslav republic of Slovenia, Russia, Belarus, Ukraine, Moldova, Armenia, Azerbaijan, Georgia, and other Central Asian countries. In sum, German *Vergangenheitsbewältigung* excels if compared to the reckoning with the past of other nations.[46]

File access, on the one hand, and screening and lustration, on the other, are the most relevant transitional justice measures for the purposes of this book, as they provide the basis for publicly

[46] Lavinia Stan, "Conclusion: Explaining Country Differences," in Stan (ed.), *Transitional Justice in Eastern Europe*, 249–270. For a varied pallet of the screening processes undertaken by several transitional regimes in the last two decades, see also Kaminski and Nalepa, "Judging Transitional Justice: A New Criterion For Evaluating Truth Revelation Procedures," *Journal of Conflict Resolution* 50, no. 3 (2006): 383–408.

identifying IMs. I shall therefore add a few additional remarks about these measures.[47] Providing an overview of the screening process in Germany (Stasi-*Überprüfung*) is extremely hard because it was carried out in an extremely decentralized fashion and because of the fragmentation of the institutions that discharged the task. Screening in Germany took place along two tracks. The first track comprises elected representatives on the local, state, and federal level. Because members of Parliament cannot be impeached or recalled for prior noncriminal misconduct, vetting parliamentarians and subsequently exposing them could produce little beyond public outcry, although as will be seen in Chapter 7, sometimes public indignation could exert pressure on "tainted" politicians to resign. The second track involved the public sector, for example a city administration, a court, a state government, or a public university, among others. Because I will have more to say about the first track in Chapter 7, the following paragraphs focus on the second track.

Screening for Stasi involvement was formalized in the Unification Treaty of 1990, although there was some ambiguity about what constitutes such involvement. Despite the decentralized nature of the process, vetting procedures across Germany roughly followed a similar pattern. A public-sector employer usually required employees to complete questionnaires about his/her political service under the GDR and, most important, about the contacts he/she had with the secret police, if any. A commission set up specifically for that purpose examined the questionnaires, as well as consulting other sources. If there was no evidence of past misconduct, the commission recommended continued employment. By contrast, if the evidence suggested the opposite, employees were offered an individual hearing to respond to the allegations (although many of the affected employees deny that their hearings were fair). Based on this further evidence, the commission made a final decision.

There was a wide variation across vetting commissions in Germany. They varied on a number of scores, such as their independence from the institutions they screened and the legitimacy they commanded, as

[47] An excellent account on file access and vetting in Germany is Wilke, "The Shield, the Sword, and the Party."

in some cases their membership was made up of members of the institution to be screened, whereas in other cases commissioners had a diverse membership, including some members who were appointed by state parliaments). They also varied in their ability and willingness to undertake comprehensive examination of the files of the SED, trade unions, and particularly those of the Stasi, instead of relying solely on self-reporting, not a trustworthy vetting mechanism.

The disparity among commissions was ammunition for those who objected to screenings. They argued that this disparity produced morally arbitrary results, and they pointed toward other flaws in the process; for example, that it lacked solid evidentiary basis; that different standards of guilt and innocence were applied from one case to the next; that different states and public agencies throughout Germany reacted differently to similar findings; and finally, especially at the beginning of the process, that the overriding concern seemed to be to find "Stasi-positive" individuals regardless of mitigating circumstances or special consideration.[48] In the emotionally charged political climate, these features of the process combined with the (false) perception among its opponents that it was as an imposition of former West Germany on East Germans and with the (accurate) perception of the ambiguity not only of the Unification Treaty but also of the Stasi Records Law about what Stasi involvement means.[49] The result was a highly contested process.

One of the points mentioned before about the examination of files bears particular relevance for this book. By far the most heavily consulted source for screenings was the archives of the MfS. It should be recalled that crowds stormed the Stasi's offices in most capitals of the nation to secure their wealth of information as citizens learned that compromising files were being destroyed. Toward the end of the regime and even earlier, the Stasi had become the most unpopular government agency. In occupying MfS headquarters, citizens were

[48] Wilke, "The Shield, the Sword, and the Party," 359, 361.

[49] A. James McAdams, *Judging the Past in Unified Germany* (Cambridge: Cambridge University Press, 2001), 73–4, 5. For an interesting criticism of screenings, see Bernhard Schlink, *Vergangenheitsschuld* (Frankfurt am Main: Suhrkamp, 2002), 61–88.

claiming "their" files. Later, after the Wall fell, and not without intense debates, public authorities entrusted the management of the files to the agency that later became the Stasi Records Office, the BStU. Without exaggeration, the agency was the institutionalization of the social movement described earlier. Thus, because its files were among the best preserved and because its authorities and bureaucrats were extremely diligent and insistent on the goal of screening (for reasons that will be touched on in later chapters), the Stasi archives turned out to be *the* source of knowledge for determining "suitability" (*Zumutbarkeit*) for public service in unified Germany. This had a remarkable impact on public debates about the legacy of the GDR in general and about IMs in particular. As Christiane Wilke points out, "public discussions about culpability, collaboration, and suitability for public office narrowed down to the question of whether someone had been an 'IM' [. . .] or not."[50] Furthermore, "What started as an early focus on the breaches of trust committed by the Stasi was soon cemented into a vetting priority through the differential treatment of the [Stasi] files in federal law."[51] As will be argued at greater length in Chapter 5, this disproportionate emphasis on IMs introduced a responsibility deficit in discussion about complicity for wrongdoing during the GDR. It is hard to establish how many people left their jobs due to screenings. What is clear, though, is that the search for IMs dominated the process.[52]

I shall now turn to one of the most important institutions in the transitional justice landscape – the truth commission. In Germany, the Federal Parliament, the Bundestag, established two Commissions of Inquiry (Enquete-Kommissionen), appointed to confront the communist past of East Germany. The first one ("Working through the History and Consequences of the SED Dictatorship in Germany") began in 1992 and lasted two years.[53] The second one ("Overcoming the Consequences of the SED dictatorship in the Process of German

[50] Wilke, "The Shield, the Sword, and the Party," 356.

[51] Wilke, "The Shield, the Sword, and the Party," 367.

[52] The Stasi Records Office had an estimate of 42,046 affected individuals as of 1997, according to McAdams, *Judging the Past*, 73.

[53] The final report is available at http://dipbt.bundestag.de/dip21/btd/12/078/1207820.pdf

Unification") was at work between 1995 and 1998.[54] Although the commissions had little direct impact on policies in addressing the communist past, they accomplished several important achievements. For example, heated discussion revolved around the question of whether the GDR had political legitimacy, which, with the exception of the PSD (the immediate successor of the SED), all parties denied. Thus, the commissions played a crucial role in the "posthumous delegitimization of the GDR,"[55] which was unequivocally designated as a dictatorship. The commissions also pursued a critical and systematic examination of the GDR; they addressed questions about German identity after unification, and they even served as a forum for debating the future of socialism. All of this does not mean that the commissions were not free of problems. They were deeply divided on partisan grounds and immersed in ideological feuds. Western conservatives, for instance, sought to discredit communists and communist ideology in general during the debates of the commissions. Postunification confrontation of the East German communist past in the commissions was not only about justice, truth, reconciliation, and so on, but also about power and ideology.

The South African Truth and Reconciliation Commission usually springs to mind when discussing the importance of truth commissions in transitional justice contexts. But the German Commission was very different from the South African body. As a commentator put it, the former was less a therapeutic commission than it was a scholarly one. Its central concern was to encourage research on the past and to evaluate the GDR on moral grounds. In contrast to what happened in South Africa, where sessions of the commission were televised and followed by a large audience, the Enquete-Kommissionen were held behind closed doors. Furthermore, whereas the latter was presided over mostly by politicians, historians, and political scientists, in the case of South Africa, victims and perpetrators had a central role. Finally, whereas the Truth and Reconciliation Commission put emphasis on individual healing and on establishing a narrative of past

[54] The final report is available at http://dip21.bundestag.de/dip21/btd/13/110/1311000.pdf

[55] Beattie, *Playing Politics with History*, 11.

events from the perspective of the individuals involved, the Inquiry Commission was more concerned about writing history from a more abstract, objective, "scientific" point of view.[56]

Let me conclude this section with the theme of victim compensation. Academic literature on transitional justice in Germany and in some other regions has predominantly focused on truth commissions, or on issues of retributive justice, that is, on how to deal with perpetrators. On this last point, for example, consider the three criteria for evaluating transitional justice efforts, mentioned before. Prosecution of communist officials and high-ranking secret police members is explicitly about meting out retribution; screening and lustration policies are also partly about retribution, although their purpose is supposed to be the restoration of confidence in public services. Finally, public access to the archives of the secret police has an indirect retributive side, although its main justification is promoting historical clarification and fulfilling victims' right to truth. In contrast, considerably less attention has been paid to the compensatory dimension of transitional justice, at least in the German case.

The Unification Treaty contained the vague notion of "appropriate" compensation to victims of the SED regime. However, as early as 1991, many political actors were skeptical about the possibility of compensating victims. One of them warned that besides the fact that it would be impossible in principle "to make good" the suffering of victims, extensive compensation would be too onerous for a country facing the challenge of unification.[57] Despite this skepticism, both the

[56] On the contrast between the German and the South African Commissions see Kora Andrieu, *La justice transitionnelle. De l'Afrique du Sud au Rwanda* (Paris: Gallimard, 2012), 214–224.

[57] In his words: "We have to openly admit: real making good cannot be achieved for the victims. It is in the nature of the matter that only a limited amount of help can be given.... Suffering cannot be undone." These are Klaus Kinkel's words, who, as we saw before, years later would be a critic of amnesty. The firm defender of prosecution had been years earlier a rather lukewarm advocate of compensation for victims. Quoted by David Clarke, "Compensating the Victims of Human Rights Abuses in the German Democratic Republic: The Struggle for Recognition," *German Politics* 21, no. 1 (2012): 20.

first democratic government of the GDR and all the governments of unified Germany have enacted legislation to compensate the victims of the GDR. According to David Clarke, the culmination of this process came with the passing of the third version of the SED-*Unrechtsbereinigungsgesetz,* or the Law for the Cleaning Away of SED Injustice, which itself consists of three laws. First, a criminal rehabilitation law offers financial support to former political prisoners of the GDR, providing a lump-sum payment based on the period of time for which they were imprisoned. Second, a career habilitation law offers welfare benefits to those whose professional careers were damaged as a consequence of political persecution, particularly in terms of calibrating how this damaged their pensions. It also provides educational funding for those still young enough to study and who would benefit from furthering their education. Third, the administrative rehabilitation law compensates those whom the state and their agencies affected through politically motivated decisions; among the beneficiaries are those forced to leave the border zone during the 1950s.[58]

Despite its virtues, the compensation scheme has at least one major flaw. As Clarke suggests, it is framed as a *welfare* measure, rather than as an *honorary* pension; it therefore withholds true recognition for victims. This has led some organizations of victims to reject it as mere "alms." In other words, victims struggled for an explicit recognition of their suffering through compensation that is understood as such. Instead they were given charity. This has been the result of the political parties taking their desire for recognition and turning it into a party–political issue. As can be seen, just as in the case of the Inquiry Commissions, the issue of compensation did not escape electoral and ideological dynamics. As David Clarke argues, this poses a problem that is relevant not only to Germany but also to other nations immersed in transitional justice scenarios. In his words, "despite the increasing frequency of calls in democratic societies for financial compensation for past political injustice, and despite the apparent moral force of such demands, the ability of victims and their

[58] Clark, "Compensating the Victims," 19.

representatives to achieve their goal of recognition will be contingent to a large extent on the strategic concerns of political parties."[59] It should be mentioned, however, that despite this criticism, and by comparison to what other nations in the region have accomplished for victims of state repression, compensatory efforts for the victims of the communist regime in Germany are remarkable.

[59] Clarke, "Compensating the Victims," 31. Although this book focuses on the retributive dimension and IMs, it should be noted that Clarke's analysis is germane to mine. Clarke argues that by being treated as welfare recipients, victims of the GDR (and the same could be true for those of Nazi Germany) were not treated with respect. They were regarded as passive beings entitled to certain benefits, but not as agents with equal standing whose suffering should be acknowledged.

3 THE CASE(S) OF THE LITIGATING SPIES: PUBLIC SHAME, REPUTATION, AND RESPECT

3.1 VEILS OF ANONYMITY AND PILLORIES OF SHAME

Jean-Jacques Rousseau was totally aware of the vilifying potential of publicity. As Elisabeth Noelle-Neumann suggests, Rousseau was among the first philosophers to use profusely (and rather unsystematically) the notion of public opinion (*l'opinion publique*). At times, Rousseau regarded public opinion as a tribunal from whose disapproval one must guard oneself because it harms one's reputation. He was "highly sensitive" to the "threatening aspect of publicity," Noelle-Neumann argues. She quotes Rousseau: "I saw nothing but the horror of being recognized, publicly proclaimed, in my presence as a thief, liar, slanderer." And again: "All this did not hinder the excited crowd [. . .] from getting stirred up against me little by little to the point of rage, insulting me publicly in broad daylight and not only outdoors and on country paths, but even in the middle of the streets."[1]

But according to Noelle-Neumann a double valence pervades Rousseau's body of work. At the same time that the private citizen Jean-Jacques dreads the reputational harm of public opinion, Rousseau the social contract theorist regards *l'opinion publique* as a sort of guardian of "public morality" (the guarantee of the "rectitude" of "manners and morals") whose institutional embodiment is the peculiar office of the censor, as Rousseau describes it in *The Social*

[1] Quoted by Elisabeth Noelle-Neumann, *The Spiral of Silence: Public Opinion–Our Social Skin* (Chicago: University of Chicago Press, 1993), 81.

Contract, an office whose role is to "honor" the "virtuous citizen" and "shame" the "man of bad mores."[2]

Why make reference to this double dimension of Rousseau's work? Chapters 3 and 4 each address these two valences of publicity in the context of the exposure of unofficial collaborators. Chapter 3 focuses on the first. In recent years, the public exposure of IMs has followed a curious path, which will be the focus of this chapter. After the fall of the GDR, many unofficial collaborators retreated into the shadows, under the rubble of the collapsed regime, preferring to conceal past deeds and hoping, perhaps, that they would slip into oblivion. Yet the laws and institutions emerging from the unified nation, as well as its leading politicians, were explicit in their resolve to turn every stone over and expose *all* individuals previously entangled with the Stasi, regardless of their current occupation, political orientation, or walk of life. Of late, however, that task has encountered some difficulties. Some private citizens who were shown to have had a tie to the Stasi, no matter how weak or how strong, how steady or how transient that link was, have invoked the right of personality (*Persönlichkeitsrecht*) in defending themselves against public exposure. According to them, that right has substantial weight and cannot be cast aside by the tides of public interest. In contrast, critics say that, in the context of informal collaboration with the Stasi, *Persönlichkeitsrecht* does not apply. Public interest shatters it.

This chapter examines the grounds for contesting the practice of public unveiling of IMs. Former collaborators themselves, first and foremost, undertake this resistance, but it is also discernible in public opinion, although far from being the dominant point of view. By invoking *Persönlichkeitsrecht*, collaborators appeal to their interest in protecting their reputation; or to their "right" to be forgotten and be exempt from stigmatization in society; regardless of whether collaborators are rightly entitled to them or not, all these interests have the value of respect for persons at their core, for they revolve around the desiderata that people should be spared humiliation or given the opportunity to pursue their life plans. The invocation to the right of personality has led a commentator to argue, with some exaggeration,

[2] Noelle-Neumann, *The Spiral of Silence*, Chapter 7. See Jean-Jacques Rousseau, *The Basic Political Writings* (Indiana: Hackett, 1987), 219ff.

that IM exposures generate a "collision" between Stasi *Aufarbeitung* and *Rechtsstaat* (roughly, government by laws), that is, between the ideals motivating the public exposure of collaborators and the respect-based principles embedded in the law in the form of reputational and privacy guarantees that presumably discourage such exposure. This chapter elaborates on this suggestion and teases out the way in which the notion of respect emerges both in legal and political discourse. A clarification is called for: In showing how public exposure of collaborators raises respect-based concerns about the potential reputational harm to IMs, I do not intend to suggest that this is a conclusive reason against such exposures. These reasons are defeasible, that is, they may be outweighed by other considerations. For instance, as we will see in this and other chapters, other interests, which may include historical clarification or respect *for victims*, may justify public exposures.

The chapter proceeds as follows. Sections two, three, and four discuss some judicial and legal cases involving the exposure of unofficial collaborators. Section two begins with the case of pastor Käbisch and informer Schubert to show how some IMs have invoked *Persönlichkeitsrecht* to protect themselves from public exposure. Sections three and four introduce similar cases and contrast German and American jurisprudence to highlight the relatively distinct way in which they balance the interests of public accountability, on the one hand, and those interests covered by personality rights on the other. The contrast is meant to reveal how German jurisprudence is particularly protective of individual reputation on the grounds that public shaming may have an aspect of disrespect toward individuals. Sections five and six shift the focus toward political discourse, where public exposure of IMs is often characterized as being disrespectful in that it prevents individuals from controlling their self-presentation, thus avoiding shaming exposures.

3.2 THE RIGHT OF PERSONALITY: SCHUBERT, TAKE ONE

During the communist era, Protestant churches became one of the staunchest and most independent bulwarks of opposition to the official regime, particularly in its final years. It is no wonder that many dissidents, particularly in the years leading up to the collapse of the regime, had close ties with these religious bodies. It is no surprise either that the Stasi had a special interest in keeping a close eye on its activities. This is, put very briefly, the background for the case of a pastor from the region of Bavaria, Edmund Käbisch, and "his" unofficial collaborator (or to be more precise, *one* of his unofficial collaborators, for the communist regime had an interest in surveying Käbisch's every move, and therefore appointed more than one informer to follow his steps): IM Schubert.[3]

In 2008, Käbisch and his religion students put together the exhibition "Christian Activities in the GDR," documenting how the Communist regime besieged religious institutions and monitored their internal life. In the exhibit, the real name of IM "Schubert" was in full display: Holm Singer. During the early 1980s, Singer had been an Inoffiziellen Mitarbeiter mit Feindberührung, an IM in close contact with the "enemy" in the *Operative Zielstellung* (Operation Goal-setting), whose target was Käbisch's religious community. Schubert had infiltrated the Church under the pretense of being a Christian to inform on several of the parishioners, including Käbisch himself. As a result of Schubert's undercover activities, for which he received rewards aplenty (paid vacations, credit for housing, money), four people were imprisoned.

One of them was Sabine Popp. She was a gardener during the day and a graffitist at night in the town of Reichenbach. As a gardener, she could move around stealthily without raising suspicions. This mobility she used to fill Reichenbach's walls with political slogans: "Class mission: Reunification;" "Down with the wall;" or "Liberty, not Socialism." Under an autocratic regime like the GDR, such laconic and seemingly harmless expressions of political nonconformity were considered highly subversive. Institutionalized spaces for the expression of political dissent were virtually nonexistent. Therefore, the outlets and the manner for manifesting political dissent had to be improvised and carried out carefully. Local authorities were genuinely alarmed by the graffiti. The police and the Stasi tried to find their

[3] Some information about the legal process can be found at Käbisch's personal website: www.dr-kaebisch.de/index.php?site=im_schubert

author but to no avail. The graffitist from Reichenbach remained on the loose until she became acquainted with the man who, she learned many years later, after reunification, turned out to be IM Schubert. Before meeting him, she had successfully exercised self-restraint and had been extremely secretive about her political activism. But IM Schubert was a charming fellow, she says. He gained her trust, and she let her secret slip. Shortly afterward she was arrested, spent two years in prison, and was finally deported to West Germany. She was forbidden to return to the East.[4]

With the help of his lawyer, not surprisingly a member of Die Linke, Germany's successor party to the old East German SED, Holm Singer brought suit to a local court, which delivered a temporary injunction prohibiting further allusion to his real name. The injunction noted that the exhibition used personal information "to degrade (*herabzuwürdigen*) the reputation (*Ansehen*) and esteem (*Wertschätzung*) of the plaintiff in the public eye."[5] The provisionary ruling relied on the right of personality and, more abstractly, on the idea of respect.

Things did not end there, of course. Pastor Käbisch remained categorical in his resolve to publicly identify IM "Schubert" as Holm Singer: "Without naming names, *Aufarbeitung* makes no sense whatsoever."[6] Members of the local Christian Democratic Union party, supporting the pastor politically and financially in his litigation against "Schubert," agreed that those who collaborated with an unjust state to harm their fellow citizens deserve to have their unjust acts reported along with the full letters of their names: "The Stasi was an essential pillar of the GDR regime. Whoever knowingly and willingly

[4] Steffen Reichert, "Verraten un Verhaftet," *Horch und Guck* 2 (2008): 60, 48–50.

[5] See Achim Beyer, "Märtyrermasche der Täter. IM 'Schubert' bemüht den Rechtsstaat," *Freiheit und Recht. Vierteljahresschrift für streitbare Demokratie und Widerstand gegen Diktatur*, August 2008, 1–2, pp. 8–9. This magazine is published by the Bund Widerstand und Verfolgung in Bavaria. There is an online version, available at: www.bwv-bayern.org/component/content/article/3-suchergebnis/27-maertyrermasche-der-taeter.html.

[6] Matthias Schlegel, "Streit um IM-Klarnamen bald wieder vor Gericht," *Der Tagesspiel*, May 31, 2008.

supported this state of injustice and harmed his fellow men must accept that this injustice is called by its full name."[7] Marianne Birthler, Gauck's immediate successor in the BStU, supported this view by stating: "*Aufarbeitung* is incompatible with anonymity; it demands clarification (*Aufklärung*)."[8]

I shall come back to the resolution of Schubert's case later in the chapter. Before that, I shall delve on the right of personality – its scope of coverage, its origin, and its concern for the protection of individual self-presentation – and explain its tense relationship with publicity.[9] *Persönlichkeitsrecht* stems from the Basic Law's (Grundgesetz) protection of human dignity, which may be regarded as the most important constitutional value in the German legal order, contained in Article 1 of the Basic Law.[10] But human dignity is a broad concept even in the

[7] Also, the town's mayor: "Wenn sich einer aus niedersten Beweggründen taufen lässt und andere ans Messer liefert, ist das für mich Grund genug, den Namen öffentlich zu nennen." ["If someone gets baptized for the lowest motives, and then hands other people to the enemy, that is for me good enough reason to make his name public."], "Die Stasi macht wieder mobil – wehret den Anfängen!" Pamphlet, n.d., www.moak.de/forum/forum_entry.php?id=1536.

[8] "Inhaltliche Entscheidung zu Klarnamen wäre besser," *Mitteldeutsche Zeitung*, April 22, 2008.

[9] There is no such thing as a constitutionally embedded right of personality in the United States. The protection of some of the interests covered by that right in the American context is based on tort law, torts such as defamation, privacy, or the infliction of emotional distress. Johann Neethling, "Personality Rights: A Comparative Overview," *Comparative and International Law Journal of Southern Africa* 38, no. 2 (2005): 210–245.

[10] Article 1 reads as follows: "(1) Human dignity shall be inviolable. To respect and protect it shall be the duty of all state authority; (2) The German people therefore acknowledge inviolable and inalienable human rights as the basis of every community, of peace and of justice in the world; (3) The following basic rights shall bind the legislature, the executive, and the judiciary as directly applicable law." Also relevant is article 2, relating to personal freedoms: "(1) Every person shall have the right to free development of his personality insofar as he does not violate the rights of others or offend against the constitutional order or the moral law. (2) Every person shall have the right to life and physical integrity. Freedom of the person shall be inviolable. These rights may be interfered with only pursuant to a law."

legal context, so much so that discussions of its precise contours rival debates over the meaning of the clause of due process in American constitutional law.[11] Given that breadth, the Federal Constitutional Court has construed its meaning more narrowly, and according to its interpretation, the right to personality encompasses the protection of private, personal, and intimate spheres; the right to one's word and image; the right to informational self-determination; and the protection of honor. It is, to put it bluntly, a right to self-presentation, that is, a right to choose how individuals wish to present themselves before the public. The right in question carves out a domain of private life where one can develop what legal doctrine calls one's "personal development." This, according to the German legal doctrine, has a direct impact on the individual's social identity. To the extent that the right guarantees that one may decide for oneself what contents of one's life one wants to disclose and what personal image one wants to convey, it prevents the person from being affected "in her social reputation (*gesellschaftliche[s] Ansehen*) [. . .] and as a consequence that her feelings of self-worth (*Selbstwertgefühl*) are undermined."[12]

The right of personality in Germany has a long history. It was born in the late nineteenth century, in a society strongly attached to norms of respectability and honor, and it embodies a complex cultural pattern of the maintenance of respectful interpersonal relations.[13] Two are its legal foundations: the ancient Roman law of insult and the law of artistic property, both of which are corpora of law that provide high sensitivity to immaterial interests. As to the first one, nineteenth-century German jurists of a Hegelian bent engaged in a large-scale reinterpretation of the

[11] The analogy comes from Donald Kommers, *The Constitutional Jurisprudence of the Federal Republic of Germany* (Durham and London: Duke University Press, 1997), 298.

[12] Ann Gosche, *Das Spannungsverhältnis zwischen Meinungsfreiheit und Ehrenschutz in der fragmentierten Öffentlichkeit* (Baden-Baden: Nomos, 2007), 43–57. For a comparative sketch of German and Canadian laws of privacy, see John Craig and Nico Nolte, "Privacy and Free Speech in Germany and Canada: Lessons for an English Privacy Tort," *European Human Rights Law Review* 1998 (2): 162–180.

[13] James Whitman, "Enforcing Civility and Respect: Three Societies," *Yale Law Journal* 109 (2000): 1282.

ancient Roman law of insult. They saw their interpretive enterprise as one of furthering the process of extending legal protections from material and monetizable interests to guarantees against immaterial, noneconomic interests (protection against verbal insult, for instance, or protection of one's name, photographed image, and correspondence), whose unfolding they traced back to the development of Roman law itself. The law of artistic property underwent a similar process of expansion, from mere copyright to including a broader right to control the use of one's work, in the name of protecting one's reputation as an artist. As a combination of these two forces and their development, by the early part of the twentieth century there were plenty of "personality" protections scattered throughout German law. Although the 1900 Civil Code did not endorse the right of personality, the protection of personality progressively flourished, in particular after the Basic Law of 1949 (the current German Constitution) embraced the German tradition of personality protection.[14]

To get a firmer handle on the values and interests involved in *Persönlichkeitsrecht*, let me draw a brief parallel between one of the aspects of this right – privacy – and the "equivalent" American notion, covered by the tort of privacy. The contrast is a foil that will help shed light on the particular aspect of the German right of personality that I have been emphasizing so far: self-presentation. Legal scholar James Whitman has insisted that the values and interests covered by the notion of privacy in Germany and the United States are not entirely the same, even though there are clear and important juxtapositions. To put it bluntly, in Germany, the protection of privacy puts *emphasis* on the right to control one's public image, whereas in the United States the *main* goal is to preserve the home as a citadel of individual sovereignty. The loss of public face seems to be the major threat under the former conception; for the latter, the main threat is the invasion of the state into the domestic sphere.[15] Thus, privacy protections in Germany are

[14] James Whitman, "The Two Western Cultures of Privacy: Dignity versus Liberty," *Yale Law Journal* 113 (2004): 1151–1221.

[15] This is not to say that under American jurisprudence, the right to control one's public persona is not protected. The development of the modern tort of privacy branches out in four different directions. Violation of privacy might

"a form of protection of a right to *respect* and *personal dignity.*" These legal guarantees are "rights to control your public image – rights to guarantee that people see you the way you want to be seen. They are, as it were, rights to be shielded against unwanted public exposure, to be spared embarrassment or humiliation."[16]

3.3 THE LIST OF INFORMERS AND THE COURTS: BALANCING PUBLICITY AND RESPECT

In the following sections I argue that the right of personality and the values associated with it have shaped the way in which courts, the law, and public opinion in contemporary Germany grapple with the phenomenon of informal collaboration, at least in very recent times. Even in those cases in which courts rule in favor of expressive and interests of the media over reputational ones, on closer inspection their decisions regarding the problem of informal collaboration reflect the importance of respect as an intractable, hard-to-dispel value. Embedded in the right of personality are logics or grammars of "self-presentation" that are deeply connected to the notion of respect in ways that will be clarified in the following lines.

The dissemination of information about an individual's past can put her reputation at risk if made public. It is usually the rule among liberal democracies like Germany or the United States that the reputational interests of the individual are not protected when the item of information that is supposed to affect them is part of, or would make a contribution to, public deliberation about issues of general interest. In a transitional justice setting such as unified Germany, it is obvious how public debate about the Stasi past would be regarded as advancing a significant interest.

mean one of the following: unreasonable publicity given to another's private life; an unreasonable intrusion on the seclusion of another; an appropriation of another's name or likeness; or publicity that unreasonably places another in a false light before the public. The first branch protects individuals' unwanted public exposures. See *Restatement (Second) of Torts* §§ 652 A-E

[16] James Whitman, "The Two Western Cultures of Privacy."

When public deliberation is conducted for the purpose of understanding public matters, and persons become the subject of investigation, an uneasy tension between privacy or reputation and what Robert Post calls "a normative theory of public accountability" is generated. According to this theory "the public should be entitled to inquire freely into the significance of public persons and events, and [. . .] this entitlement is so powerful that it overrides individual claims to the maintenance of information preserves," information preserves being a kind of "territory," which contains a "set of facts about [oneself] to which an individual expects to control access."[17] In other words, the public is entitled to unveil certain information about individuals, who would rather keep it to themselves, even if that might affect their standing to command respect from others.[18]

Courts in Germany often endorse a version of this theory. However, they seem to embrace it less ardently than American courts. German and American courts approach defamation and privacy cases in different fashions, the former being, in general terms, more restrictive than the latter.[19] In deciding defamation or privacy cases, courts in the United States will assume at least two things: that free speech is fundamental for the public realm, and that the purported injury to the individual will be cured by "more speech," as Justice Brandeis famously argued.[20] In contrast, German courts will not favor speech a priori and instead engage in an ad hoc balancing process. Thus, the American principle is one of priority, whereas the German one is a principle of balancing.[21] And the latter methodological approach to deciding cases of

[17] Robert Post, *Constitutional Domains. Democracy, Community, Management* (Cambridge: Harvard University Press, 1995), 80.

[18] Robert Post, "Three Concepts of Privacy," *Georgetown Law Journal* 89, no. 6 (2001): 2092, and "The Social Foundations of Defamation Law: Reputation and the Constitution," *California Law Review* 74 (1986): 691–742.

[19] This is the case even if there are converging tendencies. See Georg Nolte. "Falwell v. Strauss: Die rechtlichen Grenzen politischer Satire in den USA und der Bundesrepublik," *Europäische Grundrechtezeitschrift* 14 (1988): 253–259.

[20] *Whitney v. California*, 274 U.S. 357 (1927).

[21] Pavel Lutomski, "Private Citizens and Public Discourse: Defamation Law as a Limit to the Right of Free Expression in the U.S. and Germany," *German*

free speech leaves room for a more careful consideration of the risks posed by the publicity of one's compromising past, and for a greater degree of protection against that publicity.

For instance, a regional court ruled in 1979 that a magazine accusing a former Nazi collaborator of being responsible for the deaths of 20 children in a concentration camp could not recover for defamation (*üble Nachrede*). Not only was the plaintiff unable to prove that the statement was false (truth is a defense, but also the burden of proof is on the plaintiff in the German jurisprudential context). More important, but related to this, the press has a legitimate interest, the court argued, "in reporting concretely the facts that are essential for evaluating a former period of time, in preserving the memory of the era of national socialist rule, in contributing to an impartial view by its readers of these horrible acts of power, and even to help toward a clarification of particular criminal acts through the publication of further details." The court admitted that, in some cases, the interest in publicity conflicts with the interest of the plaintiff in remaining "undisturbed" and in being able "to develop his personality." The court argued that it had not overlooked the fact that the former Nazi, "now seventy years old, for whom the alleged wrongs lie over thirty years in the past, has a strong interest in not having to confront these horrible reproaches which must distress him and bring him into contempt in the eyes of his friends and acquaintances and the public." But the court affirmed that because the former Nazi collaborator had not proven the falsity of the accusation, the interest in

Studies Review 24, no. 3 (2001): 571–592. On the differences in the methodological approaches (and also the substantive ones) between the two cases see also Frederick Schauer, "The Exceptional First Amendment," in Michael Ignatieff (ed.), *American Exceptionalism and Human Rights* (Princeton, NJ: Princeton University Press, 2005), 29–56; Frederick Schauer, "Freedom of Expression Adjudication in Europe and America: A Case Study in Comparative Constitutional Architecture," in Georg Nolte, *European and U.S. Constitutionalism* (Cambridge: Cambridge University Press, 2005), 49–69.

publicity, for the reasons mentioned earlier, outweighed his interest in developing his personality.[22]

When we turn to the case of former informal collaborators, the balance between expressive and reputational rights holds constant. The following example, which I develop in the rest of this section, illustrates this continuity. The case in this example is one of the first instances in which a former IM brought suit arguing that a public unveiling affected her right of personality, although the argument of the plaintiff in this case was that the information was inaccurate, and she denied she had been an informer. The New Forum was a civic/political movement formed in East Germany shortly after the collapse of the GDR in 1989. It was critical of the regime and relatively successful at mobilizing the citizenry. Having initially been described by the communist regime as an organization contrary to the GDR, the New Forum was given official recognition in the months leading up to the German reunification. One of its postreunification activities in the city of Halle in 1992 was to make available for public consultation a list of about 4,500 names of former IMs. The purpose, according to one of its members, was to have the town undergo an episode of "psychological cleansing."

Before the Halle case made it to the highest tribunal of the land, the Federal Constitutional Court (Bundesverfassungsgericht), other lower courts had ruled in favor of the plaintiff. One stated that "mentioning that the plaintiff had been active as an unofficial employee is enough to ruin her public reputation and to pillory her [...] Through this 'branding' the plaintiff was largely affected in her claim to social reputation (*soziale Geltung*) and hit in the core of her personality." Briefly put, the plaintiff's outing had put her at the pillory and thereby had tarnished her reputation, degraded her public esteem, and compromised her social image.[23]

[22] James Gordley, *An Introduction to the Comparative Study of Private Law; Readings, Cases, Materials* (New York: Cambridge University Press, 2006), 295.

[23] Decision of the Federal Court of Justice (Bundesgerichtshofs) of July 12, 1994, VI ZR 1/94.

The Federal Constitutional Court objected to the rulings of the lower courts. First, it argued that those courts had "misjudged" the interest of free speech of the defendant. The highest court listed a number of reasons why the publication of the list should be considered as a part of the "public debate of ideas" on the Stasi question. In particular, it stressed the fact that the protection of free expression requires that not only the content of an expression be protected but also the way in which it is delivered. Thus, the court argued, the constitution protects the expressive vehicle (outings) that in this particular case the defendant used to advance a subject of public interest. In other words, the court protected the view of the defendant that, "The reality of the Stasi oppression can only be understood when the phenomenon 'Stasi' is pulled away from the abstraction of official documentation and statistics, and is presented to the affected person in a concrete and understandable way." The court also argued that it was *not* its task "to bring public discussions to a close or to declare that a debate has ended."[24]

But the Bundesverfassungsgericht also admitted that some public statements, even if made in the interest of public discussion and even if amounting to truthful remarks about particular facts, were not constitutionally protected. Such is the case of remarks that may "stigmatize" the accused: "The protection that is granted by *Persönlichkeitsrecht* is also effective even if the statement is true and therefore becomes a point of origin for social exclusion and isolation." In light of this limitation to free expression, the court took pains to explain why in this particular case there is no threat that the plaintiff may become socially ostracized. First, it argued, strictly speaking, IMs did not commit criminal deeds. Second, and important for the court, the list was not widely distributed, which mitigated the list's potential exclusionary effects: "The publication of the list did not reach a broad audience. The appellant [who published the list] did not make it accessible through the media [. . .]. Only a relatively small number of people got to see the list." In other words, the identity of the plaintiff was not exposed to a large number of citizens, the ruling

[24] BVerfG, 1 BvR 1582/94 of February 23, 2000, Absatz-Nr. (1 – 39), www.bverfg.de/entscheidungen/rk20000223_1bvr158294.html

further affirmed, and therefore the plaintiff's reputation was not unduly affected. Third, the court asserted that past unofficial collaboration did not lead to a "withdrawal from social recognition (*Anerkennung*)," as would be the case, for instance, of child molestation (in the court's example). Informal collaboration with the Ministry for State Security was, the court continued again without further argumentation, "a mass phenomenon" and therefore could not earn a single individual "a sustained exclusionary isolation." Finally, the court argued that the plaintiff was not singled out as a sole collaborator. Her name was buried among 4,499 other names, a fact that further dispels the possibility of "an exclusionary stigmatization" for the plaintiff.

I reproduce in some detail the Court's line of reasoning to illustrate the care with which it grapples with the phenomenon of collaboration. The Stasi is a subject whose importance for public deliberation is beyond dispute. Yet the court goes through the work of explaining why, given the particularities of the case, this is not a case in which the personality right of the plaintiff has been affected. It considers it is important to note that the list only reached a limited audience, thus mitigating the potential harm to her reputation. This invites the question: Had her public disclosure reached a wider audience, as happened in other case, some of which will be examined later, would its decision have been any different? The name of the IM was not singled out in the list, which further mitigates the potential harm to her reputation, the Court continues. But again, had it been singled out, like other IMs have had their names singled out, what might the Court's ruling have been? Moreover, it is hard to fathom what the Court means by designating informal collaboration as a "mass phenomenon." How many citizens does it take for a "phenomenon" to be "massive"? Only a minuscule percentage of the population was active as an IM. The factual inaccuracy is noteworthy because it furnishes the basis for the court's argument that the list could not produce "a sustained exclusionary isolation." Here the implication is that, had informal collaboration not been a mass phenomenon, then the risk of sustained isolation of the former IM might have been real and an element worth serious consideration.

I do not wish to keep piling counterfactuals. What I want to point out is that the Court moves extremely carefully through its subject because the reputation of an individual is at stake, even if the individual is a former collaborator for the Stasi. Although the uneasy tension between free expression and reputation is often resolved on the side of publicity in cases related to IMs, the claim about reputational harm has considerable weight, and the Federal Constitutional Court is careful to explain it away. It is represented as an important issue, a valid claim that must, however, be sacrificed for the sake of public debate.

This is a good point to return to Schubert's case, with which this chapter began. After two years, the regional court of Zwickau ruled in favor of Käbisch. As in the Halle case, just described, in balancing Käbisch's right to free expression and Singer's right to personality, the former, the court found, outweighed the latter. A detailed representation of Schubert's actions, as well as his identity, made it possible to understand to the fullest extent the ability of the Stasi to infiltrate and manipulate oppositional circles during the period of the GDR.[25] In other words, assuming that IM Schubert has a valid reputational claim, an assumption that his critics dispute, the goal of historical clarification overrides it. If instead of a collaborator, a victim were the subject of public scrutiny, the balance would be different. The latter does not lose her right to withdraw her identity, as it were, from the public debate of ideas, but the former does. Furthermore, to the extent that historical clarification is substantively connected to the right of victims to know which citizens contributed as denunciators to the oppressive surveillance cast on them, the notion of historical clarification carries a respect-based justification. In this case, public exposures are the manifestation of and the conflict between two claims to respect; through their actions, collaborators weakened theirs.

[25] Hans-Jürgen Grasemann, "Täter haben ein Gesicht. Die Notwendigkeit zur Benennung von Täternamen bei der Aufarbeitung des SED-Unrechts," *Freiheit und Recht* 2(2009). Available at www.bwv-bayern.org/component/content/article/3-suchergebnis/69-taeter-haben-ein-gesicht.html; see also Hans-Jürgen Grasemann, "Gerichte geben Tätern ein Gesicht. Wegweisende Urteile gegen Stasi-Spitzel," *Freiheit und Recht* 3/4(2010). Available at www.bwv-bayern.org/component/content/article/3-suchergebnis/104-gerichte-geben-taetern-ein-gesicht.html

3.4 THE LAW OF THE ARCHIVES: REPUTATION'S WEDGE

Schubert's case was just one among many cases involving unofficial collaborators who did not wish to be publicly identified and for this reason used, usually unsuccessfully, legal resources to remain anonymous. In one case, a researcher was taken to court in Hamburg, for having footnoted the name of two former denunciators. In another, the editor of a publishing house (Propylaeen Press) exercised what he called "preemptive obedience" (*vorauseilender Gehorsam*), and as a consequence, one of its books, *Die Fluchttunnel von Berlin* (*The Escape Tunnels of Berlin*), left out the identity of some individuals involved in those crimes; this was, in his words, an act of excessive prudence (*überzogene Vorsicht*) to avoid delays or reimpressions of the book based on judicial order.[26] Finally, a Berlin tribunal ruled against *SUPERillu*, a widely read magazine based in Berlin, for running a piece on the partner of a famous actress, a former policeman who as IM Wilfred had informed on several colleagues.[27] In most of these cases and others similar to them, collaborators end up losing at higher judicial instances. Despite their lack of success, the point to be made is that cases of this kind can only emerge in an environment in which reputational claims exercise moral force and factor into the considerations of decision makers, including judges. How is this possible?

The *Stasi-Unterlagen-Gesetz*, which has been amended several times,[28] is the law that governs the access and use of information contained in the Stasi archives.[29] For the purposes of this chapter, I need only underline its main goal, which is to make sure German

[26] Peter Von Wensierski, "Recht Auf Vergessen?," *Der Spiegel*, November 17, 2008.

[27] Thomas Starke, "'Ach wie gut, das niemand weiß ...' Darf man die Namen von Stasi-Mitarbeitern nennen?" *Deutschland Archive* 2 (2009): 197–206.

[28] "Gesetz über die Unterlagen des Staatssicherheitsdienstes der ehemaligen Deutschen Demokratischen Republik," Available at www.gesetze-im-internet.de/bundesrecht/stug/gesamt.pdf

[29] A good analysis of the law may be found in John Miller, "Settling Accounts with a Secret Police. The German Law on the Stasi Records," *Europe-Asia Studies* 50, no. 2 (1998): 305–330.

(or non-German) citizens receive, on request, a detailed account of all the information about them that the communist regime collected and the uses to which it was put. The law calls this the "clarification" (*Aufklärung*) goal. Such guarantees form part of a broader right that citizens have to know who collected, kept, and used what information about them and for what purposes. Subject to public interest and the rights of other individuals, a breach of these rights is a breach of the right of personality. The problem with this is that it raises a conflict between two right-of-personality claims because the vindication of the personality rights of Stasi victims cannot be done without disclosing the names of former IMs and hence infringing *their Persönlichkeitsrecht*. The Gesetz itself gives a clear indication of how the tension should be settled: There is a public interest in the *Aufklärung* purpose, and before such public interest, some personal rights of former Stasi employees must give way.[30] So the victim's privacy is protected, not the perpetrator's.[31] The interest of the perpetrator to hide his or her complicity with the secret police is, according to the law, not worthy of protection. The statute seems to assume that, through his or her former contact with the Stasi, the perpetrator forfeited much of his right to personality. IMs can ask no more than that their privacy interests be balanced against the victim's right or the researcher's interest in learning about the secret police. The BStU, the government agency that controls the balancing process, is, by its own admission, more solicitous of the victims' rights than of the collaborators.'[32] Even some courts, the examples offered

[30] An important proviso is that Stasi activity must not have taken place when the "perpetrators" in question were under eighteen. Those who were minors at the time when they got involved with the Stasi are protected today.

[31] Hence Helmuth Kohl's legal battle to prevent his Stasi file from becoming public, after accusations that under his leadership the CDU had received illegal funding, some of which had been under the radar of the Stasi, even in the face of increasing public pressure and arguments that a disclosure of his file could confirm or dispel the charges of corruption against him. On this, Annina Pollaczek, *Pressefreiheit und Persönlichkeitsrecht am Beispiel des Stasi-Unterlagen-Gesetzes* (Saarbrücken: VDM Verlag, 2007).

[32] "Gesetz über die Unterlagen des Staatsicherheitsdienstes,"§34

before notwithstanding, have ruled that scientific works may name names of former IMs.[33]

But even the Gesetz is not completely inattentive to the rights of personality of former IMs, insofar as it proposes a (timid) guideline to guarantee them whenever possible. Thus, for instance, it establishes that when the quality and the nature of an academic investigation related to the Stasi are not affected by the omission of specific names, the author should instead use aliases, informer X, for instance.[34] This is certainly a low standard of protection for IMs. However, even this standard would have hardly survived the scrutiny of an American court. Consider two illustrative landmark cases in American jurisprudence. They involve situations in which individuals were denied privacy and reputational guarantees with regard to information that would have appeared to be private because courts ascribed political significance to it, hence making it susceptible to public scrutiny. In one case, an author faced libel and privacy suits for publicizing a man's "failure as a worker and a husband through drunkenness, bad temper, and adultery,"[35] and for describing the subsequent breakup of his marriage (the man had later remarried, had a steady home and job, and was even a deacon of his local church) in a book that narrated the history of the migration of millions of blacks from impoverished rural areas to more urban sites under the auspices of the U.S. federal government in its efforts to eradicate poverty, particularly in the late 1960s. The Court ruled against the plaintiffs, arguing that readers of the work had a "legitimate interest" in those aspects of the protagonist's behavior because one of the major themes of the book

> was the transposition virtually intact of a sharecropper morality characterized by a family structure "matriarchal and elastic" and

[33] See, for instance, the ruling discussed in Johannes Weberling, "Zur Veröffentlichung der Namen ehemaliger Stasi-Mitarbeiter in einem wissenschaftlichen Bericht," *AfP – Zeitschrift für Medien –und Kommunikationsrecht* 3 (2006): 272–273.

[34] Philipp Hasso Andreas Rein, *Zugang zu Stasi-Unterlagen und Persönlichkeitsrecht* (PhD Diss, University of Bonn, 2008), 111–127.

[35] *Haynes v. Alfred A. Knopf, Inc.* 8.3d 1222 (7th Cir. 1993).

> by an "extremely unstable" marriage bond to the slums of the northern cities, and the interaction [. . .] of that morality with government programs to alleviate poverty. Public aid policies discouraged [the couple] from living together; public housing policies precipitated a marriage doomed to fail.[36]

From that point of view, the Court continued, the book "tells a story not only of legitimate but of transcendent public interest." Before it, the plaintiff's right to privacy or reputation was overridden.

Or take the case of Oliver Sipple, the man who frustrated an assassination attempt against President Gerald Ford in San Francisco in 1975. Several publications reported Sipple's "heroic deed" but also his homosexuality (filtered to the media by Harvey Milk, the first openly gay mayor in the United States), which he had struggled to keep secret and the disclosure of which had estranged him from family and relatives and, he claimed, brought embarrassment and humiliation upon him. Sipple brought suit for disclosure of private facts. A California appellate court rejected the claim on the grounds, first, that his story was "newsworthy." The publications reporting it, the court said,

> were not motivated by a morbid and sensational prying into appellant's private life but rather were prompted by legitimate political considerations, i.e., to dispel the false public opinion that gays were timid, weak, and unheroic figures and to raise the equally important political question whether the President of the United States entertained a discriminatory attitude or bias against a minority group such as homosexuals.[37]

The court ruled that contributing to the task of dismantling entrenched stereotypes against homosexuals and dispelling doubts about the president's attitude toward homosexuality were legitimate reasons for publicizing information that would otherwise be private. I am very aware of the fact that domestic abuse and sexual preference are not private matters. To argue so would be to endorse a dichotomy that has been widely discredited, especially among feminist scholars.

[36] *Haynes v. Alfred A. Knopf, Inc.* 8.3d 1222 (7th Cir. 1993).

[37] For an analysis of this case see William Jones, *Insult to Injury: Libel, Slander, and Invasions of Privacy* (Boulder: University Press of Colorado, 2003).

My point, rather, is that personal information of the sort described earlier (sexual orientation, drinking habits, etc.) usually falls within the "informational preserves" whose protection is a matter of respect for the individual. And yet, in the United States, publicity claims override such information preserves in the name of public interest. There is more room for maneuvering in Germany, even in a case of clear public concern such as Stasi collaboration, as a result of personality rights.

3.5 *RESOZIALISIERUNG* AND THE RIGHT TO FORGETFULNESS: SCHUBERT, TAKE TWO

Two notions associated with the right of personality have made their appearance in the context of political and legal discussions about former collaborators – *Resozialisierung* and the informal right to forgetfulness. Both lead back to the logic of self-presentation, a logic that is intertwined with the concern for respect. I shall introduce them through an example. As was mentioned in the previous chapter, upon enrollment with the Stasi, unofficial collaborators reported under an alias. The aliases they used were usually of their own invention (and they could range from the ridicule to the dull). For this reason, it was rare that two unofficial collaborators bore the same code name, but it happened at least once, and the duplicate alias was none other than Schubert. Like the first Schubert, the second, Herbert Gräser, was an IM "in contact with the enemy" during the GDR, which means that among other things he participated in *Zersetzung* measures. He infiltrated oppositional circles in the city of Erfurt, wrote long and detailed reports on dissidents (his record in the Stasi archives has more than 3,000 pages), and received compensation for his work. As a result of his activities, numerous dissidents were apprehended and imprisoned, one of them for organizing a protest against electoral fraud in the final years of the regime.

Again, like the first Schubert, the second one tried to preserve his anonymity in unified Germany by invoking his right to personality. Joachim Heinrich, a victim of Stasi surveillance, created an Internet website (www.stasi-in-erfurt.de) that localized the houses where the

Stasi held meetings with their informers. On the website he also posted the name and photograph of Gräser and identified him as a collaborator. Gräser brought suit before a court of München, asking that his name and photograph be removed from the website.[38] The claim he made, via his lawyer, was that he had a right to being forgotten, one that would allow him to be "resocialized."

Again like Schubert I, Schubert II lost his case. But it is interesting to examine the ideas and values that were invoked in the process, such as *Resozialisierung* (resocialization). In German legal culture, that notion is a term of art that captures the expectation that citizens should not be "ostracized" as a result of crimes or activities they committed in the past and should instead be given the opportunity to be "reincorporated" into society.[39] The notion has been evoked explicitly in several IM outings. It also made its appearance in the famous Stolpe Case. Manfred Stolpe was a prominent German politician. He contributed both to the rapprochement and ulterior reunification of the two German Republics. After the reunification, he became Prime Minister of Brandenburg with the SPD and then Minister of Transport at the federal level under the Schröder government. During the GDR years, Stolpe was an active member in the Protestant Church and held several posts within its governing bodies, a position that put him in close contact with Stasi officials. He became the representative of the church vis-à-vis GDR authorities, largely because he was prepared to negotiate with those in power, something that others within Protestant circles were not prepared to do. As the Stasi files became public, he faced the accusation, which he denied, of having been a Stasi collaborator all along (IM *Sekretär*) and came under pressure to resign from public office, which he did not do. Before a parliamentary commission, formed to investigate the nature

[38] See Rainer Berger, "Vorbei, vergangen, vergessen?," *Frankfurter Allgemeine Zeitung*, December 23, 2008.

[39] For instance, Matthias Platzeck, the Minister President of Brandenburg, argued late in 2009 that former Stasi collaborators deserved a chance to "resocialize." Constanze von Bullion, "Platzeck kennt keine 'Jammer-Ossis,'" *Süddeutsche*, May 17, 2010. Available at www.sueddeutsche.de/politik/33/488429/text/. This case will be discussed thoroughly in the last chapter.

of Stolpe's Stasi past,[40] and which in the end controversially accepted his version of the events in a decision made along party lines,[41] Stolpe argued that he had never acquiesced to work for the MfS even if the secret police considered him one of its informers, and that, in any case, his "pact" with the Stasi had been one of necessity, what he envisioned as the only way to protect the church. I will have more to say about Stolpe later. For now, I simply note that one of the arguments used in the Stolpe Committee was "No one should be denied the chance of personal development and the desire to redirect their life."[42] This is the spirit captured by the concept of *Resozialisierung*, a notion with considerable political–rhetorical purchase.

The notion of Resozialisierung implies that if the publicity of sensitive information might create obstacles for the successful "reinsertion" of an erstwhile criminal into society, such publicity should be curtailed. The most salient illustration of this restriction in German constitutional jurisprudence is the so-called *Lebach*[43] case, a landmark judicial ruling of the Constitutional Tribunal that has been explicitly deployed as a relevant precedent in the *Halle* case, but also, more vigorously, in some of the cases mentioned in the previous section and also in the case of Schubert II. In *Lebach*, the Federal Constitutional Court decided on a case where a convicted robber was able to stop the broadcasting of a documentary depicting, accurately, his participation in a notorious armed robbery of an army munitions depot that resulted in the death

40 The commission was formed in virtue of Stolpe's standing as a prominent politician. Obviously, parliamentary commissions are not formed to investigate the Stasi past of every ordinary German citizen.

41 Barbara Miller, *Narratives of Guilt and Compliance in Unified Germany. Stasi Informers and Their Impact on Society* (New York: Routledge, 1999), 80.

42 Protocol of the Debatte zum Bericht des Parlamentarischen Untersuchungsausschusses 1/3 des Landtages: 'Aufklärung der früheren Kontakte des Ministerpräsidenten Dr. Manfred Stolpe zu Organisationen des Staatsapparates der GDR der SED sowie zum Staatssicherheitsdienst und der in diesem Zusammenhang erhobenen Vorwürfe', 16 June 1994, Schriften des Landtages Brandenburg, 2 (1994). Quoted by Barbara Miller, *Narratives of Guilt and Compliance in Unified Germany*, 83.

43 Decision of the Federal Constitutional Court (Lebach Case), BVerfGE 35, 202 (1973).

of four soldiers. Lebach had already served his term in prison by the time the film was supposed to air. Lebach obtained injunctive relief against the distribution of the film, a decision that in American jurisprudence would constitute a very strong form of prior restraint. The Federal Constitutional Court affirmed that there were two interests in conflict. On the one hand, a public interest in receiving information about the commission of a crime, including the identity of the criminal and the events leading to the criminal act, whose presentation is the "quintessential" task of the media. On the other hand, the interest of the accused of the crime, whose "intimate sphere" might be intruded on as a consequence of the negative image of his person conveyed by the public report of the crime in which his identity is provided. In balancing these interests, the court argued that a crucial standard in figuring out the limits to broadcasting is "the criminal's interest in rehabilitation or in recovering his position in society." In more detail: "The criminal's vital interest in restoring him to his social position must generally have precedence over the public's interest in a further discussion of the crime." Put in slightly different terms, beyond a certain temporal threshold, albeit an admittedly imprecise one, "perpetrators" have a right to have their past deeds thrust into oblivion. They have, in other words, a *right to forgetfulness* (a notion that is neither the Court's nor a legal term, but which certainly captures the spirit of what the Court does say). *Resozialisierung* and the right to forgetfulness thrive on logics of self-presentation that are geared toward protecting citizens from receiving an undignified treatment, even if this protection constrains public discourse.

Let me once more compare the jurisprudence of Germany to that of the United States and briefly discuss a case that on the surface has little to do with the Stasi and its informants but that touches on the issue of resocialization and self-presentation. *Melvin v. Reid*[44] is a judicial case about a former prostitute who brought suit against the producers of a film for accurately depicting the facts of her life and using her name. Melvin, the plaintiff, who claimed she had abandoned her previous life and tried to "rehabilitate" herself, alleged that

[44] *Melvin v. Reid*, 112 Cal. App. 285, 297.

this caused her harm and ridicule and exposed her to obloquy. A local court agreed that it was unnecessary to use the plaintiff's real name in connection with the facts of her case. "One of the major objectives of society as it is now constituted, and of the administration of our penal system, is the rehabilitation of the fallen and the reformation of the criminal." The court put emphasis on the importance of an individual's ability to rehabilitate and felt that the unnecessary use of Melvin's real name inhibited this right. Although, not phrased in this way, the rehabilitation of the individual hinges, in the *Melvin* court's view, on her ability to control her self-presentation. Although similar to *Lebach* in its concern for the "resocialization" or "rehabilitation" of the culprit, *Melvin* is of doubtful validity[45] after *Cox Broadcasting Corp. v. Cohn,*[46] however. In *Cox*, the Supreme Court laid down a standard favorable to publicity, ruling that once information (in this case, the name of rape victims) is available in a public document, the state cannot prohibit its dissemination by the media.[47] In other words, the argument for restricting publicity to guarantee the resocialization of individuals is discredited in the United States. In the German case, by contrast, the argument seems to persuade some courts; the Stasi files are public documents, and yet the latter place some restrictions on their diffusion. Critics of IM outings, in other words, defend an informal right to forgetfulness, on the grounds that it will help the individual to be resocialized.

With this background in mind, let me get back to the case of Schubert II. The reaction of the online readership of the newspaper *Die Welt* before and after the ruling of the court illustrates the terms of the public debate around cases like this one. Some readers believe

45 Richard Posner, *Overcoming Law* (Cambridge, MA: Harvard University Press, 1995), 542.

46 *Cox Broadcasting Corp. v. Cohn*, 420 U.S. 469 (1975).

47 The majority in *Cox* writes: "We are reluctant to embark on a course that would make public records generally available to the media but forbid their publication if offensive to the sensibilities of the supposed reasonable man. Such a rule would make it very difficult for the media to inform citizens about the public business and yet stay within the law. The rule would invite timidity and self-censorship and very likely lead to the suppression of many items that would otherwise be published and that should be made available to the public."

IMs do not have such a right and wonder how informers can be so "shameless" to claim for themselves what they "denied" to other citizens ("It is remarkable that ex Stasi persons claim rights that they actively refused to citizens of the GDR. How messed up and blind must a person be to not feel ashamed for that?"). Others believe that not a single one of those who willingly worked for a "wicked" regime should be forgotten ("Each one must be clear that he worked for evil by betraying independent individuals within society. That is why one can never forget and each victim must decide whether he can forgive.").[48] Yet some readers believe that ex-IMs do have a right to be forgotten and advance arguments that, in a nonjuridified fashion, are reminiscent of the notions contained in the Court opinions sketched earlier, in particular the following one:

> What would be the benefit of continuing to denounce the informants of the Stasi after thirty or twenty years [. . .] Some people can't draw the line: they just want to get revenge, and not only once, but repeatedly. That's sick and hardly tells them apart from the perpetrators. I would not want to publicly destroy the life of a person by openly calling for her verbal lynching.

Others contend that too long a period of time has already elapsed ("People, 20 years have gone by. Worrying about these hideous small informers after all those years is nonsense.") or that the number of people who collaborated or turned a blind eye is so high that pointing fingers is simply absurd and rather a problematic enterprise ("They simply want to criminalize a whole generation of GDR citizens.").[49]

The reaction of the same readership to the decision of the regional court, ruling against this IM, shows the same pattern. There are satisfied and enthusiastic readers who would go so far as to expel once unofficial collaborators ("All denunciators must get out of Germany!"), but there are also disapproving ones, whose arguments decry the exclusionary dimension of outings and take them to be

[48] Or this one: "This man stepped on the personal rights of his fellows GDR, so he should not make such a fuss. All of those who support the powers that be in a dictatorship, cannot present themselves as innocent lambs afterwards."

[49] These are actual quotes from online readers of following the article: Uwe Müller, "Haben Ex-Stasi-Spitzel ein Recht auf Vergessen?" *Die Welt*, March 18, 2009.

manifestations of the *Siegerjustiz*, or "justice of the victors" ("This ruling stirs up hatred towards, and calls for the exclusion of, those who over forty years ago protected us from the dismantling of democracy and social welfare, and from the adventures of German militarism. Down with victor's justice!"). Others even draw comparisons between denunciators and other criminals that intimate some legal savvy and suggest the detrimental effects of outings ("Why then couldn't child molesters and rapists also be publicly placed in the pillory on the Internet?"), and yet others ask questions about the extent to which "coming to terms with the past" actually requires that actual names be named ("How would *Aufarbeitung* be hindered if, for instance, only the initials of former members of the MfS were disclosed?").[50]

These exchanges document the perception that, according to some people at least, outings lower the social standing of those who collaborated with the Stasi in the eyes of others. They prevent wrongdoers from being rehabilitated or "resocialized."

3.6 A TALE OF TWO (HARMFUL) BROTHERS

In the previous sections I illustrated how concern for the reputation of individuals influences judgments about, and sometimes even modestly circumscribes the scope of, the publicity of the identity of former informal collaborators. I paid particular attention to a few legal cases that were widely discussed in public debates. This section focuses on a case that did not reach any court of law but that reflects some of the stakes involved in the public unveiling of IMs.

A recurrent theme in public discourse in Germany is that outings are forms of pillorying and are therefore disrespectful. The image of the pillory, which is a typical representation of shaming punishments[51] and is recurrent in public discussion,[52] captures the perception of outings as

[50] "Ex-Stasi-Spitzel muss Identifizierung hinnehmen," *Die Welt*, April 15, 2009.

[51] On this, Jon Elster, *Alchemies of the Mind: Rationality and the Emotions* (New York: Cambridge University Press, 1999).

[52] See, for instance, Albrecht Schönhofer (ed.), *Ein Volk am Pranger? Die Deutschen auf der Suche nach einer neuen politischen Kultur* (Halle: Aufbau, 1991). The title of the book (*A People at the Pillory*), published two years after the fall of the wall and

practices that trigger what one may call the mechanism of shame. Scholarly literature on shame might be helpful in capturing what this means. David Velleman, for instance, argues that individuals are self-presenting creatures who compose a persona for an audience in social life; they display an outward face, an overt self.[53] If the individual loses her ability to control her public persona, her social standing might be compromised: "Threats to your standing as a self-presenting creature are [. . .] a source of deep anxiety, and anxiety about the threatened loss of that standing is [. . .] what constitutes shame." In a sentence, "shame is the anxious sense of being compromised in one's self-presentation in a way that threatens one's social recognition as a self-presenting person."[54] Thus, as Thomas Scheff argues, shame is "a threat to the social bond." It produces a "fear of social disconnection," of "being adrift from understanding and being understood by others."[55]

I want to illustrate the mechanism of shame through a very concrete example drawn from the media annals of IM exposures, a particularly interesting indicator of the set of beliefs that mirror, inform, or shape the way in which citizens evaluate that practice. Tales of familial betrayal of Stasi informers (husbands informing on their wives, parents telling on theirs sons, brothers or sisters spying on their siblings) are not numerous, but there are some famous cases. That of the Schädlich

whose goal was to weigh in on the debates about the GDR legacy and propose ways to grapple with it, uses the metaphor under discussion.

53 This is the general thesis of the so-called symbolic interactionism school. Its main insight is that individuals do not engage in social action simply for the sake of that action, but that, instead, all actions are social performances whose goal is not only achieving whatever "inherent" purposes the action may have had, but also giving off and maintaining certain desired impressions of one's self to others. See Erving Goffman, *The Presentation of the Self in Everyday Life* (New York: Doubleday, 1959), which is the seminal study; and Erving Goffman, *Stigma: Notes on the Management of Spoiled Identity* (New York: Simon & Schuster, 1963).

54 David Velleman, "The Genesis of Shame," *Philosophy and Public Affairs* 30, no. 1 (2001): 37, 50.

55 Thomas Scheff, "Shame and the Social Bond: A Sociological Theory," *Sociological Theory* 18, no. 1 (2000): 95.

brothers (the last name is the German word for "harmful," an ominous sign as it turns out) bears more than a passing mention.

In 1992, very shortly after the Stasi files became public, Hans-Joachim Schädlich, an acclaimed German writer, learned on reading his Stasi act that his brother Karlheinz, a historian, had spied on him during the GDR years. In 2007, only a year after he was outed a second time for informing on novelist Günter Grass, Karlheinz shot himself in the head at a Berlin park in the Prenzlauerberg district. Not surprisingly, the gruesome death received widespread press coverage, in particular by newspapers in Berlin, which reported on the suicide in a very peculiar way. First, they portrayed Karlheinz as a victim of "the system," which turned him into a *Spitzel*(informer). Then they depicted his life after his outing as a progressive but inexorable demise. Thus, the *Berliner Morgenpost* talks about "the perversity of the Stasi denunciator system," which, through threats and blackmail, injected fear into his life and forced him to cooperate: "The traitor [the IM] was not only a perpetrator. He was also a victim." And more: "his tranquility Karlheinz Schädlich did not find. He had to live with the shame of having betrayed friends and relatives to the Stasi. Now he publicly ended his life."[56] The *Berliner Zeitung* voices (and apparently sympathizes with) the opinion of an anchor for ZDF, one of Germany's largest public television broadcasters: "I think that Karlheinz had two faces, like a Janus [. . .] He was in many ways a traitor, but at the same time he was also a victim of the dictatorship." The newspaper then describes the aftermath of his outing:

> he tried to be unreachable for anyone and again fled to a friend's weekend house in Bad Saarow. [This friend] remembered that "he was totally hysterical and in panic." Schädlich had called several people to apologize. He wanted to restore relationships, build bridges – without success. He said he didn't hurt anyone. That's what everyone says who is exposed.[57]

[56] Axel Lier et al., "Grass' Stasi-Spitzel erschießt sich auf Parkbank," *Berliner Morgenpost*, December 18, 2007.

[57] Andreas Kopietz, "Der Gentleman IM," *Berliner Zeitung*, February 2, 2008. See also Rolf Schneider, "Vielleicht war es Scham," *Die Welt*, December 19, 2007.

Even the tabloid *Bild-Zeitung*, bending the story to fit it into its salacious molds, as it often does, puts a relatively empathetic spin to Karlheinz's life: "His life – a mixture of resistance and Stasi, between treason and self-commiseration." And: "He rushed into obedience to come to a pact with the Stasi, and delivered others to the knives. His victims did not forgive him. A former friend: 'probably because he did not show any regrets.'"[58]

The editorializing of Karlheinz's story conveys to the reader a very clear lesson: He was the perpetrator/victim, whose outing compromised his ability to control his self-presentation, put him in a state of anxiety, and thrust him into a sea of shame and panic in which he eventually drowned. The bridges Karlheinz tried to build crumbled into that sea: He became a castaway, ostracized himself, lost face. His standing in the eyes of others was lowered, and his efforts to reassert his place in the community were useless.

The media framing of Karlheinz's (or of any other informer's) outing has the elements of what one might call an emotional economy of honor. Viewed from this honor-based perspective, the media coverage seems to convey the following message. First, Schädlich "dishonored" (i.e., disrespected) himself through his past conduct. He was no longer the honorable Herr Professor Schädlich, but simply a dishonest man. And because he dishonored himself through his past collaboration, he thereby lost, to an extent, any claim to respectful treatment. Schädlich's suicide can be interpreted as a modern version of an honor suicide – because his reputation had been severely damaged, and because he had been utterly incapable of reacquiring it and thus restoring his honor, he preferred dying to living without his honor.[59]

[58] "Tod eines Spitzels," *Bild-Zeitung*, December 19, 2007.

[59] Take, for instance, Kant's "forfeiture principle": "If a man cannot preserve his life except by dishonouring his humanity, he ought rather to sacrifice it [. . .] if he can no longer live honourably, he cannot live at all; his moral life is at an end [because] it is no longer in keeping with the dignity of humanity [. . .] Thus it is far better to die honoured and respected than to prolong one's life for a few years by a disgraceful act and go on living like a rogue." Immanuel Kant, *Lectures on Ethics*, trans. Louis Infield (Indianapolis: Hackett, 1979), 156. Quoted by Anderson, "Emotions in Kant's Later Moral Philosophy."

Second, even though Schädlich did something that did not suit his role as a citizen, let alone his social position as a "learned scholar," to use Kant's term, he nevertheless had a legitimate honorific claim to avoid shame, even more so because his moral culpability is partially mitigated, according to the media reports I described earlier, by the fact that Karlheinz himself had been a victim of the Stasi. To be sure, there is a legitimate publicity interest that would trump Schädlich's interest in safeguarding his honor. None of the newspapers objects to the declassification of the Stasi archives. In fact, they all make good and profitable use of them. But they also spell out a concern for the consequences of the outing. Safeguarding individuals from shameful exposure is part of what protecting one's honor is about. Even a moral philosopher like Immanuel Kant admitted, after all, that the avoidance of shame is a legitimate human concern, a point he illustrates in the *Metaphysics of Morals* (*Rechtslehre*), where he argues that filicides, although morally unacceptable, are, at the same time, motivated by shame-avoidance drives (namely, the desire to avoid the embarrassment of giving birth out of wedlock), whose legitimacy flows from a moral source – self-regard. In view of this, the state should hesitate before punishing mothers who are trying to reassert their honor.[60] Karlheinz probably wanted to brush his collaboration with the Stasi under the rug and see to it that the evidence of his past activity would vanish, so he could escape "social (and eventually actual) death." But after he was publicly identified as an IM, he was no longer able to hide his own misbegotten child.

Schädlich did not appeal to his *Persönlichskeitsrecht* to prevent his public identification as a collaborator. But his example is, I think, an instance of what the right of personality could be

The indelible trace of the ethics of honor in Kant's ethical system surfaces here. There are circumstances in which it is no longer worth living when one's honor has been tarnished.

60 On this, Anderson, "Emotions in Kant's Later Moral Philosophy;" Mika LaVaque-Manty, *Arguments and Fists. Political Agency and Justification in Liberal Theory* (New York: Routledge, 2002); Mika LaVaque-Manty, "Dueling for Equality: Masculine Honor and the Modern Politics of Dignity," *Political Theory* 34, no. 6 (2006): 715 – 740.

seen as trying to protect: claims that have an honor-based grounding. It is no wonder that the genealogy of the right of personality, as I argued in the previous chapter, reaches back to guarantees protecting honor that were associated with aristocratic privilege in the eighteenth century but were later generalized, subject to egalitarian pressures.[61]

To sum up, when the issue of informal collaboration comes to the forefront in public debates, we find some doses of skepticism in relation to IM outings. Part of that skepticism is rooted in the rejection of the mechanism of shame that public exposures often trigger in the present context, as is illustrated in the extreme case of Karlheinz Schädlich. Although priorities have been set in German society today, and the goal of "coming to terms with the past" seems to legitimate outings, one can discern social grammars of self-presentation that pose a caveat to freewheeling public exposures.

3.7 CONCLUSION: THE POLITICS OF SHAME

In this chapter I argued that when courts and the general public address the outing of IMs, the question of respect for former IMs is central, even more central than in the United States, which has been the contrast category throughout the chapter. Legal and political discussion about the public identification of Stasi collaborators in

[61] One should be careful about drawing extremely liberal analogies between moral and legal themes. However, there is a point to be made about the insightful parallel between the honorific grounding and subsequent egalitarian transformation of both Kant's ethics and the right of personality. Kant's ethics, like the legal doctrine that underpins the right of self-presentation, radically transform ethics of honor in the service of universal and egalitarian values. Although the ethics of honor reserve respect exclusively for people of superior social rank, Kant's ethics, by contrast, universalizes respectful standing to all rational agents, who are thereby entitled to rights. Yet that transformation is not fully and thoroughly achieved, and some features of Kant's ethics still bear the imprint of the ethics of honor.

Germany emphasize the worry that some information, even when of public concern, might be detrimental to the standing of individuals in society, and that risk motivates courts and media outlets to approach the issue the publicity of information regarding informers with caution. In the United States, even sexual preferences or drinking habits may be framed in such a way that they are subject to public scrutiny, claims to individual respect notwithstanding. By contrast, in the German case, information that clearly touches on a public issue of historical and contemporary relevance (the Stasi and its collaborators) may be restricted, even if not fully, to protect the individual from threats of public shaming and from threats to the person's standing and reputation.

4 CIVIC INTERPELLATIONS: DENUNCIATION AS SELF-DISRESPECT

4.1 THE RHETORIC OF *ZIVILCOURAGE*

Chapter 3 pointed out some of the concerns (reputational harm, loss of social standing, etc.) with public exposure of collaborators. This is the negative dimension of Rousseau's views on publicity. This chapter addresses its positive dimension: *l'opinion publique* as the guardian of "public morality" that "honors" the "virtuous citizen" and "shames" the "man of bad mores." From this perspective, exposures are practices that contribute to the process of setting up and upholding a standard of ideal citizenry, whereby public honor is bestowed on the righteous citizen, and public shame on the collaborator. In this chapter, I argue in favor of the conclusion that public identifications of unofficial collaborators are part and parcel of a process that is aptly captured by the notion of shaming interpellation, the construction of a deviant "other," whose status as such helps to consolidate the position of the "proper" citizenry. IM exposures, in other words, are part of a process to embed a political ideal in German public opinion. They provide the model of the corrupt citizen, the noncitizen, or the citizen of lesser degree, which contrasts with that of the proper citizen, who behaves courageously in the context of nondemocratic regimes and is therefore the standard of political agency in the new polity. The interpellation of public unveilings does not go unchallenged, of course, as the chapter will show.

The ideas of respect and self-respect are implicit in the interpellation process. The ideal of proper citizenship is constructed opposite the presupposition that "citizens" of the GDR somehow "degraded" themselves, that is, that they lacked self-respect. According to this view, unofficial collaborators were the utmost instantiation of the degraded citizen: They could have refused to collaborate, and yet they did not. They became "barbarians," in the words of Joachim Gauck, the first Federal Commissioner of the Stasi Records Office. And barbarians, to follow this rhetorical excess, should be subject to public dishonor (the general and open disapproval of many citizens and public officials) for having relinquished their status as citizens on account of their behavior. Put in the terms that were introduced in Chapter 1, under the GDR, collaborators disrespected themselves in the recognition sense because they did not defend their entitlement to be treated with dignity and because they abandoned their commitment to valued civic ideals. On account of this lack of self-respect, which had severe consequences for the rest of the citizenry – the contribution of collaborators, so the argument goes, contributed to the survival of the regime – many citizens refrain from engaging IMs with respect in the appraisal sense, that is, they negatively evaluate their lack of civic virtue and publicly dishonor them on that account. Now, as I said before, shaming interpellations are sometimes contested, and this is because, among other reasons unofficial collaborators, at whom they are targeted, as well as those who in a loose sense feel represented by IMs, can experience interpellations not as justified criticism of their actions or omissions, but as an expression of contempt and arrogance toward them. Shaming interpellations are for some a legitimate condemnation of an individual's moral qualities or character; based on an accurate retrospective assessment her conduct deserved public dishonor. For others, they are an unjustifiable display of superiority – *undeserved* public dishonor. These conflicting understandings illustrate the relative frequency with which expressions of respect, as was mentioned in Chapter 1, can be interpreted differently; unavoidably, relations of respect are immersed in a universe of symbolic interaction.

The structure of the chapter is as follows. Section two develops the notion of shaming interpellation and shows how it is put to work in the context of post-Stasi Germany. Section three explains how exposures are premised on the belief that IMs lacked civic courage, for which they must be publicly condemned. A shared understanding seems to be that because such individuals behaved in self-disrespectful ways, they lost the standing for preventing such exposure. Section four discusses the famous and controversial case of Manfred Stolpe, a high-level politician who had very close contacts to the Stasi but claims to have collaborated with the Stasi only for the common good. This section shows that even in a situation of "dirty hands" (an agent does something that would be considered wrong under normal circumstances but only in order to advance a greater good), the shaming interpellation of public exposures is at work. Finally, section five explains how public exposures do not always achieve their purpose. The process of consolidation of an ideal of proper citizenry is often contested and open to resignification.

4.2 THE FILTH OF DENUNCIATION: SHAMING INTERPELLATIONS

In 2009, Susanne Schädlich, the daughter Hans-Joachim Schädlich, the writer who made his appearance in the previous chapter, wrote a memoir about her father and her uncle.[1] The purpose of the memoir, she says, is to bring some clarity to the background and the events leading to the suicide of Karlheinz, Hans-Joachim's brother. In an interview with *Der Spiegel*, which the magazine entitled "The Filth Remains," she claims that with the memoir she wants to set the record straight and correct the false representation that the "Berliner press" spread about Karlheinz Schädlich. "The poor uncle," she quips, "was always the uncle, but also a traitor – the latter had more weight in the end." Karlheinz was an opportunist and became an IM voluntarily she says ("He thought only of himself. He received benefits from his work as an informer, and he also protected himself."). Furthermore, she adds, the memoir sets out "to rehabilitate my family, that was put in the pillory. All of a sudden he was the victim and we the villains, because we did not forgive him." She is skeptical about the suggestion that her uncle's intention in committing suicide was to die a victim, but complains that newspapers in Berlin certainly did take his death as

[1] Susanne Schädlich, *Immer wieder Dezember* (Droemer: München, 2009).

proof of his "innocence."[2] The filth remains, Susanne concludes, even now that he is dead.

The notion of "filth" evokes the oft-used trope in postcommunist rhetoric that the nation needs to be "cleansed" or "purified"[3] of its communist remnants. This rhetoric should be borne in mind in the context of our discussion because many outings are precisely social practices that help identify and expose the kind of "filth" that denunciators were, or so claim many civil and political activists. Like Karlheinz, most unofficial collaborators are considered to be individuals to whom a high degree of guilt may be ascribed because their actions were, ultimately, of their own choosing. In this bleak diagnosis, informers, particularly those who are unrepentant about their actions, are no longer considered full-fledged citizens. Rather, their status is that of abject, "filthy" individuals. And precisely on account of such status they deserve the treatment they get: to be publicly exposed as wrongdoers.

Thinking of IM exposures in terms of William Miller's understanding of shaming and humiliation rituals might be useful in supplementing these points. For Miller, the two rituals, although usually conflated in the literature on the subject, are not the same. Rituals of humiliation, on the one hand, are a sort of test or rite that paves the way for the attainment of good standing as a group member. Shaming rituals, on the other hand, hold the opportunity for reintegration into the group at a lower status than was previously held, if they allow reintegration at all. In both cases, then, social status or standing is at stake. The former type of ritual is usually a practice that might earn you a desirable status; the latter is a practice that calls into question a standing you presumably had before your own actions put it at risk.

[2] "Der Schmutz bleibt," *Der Spiegel*, March 9, 2009.

[3] The language of cleansing is very common in the context of several postcommunist European countries (for instance, Eastern European nations like Poland or the Czech Republic), where communism is portrayed as an alien force (the ideological manifestation of Soviet influence), making nationalism a continuing political process necessary for the purification of the nation. To the extent that the GDR was relatively autonomous from Soviet dominance, this deployment of the notion referred to "indigenous actors" in the German context.

Outings can be shaming rituals in that they brand IMs as filth and assign them a lower status than they previously possessed.

But there is an additional dimension of IM exposures that the notion of a shaming ritual, to my mind, does not fully emphasize, and that the concept of shaming *interpellation* does underscore. Succinctly put, a shaming interpellation is the process in which some individuals are constituted as deviant to underwrite a community of people whose identity is constructed or reaffirmed against these deviant "others." Shaming interpellations, in other words, intend to provide a form of cohesion and of common identification. Relying on this category, Jill Locke's work, for instance, studies the reemergence of "chain gangs" in some southern states in the United States and argues that such punishment provides a social bond for Americans who are anxious about American identity. The criminals of the chain gang form an ostensible, visible, and abject "other" whose status reaffirms the identity of upright, hardworking, and honest American citizens.[4] Public identifications of unofficial collaborators can be understood in similar terms.

Shaming interpellation operates through the use of legal and other informal or extralegal forms of *categorization* advanced in public discourse, particularly government discourse; in the discourse articulated in mass media; and in informal social networks. The interpellation also works through reiterated *public performances*. I now turn to explaining these two aspects of interpellations in the context of IM exposures and show how they create what one might call civic "publics" – open-ended and loose segments of the public that are constituted precisely in virtue of the process of reckoning with the issue of unofficial collaboration.[5]

[4] The notion comes from Judith Butler and is applied by Jill Locke, "Work, Shame, and the Chain Gang: The New Civic Education," in Jason Frank and John Tambornino (eds.), *Vocations of Political Theory: Political Imagination in an Age of Uncertainty* (Minneapolis: University of Minnesota Press, 2000), 284–304.

[5] Michael Warner, "Publics and Counterpublics," *Public Culture* 14, no. 1 (2002): 49–90. The idea of the publics that I have in mind is Michael Warner's. When one makes reference to the concept of public, Warner argues, the referent is usually "a kind of social totality" (the people in general) or a concrete

Categorization

The figure of the "denunciator" is not a mythical invention of reunified Germany. As was already mentioned in Chapter 2, there existed under the GDR a small army of informers who denunciated fellow citizens. What the interpellation does, however, is simplify taxonomies of complicity and resistance that are in fact complex, in order to create the abject individual that is interpellated. Jon Elster identifies as many as seven categories of wrongdoers. They include opportunists pursuing material gain; losers seeking the psychic benefits of appearing important in their own eyes and those of others; the malicious, seeking the satisfaction of watching their enemies or rivals go down; conformists, whose motivation is fear of material loss; fanatics and principled actors, who serve "the cause," the latter differing from the former in their willingness to change course once they discover that the cause is worthless or badly served; and finally the thoughtless, who have no motivations at all.[6] Along similar lines, a study on the GDR proposes four categories of wrongdoers: on one hand, opportunists and conformists, that is, those who acted in the knowledge that what they did was wrong, the former taking the initiative, with the latter merely succumbing to pressure; on the other hand, those who acted in good faith and those who embraced wrongdoers, thinking it was the lesser evil.[7]

The relevant law in Germany creates legal categories that erase these nuances. The Gesetz über die Unterlagen des

audience. But the idea of *a* public is distinct from *the* public or from any bounded audience. Publics, as Warner understands them, are partial (there might be an infinite number of publics within the social totality); open-ended (they exist by virtue of their address); impersonal (their primary orientation is reaching out to strangers); and, finally, are constituted through attention (as they commence with the moment of attention and cease to exist when attention is no longer predicated).

[6] Jon Elster, *Closing the Books. Transitional Justice in Historical Perspective* (New York: Cambridge University Press, 2004), 141–142.

[7] Lothar Fritze, *Täter mit gutem Gewissen: Über menschliches Versagen im diktatorischen Sozialismus* (Cologne: Böhlau Verlag, 1998). Referenced by Elster, *Closing the Books,* 2004, 137. See also Karsten Dümmel, "Motive, Motivketten und Kriterien für die Mitarbeit bei der Stasi," in Dümmel and Schmitz (eds.), *Was war die Stasi?*, 92–94.

Staatsicherheitsdienstes considers four categories of actors (affected persons, collaborators, advantaged persons, third parties) but ultimately, when it comes to their respective rights, boils it down to the dichotomy of victims/wrongdoers.[8] As soon as a tie with the Stasi is presumed, regardless of the particularities of each case, actors instantly fall within one of these two categories. The absence of a more fine-grained categorization of complicity might in part be attributed to the difficulty of translating the complexities of social and political realities into the language of the law. However, a pull toward some smaller, more precise categories of complicity would not have been difficult to imagine. In fact, in some of the so-called screening cases, discussed in Chapter 2, courts narrowed down the grounds for the dismissal of unofficial collaborators, for which they created subcategories of IM complicity that factored in the varying degrees of involvement with the Stasi.[9]

Extralegal categories of the abject informer are found in public discourse, where Stasi collaborators are often represented as individuals who are prone to lying, who are shameless and cynical, and who proved to be cowards through their actions. To illustrate in greater detail, consider the book *Die Täter sind unter uns [The Perpetrators Are Among Us]* by Hubertus Knabe, head of the former Stasi prison memorial site at Berlin-Hohenschönhausen.[10] Knabe is an activist who could be best described as a "moral entrepreneur"[11] who draws the attention of public opinion toward presumably neglected issues.[12] The text is a political tract addressing the legacy of the

[8] John Miller, "Settling Accounts with a Secret Police. The German Law on the Stasi Records," *Europe-Asia Studies* 50, no. 2 (1998): 305–330.

[9] On the "pull" toward smaller legal categories in law, see Frederick Schauer, "Categories and the First Amendment: A Play in Three Acts," *Vanderbilt Law Review* 34 (1981): 265–307.

[10] *Die Täter sind unter uns. Über das Schönreden der SED-Diktatur* (Berlin: List, 2008).

[11] The notion comes from Jürgen Habermas, "Hat die Demokratie noch eine epistemische Dimension? Empirische Forschung und normative Theorie," in *Ach, Europa* (Frankfurt am Main: Suhrkamp, 2008), 166f.

[12] Knabe is the author of several books on the Stasi and makes regular media appearances to discuss anything related to the secret police. His activism has

communist regime. It is worth more than a passing mention because it is an eloquent lamentation illustrating the tenor of public discourse around the outing of former Stasi collaborators in Germany. *The Perpetrators Are Among Us* warns against the attempt by the cadres of the old regime to trivialize the GDR dictatorship and explain away its injustices. The book discusses the "spectacular exposures" of former IMs with political ambitions. The author concludes that these outings were acts of *symbolic self-purification* of individuals who lent themselves to the "degrading" (*entwürdigenden*) double-dealing of denunciation. He adds, "The whole nation participated in the collapse of betrayal and lies. The perpetrators were not sent to prison, but they resigned office and lost their *social status*. After forty years of denunciations, moral standards were thus restored." He adds that those who refused to cooperate with the regime during the "dictatorship" saw confirmation of the integrity of their behavior. "Society reencountered its *values*, one of which says, 'the greatest scoundrel in the whole land is and remains the denunciator.'"[13]

The diagnosis is quite incisive in many ways. Three remarks are worth noting for now. First, in the passage public exposures are a *collective* practice: The whole country "participates" in them. Second, they stand in place of a criminal sentence: Collaborators are not branded criminals, but they are socially *disqualified* or demoted. Third, outings are *restorative*: They trigger a process of collective evaluation of Stasi collaboration that presumably leads to its public disapproval and an endorsement of a set of values defined in opposition to such collaboration. The accuracy of some of these points is disputable. For instance, as we will see later, it is not clear that the whole nation participates enthusiastically in and approvingly of public exposures. At any rate, the point to bear in mind is that informers are,

earned him aliases like "Opfer Messiah" (Messiah of victims) or "Hassfigur aller DDR-Nostalgiker und verharmloser." (roughly, the hate figure of those who are nostalgic of the GDR and trivialize its flaws). See for instance "Muntere Stasi-Aktivisten. Eine Abrechnung mit allen DDR-Nostalgikern," *Süddeutsche Zeitung*, April 16, 2006.

[13] Knabe, *Die Täter sind unter uns*, 167. The emphasis throughout is mine.

in this narrative, degraded "scoundrels" who have lost their social status, a category created by the shaming interpellation.

Public Performances

Go back to Jill Locke's claim that the reemergence of chain gangs in some southern states in the United States provides a social bond for Americans who are anxious for American identity. The criminals of the chain gang form an ostensible, visible, and abject "other" whose status reaffirms the identity of upright, hardworking, and honest American citizens. Chain gangs are always there, in the eyes of the public, and every glance cast on them is likely to spark a judgment of reprobation, as their promoters expect. Public exposures resemble chain gangs, at least partially: They too follow the logic of public reiteration that is typical of shaming interpellations, for the reasons and with the consequences I now turn to develop.

Although not without controversy, public officials in the newly unified German nation were committed to grappling with the communist past from the outset *and* sustained that policy unremittingly throughout the years. For this reason, outings of all sorts kept stirring public opinion even decades after the East German Parliament authorized the opening of the files in 1990. Several factors explain the "eagerness" of Stasi *Aufarbeitung*. For one, the precedent of Nazi *Aufarbeitung*, which garnered many critics, who argued that the latter had been too lenient and mild, made current public officials and activists more reluctant to avoid following in their predecessors' footsteps.

But at least as important as historical variables are structural ones, especially those regarding the manner in which, per law, the Stasi Records Office (BStU) declassified the Stasi archives, which in turn created the conditions for frequent public exposures of IMs and steadfast, undeterred coverage of them.[14] First, for the BStU, sufficient grounds for releasing a file containing the identity and

[14] For a good overview: Bärbel Broer, *Die Innere Struktur der Behörde für die Unterlagen des Staatssicherheitsdienstes der ehemaligen DDR* (Master Thesis, University of Hannover, 1995), 148–158.

further information about IMs is the request of a citizen for her own file. The number of such requests has steadily risen over the course of the years, as some of the citizens who in the past had hesitated before asking for their files, have eventually done so. Second, the BStU also declassifies the files per request of other government agencies and, to a lesser extent, of private organizations carrying out screening processes for past Stasi involvement. This process goes on to date. Third, the media may request from the Stasi Records Office information regarding suspected IMs, and as I have illustrated in the first chapter, in many instances it has a reasonable chance of broadly disseminating information regarding former denunciators, either on grounds of public interest or for purely sensationalist interests. Fourth, there is an academic division within the BStU, which, as I also mentioned in Chapter 1, carries out historical research, with the tempo proper to the nature of the academic profession (parsimony) and with the additional burden of organizing, this is the fifth point, a daunting archive. Indeed, the Stasi Records Office organizes and examines an overwhelming number of files (more than 100 kilometers).[15] It is even committed, with uncertain prospects of success, to reconstructing more than 15,000 sacks of material that MfS officials shredded at the last minute in an attempt to wipe out incriminating evidence. All these procedures can only be made in a piecemeal fashion.[16] In sum, the outcome at the aggregate level is an ever-present supply

[15] The office works through what it calls "the legacy of the Stasi," by which it refers to the 112 km of material (including photos, films, video, and sound recording, even shredded documents intended to be destroyed) that were in the archives of the Stasi.

[16] Some findings are casual. A case illustrating this last scenario involves the infamous Karl-Heinz Kurras who shot Benno Ohnesorg, a student participating in a West Berlin demonstration against the Shah of Iran (Ohnesorg's death contributed to the radicalization of the student movement and the rise of urban terrorism in the nation in the late 1960s). More than 40 years after the incident, 20 after the fall of the wall, an accidental finding in the Stasi archives revealed that the policeman who was tried and absolved of the murder of Ohnesorg was a Stasi denunciator. The news made it to the headlines of most national newspapers, which reiterated the abjection of denunciation.

of opportunities for exposing one or another IM. And the continued occurrence of exposures throughout time makes possible the sort of reiteration that is part and parcel with the process of shaming interpellation.

At the risk of depriving *Aufarbeitung* and outings of their gravity, it might be useful to analogize them to a more (apparently) trivial human pursuit: gossip.[17] The analogy is useful not only because sometimes the motivation to out collaborators seems to be propelled by an interest in revealing sensational facts about individuals (such as their past as denunciators) to disseminate these facts and "manufacture news," a profitable endeavor at the expense of the infamous secrets of IMs. That is, the interest is not historical or political, but rather strictly commercial. There are several interpretations regarding what gossip is and, more important, what gossip does. From one vantage point, it is low-value speech, to borrow a judicial term, a parasite to serious public discussion that can only entrench prejudices, feed the mills of media sensationalism, and lead to defamation and invasion of privacy. In a nutshell, gossip is an impoverished form of public discourse that can be dispensed at no cost and without much loss. But from a more sympathetic view, one that does not necessarily turn a blind eye to the sleaze that usually accompanies it, gossip plays a crucial role in enforcing social norms on proper civic behavior, and insofar as it does so, it ought to be tolerated. What is one to do if the cement of social order is mixed with some sleazy materials? To suppress gossip would be to hinder the functioning of one mechanism – gossip – that structures rules of civility in a society, so the argument goes. One may portray *Aufarbeitung*, in relation to informal collaboration, as massive and well-orchestrated gossip. It "operates" to endorse certain forms of behavior, namely civic ones, and condemn others. Putting obstacles such as personality rights in its way would be problematic because this would stifle the spontaneous dissemination

[17] Edwin C. Baker, "Autonomy and Informational Privacy or Gossip: The Central Meaning of the First Amendment," *Social Philosophy and Policy* 21, no. 2 (2004): 215–268. See also Jeanne M. Hauch, "Protecting Private Facts in France: The Warren & Brandeis Tort is Alive and Well and Flourishing in Paris," *Tulane Law Review* 68 (1994): 1219–1301.

and enforcement of social norms. Likewise, gossip is a practice that allows people to have informal conversations with others about how one would respond to certain concrete moral dilemmas. In this way, civic relationships may be developed through communication on ethics. Public exposures trigger just this process.

4.3 CITIZENS AND BARBARIANS: ENCOURAGING CIVIC COURAGE

The Stasi Files: Archives of *Zivilcourage*

Civic courage is the antithesis of denunciation. "Memory managers" in many postauthoritarian settings know that for the purposes of advancing and consolidating a set of political virtues, citizens should relate to heroic narratives, particularly those involving acts of courage, solidarity, and so on.[18] The subject of this section is precisely this narrative, and how it is constructed in political discourse through the ideal of civic courage. The following vignette will serve as a starting point.

A Stasi past runs counter to the aspirations of the new democratic regime, according to the rules of the Bundesrepublik, and therefore screening for Stasi complicity in German public service is considered to be a crucial task in the new era. Stasi-*Überprüfung* extends not only to key government positions but also to every bureau funded with taxpayers' money. Even agencies in charge of the promotion and organization of sports events are not exempt from the painstaking screening process. Such was the case of the German Ski Union (Deutscher Skiverband or DSV), which confronted the Stasi past of one of its trainers, Harald Böse, whom the Stasi files showed to have been an informer. Although he claimed he had been blackmailed into

[18] Walter Ch. Zimmerli and Joachim Landkammer, "Erinnerungsmanagement und politische Systemwechsel: Kleine Versuche zur Erklärung eines grossen Problems," in Joachim Landkammer, Thomas Noetzel, and Walter Ch. Zimmerli, *Erinnerungsmanagement. Systemtransformation und Vergangenheitspolitik im internationalen Vergleich* (München: Wilhelm Fink Verlag, 2006), 268.

service, the regional bureau for the BStU pleaded for dismissing Böse in 1998. Despite the petition, he remained in his post. Complaining that the DSV had shown very little involvement and concern for athletes who had been victims of the communist regime, a commentator added: "The taxpayer-funded elite sports should be decisively separated from those tainted Stasi people who represent no role model for young people. Otherwise, politics, with its songs of praise for moral courage, will also be untrustworthy."[19] I want to emphasize that the reason for advocating Böse's dismissal according to this view is that he set a negative example for the "youth," and that Böse's permanence within the ski union would call into question the government's commitment to publicly acknowledging the value of civic courage.

Praising instances of civic courage during the GDR era has been one of the missions of the Stasi Records Office. According to a leaflet for public dissemination, the explicit goals of the bureau are: giving citizens "the right to examine Stasi documents relating to oneself and to find out the extent to which the State Security Service of the GDR influenced one's own life;" promoting "the examination and reappraisal of the MfS's activities" and "the ruling mechanisms of the former GDR and the National Socialist past," to which ends the bureau makes documents available to scholars, the media, and private organizations dealing with the past; assisting public and nonpublic offices in screening requests, that is, in finding out "whether people occupying high positions in politics, sports, and administration worked for the State Security Service." Likewise, the bureau processes inquiries from the agencies responsible for the rehabilitation and restitution of victims of the communist regime, as well as those responsible for clarifying pension matters.[20] But the point I wish to

[19] Thomas Purschke, "Nur die üblichen Berichte," *Gerbergasse 18* 1(2003): 9.

[20] The results, as of May 2008, indicate that since 1991, about 6.2 million applications have been made to the Stasi Records Office. Around 2.5 million have been personal reviews of files; 3.2 million, screening requests; 20,600 requests have come from the media or research institutions; and 442,000 have served the purpose of rehabilitation, restitution, and criminal prosecution. Federal Commission for the Records of the State Security Service of the

underscore is that the leaflet also includes a message from the head of the office and Gauck's successor, Marianne Birthler. In her message, she draws attention to the fact that in the records of the MfS one finds not only "reports about people who spied on and betrayed their fellow citizens at the service of the Stasi, but also examples of civic courage, of many people's bravery and their longing for freedom."[21] This is a point she makes constantly.[22] Her predecessor, Joachim Gauck, set the example when he claimed that the files of the BStU not only contain "the protocols of oppression," but also testify "to the courage and determination of many who refused to be the henchman of this [GDR] dictatorship." This behavior, Gauck claims, was extremely risky, for those citizens did not know what to expect as a result of their refusal. Nevertheless "thousands of people refused to work with this system of oppression. The open files testify to this, and it is something of which the East Germans can be proud."[23]

Besides the public celebration of *Zivilcourage*, the further rhetorical move in public discourse that I wish to draw our attention to is the connection between civic courage (or absence thereof) and respect (or lack thereof). More concretely, the claim is that IMs did not act courageously and therefore failed to respect themselves. In other words, unofficial collaborators performed very poorly on the evaluative scale of citizenship[24] and thus lacked self-respect.

Former German Democratic Republic, "BStU. The Stasi Records Office," Pamphlet, n.d.

21 "BStU. The Stasi Records Office."

22 See, for instance, an interview given to the Spanish newspaper *El País* (Lola Huete Machado, "Un archivo guarda el horror y el coraje de muchos," May 23, 2010) in the context of the discussion of the law of historic memory in Spain.

23 Joachim Gauck, "Opening of Files and Public Access to Them: An Important Contribution to Dealing with the Communist Dictatorship," in Jerzy W. Borejsza, Klaus Ziemer, and Magdalena Hułas (eds.), *Totalitarian and Authoritarian Regimes in Europe: Legacies and Lessons from the Twentieth Century* (New York: Berghahn, 2006), 432–33.

24 Consider the following rough template defining the notion of citizenship as a form of *political agency* aimed at (a) a *common good* within (b) a *bounded community* in which the agent can claim (c) the *status of membership*. The exercise of this agency expresses (d) a *public role* of the citizen, fulfilled by the

In turn, this manifestation of self-disrespect made them subject to well-deserved public dishonor. But such dishonor is ultimately a form of disrespectful treatment. The claims are obviously never stated in such an explicit way, but these formulations capture the crucial issues that are at stake. I now turn to developing them more fully.

The Barbarization Thesis

Key in addressing the first point is the notion of degradation. Elaborating on a different subject, Elizabeth Anderson describes degradation as treating someone or something "in accordance with a lower degree of valuation than he is owed. We value things not just 'more' or 'less,' but in qualitatively higher and lower ways."[25] The definition is useful in making sense of what Marianne Birthler, Gauck's successor, might have in mind when she says that there "is a lot of shame in the East [. . .] Shame about the fact that we accepted [life under the Stasi], that we lived under such degrading (*entwürdigenden*) conditions." She continues, "Citizens from East Germany are ashamed," and want to forget "that they were afraid and did not open their mouths when it was necessary to do so."[26] Joachim Gauck

performance of (e) *activities or functions* characterized by (f) a set of *virtues*, where virtues are evaluative criteria for distinguishing better performances of the roles and practices of citizenship from worse. Melissa S. Williams, "Citizenship as Agency within Communities of Shared Fate," in Steven Bernstein and William D. Coleman (eds.), *Unsettled Legitimacy. Political Community, Power, and Authority in a Global Era* (Vancouver: University of British Columbia Press, 2009): 33–52.

[25] Elizabeth Anderson, "Is Women's Labor a Commodity?" *Philosophy and Public Affairs* 19, no. 1 (1990): 77. Respecting someone means valuing her in a higher way than one would if one merely used her. Treating a citizen as an informer means, under a Kantian light, treating her as an instrument (of governance) rather than holding her as a citizen worthy of respect. The fact that IMs were often remunerated is often presented as evidence that IMs acted on selfish grounds, but it would also be evidence that some citizens were used as means for accomplishing the state's ends. This is not viewing citizens as ends-in-themselves, but as instruments of socialist society.

[26] "Unterm Strich," *die tageszeitung*, April 14, 2006. See also "Viele wollen nicht daran erinnert werden," *Frankfurt Allgemeine Zeitung*, May 18, 2009.

argues along similar lines when he affirms in rhetorical but telling excess that, "The records indicate that oppression, war and hardship not only turn people into barbarians, but also into people willing to overcome hardship, into martyrs, and into dignified citizens (*würdevolle Bürger*)."[27] When Birthler says that the people under the communist regime yielded to living in degrading condition, and when Gauck argues that some individuals let themselves be turned into barbarians, what they mean is that they accepted being valued and treated in a less than dignified manner; they lacked self-respect.

The statements of Gauck and Birthler are fully Arendtian. Consider one of the most interesting aspects of Hannah Arendt's work: her focus not on the gross war criminal or the grand perpetrator, but on the average man during Nazi Germany.[28] Her famous characterization of the "family man" goes in this direction. Arendt describes him as a "bourgeois," a devoted "*paterfamilias*" and laments the "transformation of the family man from a responsible member of society, interested in all public affairs, to a 'bourgeois' only concerned with his private existence and knowing no civic virtue."[29] She adds: "It became clear that for the sake of his pension, his life insurance, the security of his wife and children, such a man was ready to sacrifice his beliefs, his honor, and his human dignity."[30] After such degradation, she concludes, this man was prepared to do anything.[31] Arendt's

[27] Quoted in Norbert Robers, *Joachim Gauck. Die Biografie einer Institution* (Berlin: Henschel, 2000), 183.

[28] Arendt wrote extensively on the subject of Nazi-*Aufarbeitung* in short pieces like "Collective Responsibility" in James Bernauer (ed.), *Amor Mundi: Explorations in the Faith and Thought of Hannah Arendt* (Boston: Martin Nijhoff, 1987): 43–50; "Organized Guilt and Universal Responsibility," in Peter Baehr (ed.), *The Portable Arendt* (New York: Penguin, 2003); in her exchange with Karl Jaspers, in Lotte Kohler and Hans Saner (eds.), *Hannah Arendt–Karl Jaspers Correspondence 1926–1969* (New York: Harvest Edition, 1993); or her influential *Eichmann in Jerusalem. A Report on the Banality of Evil* (New York: Penguin, 1963).

[29] Arendt, "Organized Guilt and Universal Responsibility," 2003, 153.

[30] Arendt, "Organized Guilt and Universal Responsibility," 2003, 152.

[31] Principled action involves a particular kind of "courage," one that does not necessarily involve the willingness to gladly risk one's life "for the sake of being as thoroughly and intensely alive as one can be only in the face of danger and

paterfamilias or bourgeois and Gauck's barbarian are similar. The point Arendt and Gauck make is that no self-respecting citizens would endure an "undignified" treatment at the hands of state officials. Such treatment should bring out one's civic courage. In the absence of such courageous action, citizens degrade themselves. The argument is roughly equivalent to Kant's objection to servility. Servility, Kant claims, is a form of self-disrespect because it amounts to showing a deferential role vis-à-vis others simply out of laziness, timidity, or a desire for some minor advantage. Such attitude shows little concern for one's moral and political status, that is, for one's rightful place in a moral and political community, which leads one to overlook the fact that one is equal to every other person. Protecting one's standing within a community requires effort and courage, the lack of which, Kant argues, might result from placing low value on one's worth.[32]

In sum, what I want to underscore about this way of understanding citizenship and of passing judgment on the "barbaric" behavior of unofficial collaborators is that it reflects the belief that dignity is tied to a performance. Dignity, in Arendt's view, is not a given, but rather something that might be lost if not exercised, an insight that is fully consistent with what Kant has to say about dignity.[33] Dignity, in other

death." Instead, what is at stake is a simpler kind of courage: "It requires courage even to leave the protective security of our four walls and enter the public realm, not because of particular dangers which may lie in wait for us, but because we have arrived in a realm where the concern for life has lost its validity." Hannah Arendt, *The Human Condition* (Chicago: University of Chicago Press, 1958), 186.

32 This interpretation of Kant's objection to servility comes from Thomas Hill Jr., "Servility and Self-Respect." In turn, the interpretation stems mainly from the Doctrine of Virtue in Kant's *The Metaphysics of Morals.* For analyses emphasizing the normative link between self-respect and courage, see also Bernard Boxill, "Self-Respect and Protest;" and Thomas Hill Jr., "Self-Respect Reconsidered," all included in Dillon, *Dignity, Character, and Self-Respect*.

33 This would be the case, in the context of Kant's epoch, of the soldier who failed to challenge to a duel someone who called his bravery into question; of the mother who refrained from taking up whatever means necessary (even immoral ones) to save her honor before losing it to an out-of-wedlock child; of

words, is for citizens, not for barbarians. And without dignity, one loses one's claim to respect.

Exposing Barbarians: On Public Dishonor

In the viewpoint under consideration, civic degradation in the past determines to a good extent how citizens ought to be treated in the present. If the past is to be remembered even against the inclination of some citizens, it is because that past shows the demeaning way in which citizens behaved, particularly unofficial collaborators. If the Stasi files were disclosed, even against the will of some individuals, it is because they show how individuals may be turned into barbarians, and how others may resist this transformation and behave like dignified (*würdevolle*) citizens. Thus, Gauck argues that there is a large group of people for whom the memory of the dictatorship is painful because "it reminds them of their lack of civic courage (*Zivilcourage*)." They don't want to be told that over and over again. They want "to forget quickly. However I lead an agency that keeps memory awake."[34]

The idea that dignity is a quasi-universal entitlement tends to obscure the extent to which practices of respect depend on an evaluation of one's actions. This is what Michael Walzer has in mind in the following passage:

> Egalitarian philosophers commonly hold that in a democratic community the citizens are entitled to equal respect. [There is] some sense in which the claim is justified; but [from a different perspective] it would make more sense to deny it. The law is no respecter of persons. When citizens petition their government, they are entitled to equal attention; when offices are available, to equal consideration; when welfare is distributed, to equal concern. But when respect is at issue, "deferential esteem,"

the woman who must fight her assaulter to death before accepting to live with the "dishonor" of rape. I am drawing heavily on the interpretations of Kant by LaVaque-Manty, "Dueling for Equality" and Anderson, "Emotions in Kant's Later Moral Philosophy."

[34] *Süddeutsche Zeitung*, April 23, 1995.

> special regard, ritual eminence, they are entitled to none at all until they have been found to deserve it.[35]

The crux of this passage is that respect is treatment or a regard to be earned, not something that can be taken for granted. Citizens are not necessarily entitled to equal respect because there is a component of respect that does not depend on an intrinsic worth of individuals but on what they deserve on the basis of what they do or fail to do.

The case of Hans Hartleb aptly illustrates how the public exposures of IMs have been socially conceived as dishonoring practices. Hartleb was a trainer at the women's national skiing team and had an honorary appointment (*Ehrenamt*) as vice-president of the skiing union of Thüringen. While in the exercise of both of his duties, a report by the weekly magazine *Der Spiegel* revealed that he had collaborated with the Stasi as IM Falun. By request of the secret police, he had written incriminating reports on some of his colleagues, as a result of which some of them had lost their jobs as professional athletes. Hartleb even delivered private information about other colleagues and received monetary compensation for all his services. One of the athletes he informed on was enraged that none of the 16 informers that had been set on him had come out and apologized to him.[36] Despite pressure from some quarters of public opinion, Hartleb was not dismissed from his job with the national team as a consequence of *Der Spiegel*'s note. What he did lose, however, was his *honorary* post. Furthermore, the fact that he did not openly acknowledge his collaboration and show signs of repentance simply contributes to his dishonor.

In sum, this section argued that unofficial collaborators are interpellated to uphold civic ideals. The narrative of civic courage as I described it points in this direction. This narrative is based on fairly transparent ideas about respect and self-respect. Unofficial collaborators lack self-respect because they did not defend their dignity as citizens who are not servile to public authorities and because their

[35] Michael Walzer, *Spheres of Justice. A Defense of Pluralism and Equality* (New York: Basic Books, 1983), 267.

[36] Purschke, "Nur die üblichen Berichte," 7–8.

behavior was beneath civic standards. On account of these uncivic attitudes and behavior, unofficial collaborators deserve to be publicly dishonored.

4.4 DIRTY HANDS AND RESPECT: WHEN IN DOUBT, OUT

The devil is in the details, but sometimes it is there regardless of the details. Shaming interpellations are, of course, based on material evidence of the complicity of informers with the Stasi; but sometimes they can ignore the moral nuances behind the motivations of some of those who collaborated with the Stasi. The case of Manfred Stolpe, introduced in the previous chapter, illustrates this. Stolpe contends that he knew the moral stakes of his rapprochement to the Stasi but cultivated it nonetheless for the sake of the common good. Reflecting on Stolpe's case, Jürgen Habermas writes: "The ambivalent nature of post-Stalinist entanglement, which has been illuminated by the Stolpe case and of which we in the West have only a vague understanding, makes it even more difficult to come to any moral judgment on individual cases."[37] This section argues that shaming interpellations circumvent rather than confront this difficulty for the purposes of demarcating the boundaries of acceptable political action, or, to be precise, of a particular conception of acceptable political action. Despite the fact that Stolpe's behavior was far from being opportunistic, and that his intentions were arguably based on considerations of public interest, he was nonetheless interpellated as an unworthy citizen who compromised with dictatorial powers, even when that required of him that he lie and betray the trust of fellow citizens.

Manfred Stolpe was an active member of the Evangelical church during the GDR years. He held several posts within its governing bodies, a position that put him in close contact with Stasi officials. He became the representative of the church vis-à-vis GDR authorities, largely due to the fact that he was prepared to negotiate with

[37] Jürgen Habermas, "Bemerkungen zu einer verworrenen Diskussion. Was bedeutet '*Aufarbeitung* der Vergangenheit' heute?" *Die Zeit*, April 3, 1992.

those in power, something others within evangelical circles were reluctant to do. Stolpe became one of the architects of a modus vivendi between the church and the state that came to be known as *Kirche im Sozialismus* (Church in Socialism), which could be characterized as a point of balance between blind conformity to the existing political conditions of the GDR and open rejection of them.[38]

Stolpe faced the accusation of having been a Stasi collaborator (IM Sekretär) and came under pressure to resign from public office, which he did not do. Like Heinrich Fink (IM Heiner),[39] who was dismissed as the president of Humboldt University, Stolpe never accepted that he had collaborated with the Stasi (although, one should note, the evidence against Stolpe was by far less incriminating than that against Fink). In his refusal to accept his complicity with the Stasi, Stolpe went as far as to sue CDU politician Uwe Lehmann-Brauns, who in a television broadcast affirmed that, to paraphrase him, the fact that Stolpe had become prime minister of Brandenburg despite his past as an informer was something that gave him a headache.[40] After a long and winding nine-year legal process, Stolpe won a defamation suit against him. The Federal Constitutional Court argued that dubious and speculative affirmations must be presented as such by the speaker, and that, to avoid a legal process, she needs to clarify the meaning of ambiguous statements. Uwe Lehmann-Brauns was not willing to do this.[41] But while the Court ruled in favor of

[38] Anne Sa'adah, *Germany's Second Chance: Trust, Justice, and Democratization* (Cambridge: Cambridge University Press, 1998), 195–196.

[39] Fink's act is very incriminating. He alerted the Stasi about a student who wanted to flee East Germany. In 1988, he reported on 19 students who wrote an open letter that criticized the SED's oppression. See Renate Oschiles, "Der Denunziant," *Berliner Zeitung*, June 16, 2005.

[40] His exact words: "Die Tatsache, dass Herr Stolpe, wie wir alle wissen, IM-'Sekretär,' über 20 Jahre lang im Dienste des Staatssicherheitsdienstes tätig war, dass er die Chance erhält, hier Ministerpräsident zu werden. . .das verursacht mir doch . . . Kopfschmerzen."

[41] Kirsten Teubel, "Unterlassungsanspruch bei mehrdeutigen Äusserungen und zweifelhaftem Wahrheitsgehalt," *Archiv für Presserecht-Zeitschrift für Medien- und Kommunikationsrecht* 1 (2006): 20–24. For a friendly reading of the Bundesverfassungsgericht's decision, arguing that it does not in any way

Stolpe, some media outlets "ruled" against him, as it were. A "black day for freedom of expression and of the press in Germany," is the way the newspaper *taz* communicated its disappointment the day after the Federal Constitutional Court reached its decision. Commentators in that newspaper[42] argued that *Persönlichkeitsrecht* in this context produced a chilling effect on the press (an argument that would have found more resonance under American jurisprudence[43]). The newspaper went on to explain that before the Stolpe decision the Federal Constitutional Court had laid down the precedent that whenever an expression was potentially threatening to another's rights of personality, in this case one's honor, but was so open-ended that it could be interpreted in several ways, then the courts should rule against the plaintiff insofar as at least one of the interpretations of the expression was not offensive to one's honor. With the *Stolpe* decision, so *taz* concluded, the Federal Constitutional Court abandoned strong judicial protection of freedom of expression. Underlying this fierce defense of free expression is, of course, a tacit reprobation of Stolpe's behavior by some groups in German society (but not all groups, as will be seen in the next section).

Stolpe denied ever having acquiesced to work for the Stasi, but he admitted to having had very close contacts with it. He did some of the things one would expect informers to do, such as giving the Stasi information about fellow members of the Evangelical church. And yet his reasons for acting in this way, he claimed, reflected his best judgment about the ideal strategy for benefitting the church. He contended that he had been a "middleman" between the church and the Stasi, and that whatever "pact" he had crafted with the Stasi

threaten freedom of expression and that it is actually consistent with precedent, mainly with the Lüth case, see Martin Hochhuth, "Kein Grundrecht auf üble Nachrede – Der Stolpe-Beschluss des BVerfG schütz das Personal der Demokratie," *Neue Juristische Wochenschrift* 59, no. 4 (2006): 189–191.

42 "In Zukunft mit Schere im Kopf," *die tageszeitung*, November 18, 2005; "Im Zweifel für die Ehre," *die tageszeitung*, November 17, 2005.

43 Under First Amendment law, *New York Times v. Sullivan* 376 U.S. 254 (1964), the press cannot be successfully sued for defamation unless reckless intention to disregard the truth is shown to be its motivating force.

during this time should be regarded as one of political necessity, what he envisioned as the only way to protect the church. In describing his reasons for working closely with the Stasi, he even put a Weberian label to his work: "Demystification of power."[44] His intention all along, he said, had been to understand the inner functioning of the system.

The parliamentary commission formed in Brandenburg to examine Stolpe's past (controversially) accepted his version of the events. In the commission, one parliamentarian turned to Kant's 1797 text on what he called the "alleged" right to lie out of love for humanity to evaluate Stolpe's involvement with the Stasi. The deputy quoted Kant:

> Thus a lie, defined merely as an intentionally untrue declaration to another, does not require what jurists insist upon adding for their definition, that it must harm another (*mendacium est falsiloquium in praeiudicium alterius*). For it always harms another, even if not another individual, nevertheless humanity generally, inasmuch as it makes the source of right unusable.[45]

Here, one of the most demanding aspects of Kant's ethics is put to the service of *Vergangenheitsbewältigung*.

What is one to make of this allegedly Kantian recrimination of Stolpe's actions? One way of explaining it is as mudslinging behind a philosophical façade: Stolpe's antagonist is not really taking sides on a complex moral issue but simply using incriminating information from the Stasi files to discredit a rival. This would be another case, so typical in transitional justice contexts, of misuse or manipulation of information about the old cadres of the *ancien régime* or simply about political opponents to oust them from the new political order.

A less cynical way of interpreting this Kantian criticism of Stolpe's actions is to see it as emerging from the clash between two types of

[44] Manfred Stolpe, *Schwierige Aufbruch* (Berlin: Goldmann Verlag, 1993).

[45] Ehrhart Neubert (ed.), *Abschlussbericht des Stolpe-Untersuchungsausschusses* (Köln: Heinrich-Böll-Stiftung, 1994), 273. The translation comes from Immanuel Kant, "On a Supposed Right to Lie from Philanthropy," in *Practical Philosophy*, Mary Gregor, ed. (Cambridge: Cambridge University Press, 1996): 612.

ethical outlooks, namely, to use Max Weber's classic dichotomy between an ethics of convictions of those who followed strict codes of conduct that prevented them from compromising with the Stasi and an ethics of responsibility of cunning political actors, like Stolpe, who were willing to relax rigid moral standards out of political necessity.

Some scholars would contend that this distinction is misleading. For example, Mary Fulbrook argues that the appeal to this distinction in the context of the GDR falsely leaves the impression that there actually was a choice to be made under the communist regime: One could either yield to the Stasi and work from within, or one could refuse to entertain any contacts with the Stasi and put up resistance, working against it from the outside. According to Fulbrook, the political circumstances in place in the GDR were such that the two courses of action were not antagonistic to each other, but symbiotic.[46]

One possible conclusion to draw from Fulbrook's rejection of the Weberian dichotomy is that the philo-Kantian recrimination of Stolpe, based on an ethics of conviction, is too dogmatic, and that he (and other political actors like him) should not be condemned, publicly or even privately, or sanctioned; after all, the fact that he worked "from within," alongside the Stasi, does not mean that he was working for it, in pursuit of *its* goal, or that he obstructed the action of those who worked "from the outside" to undermine the communist regime. All things considered, one could argue, he was working toward the common good.

This might very well be the case. But our parliamentarian's insistence that Stolpe be condemned and sanctioned (i.e., lustrated) may not be all that unwarranted and dogmatic, as it may seem. His central message may be interpreted as follows: even if Stolpe did indeed collaborate with the Stasi to consolidate the position of the church and the community vis-à-vis political authorities through the *Kirche im Sozialismus* doctrine, he did something that rubs against ordinary morality. Stolpe might have deemed it inevitable to lie to some of his church colleagues, believing political necessity dictated he do so.

[46] Mary Fulbrook, *Anatomy of a Dictatorship. Inside the GDR 1949–1989* (New York: Oxford University Press, 1995), 87–128.

But political necessity, our Kantian parliamentarian seems to imply, is not morally redeeming. Reprobation of Stolpe's immoral actions needs to be socially expressed, our parliamentarian believes. They warrant neither indulgence nor absolution, but deserve some form of condemnation. This condemnation, which is precisely what shaming interpellations provide, need not be the result of an "absolutist" and rigid position.

Michael Walzer's formulation of what he called the problem of "dirty hands," inspired by Sartre's homonymous play, captures these concerns about Stolpe's collaboration with the secret police. The problem of dirty hands begins with a moral dilemma: a situation in which a political actor must choose between two courses of action, both of which would be wrong for her to undertake, for example, choosing between honoring a moral principle and averting a looming disaster or helping to moderate its harm. Walzer identifies two ways in which political actors can confront the dilemma. The first one is the way of Hoerderer, the Communist leader in Sartre's play: "I have dirty hands right up to the elbows. I've plunged them in filth and blood. Do you think you can govern innocently?"[47] Hoerderer poses this question, rhetorically. He believes, as does Walzer, that it is not possible to govern, or simply engage in politics, innocently. However, Walzer adds, "This does not mean that it isn't possible to do the right thing while governing. It means that a particular act of government […] may be exactly the right thing to do in utilitarian terms and yet leave the man who does it guilty of a moral wrong. The innocent man, afterwards, is no longer innocent."[48] The alternative to this position is the "absolutist" one, as Walzer calls it. The political actor can decide to remain innocent, but in so choosing "he not only fails to do the right thing (in utilitarian terms), he may also fail to measure up to the duties of his office (which imposes on him a considerable responsibility for the consequences and outcomes)."[49] Briefly put, a political agent has two options: she can do the right thing by transgressing important moral norms, thereby losing her

[47] Michael Walzer, "Political Action: The Problem of Dirty Hands," *Philosophy and Public Affairs* 2, no. 2 (1973): 161.

[48] Walzer, "Political Action," 161. [49] Walzer, "Political Action," 161.

innocence; or she can refrain from moral transgression, thus retaining her innocence, but failing to do the right thing. This is the dilemma and the alternatives to confront it, according to Walzer, who embraces the former.

But in endorsing this alternative, he adds a crucial proviso: when a political actor dirties her hands, she should *not* be allowed to go scot-free, for that would simply set everyday morality aside, at a great cost for all. Some sort of punishment or penance needs to be imposed on those who break the moral code, even if they do it for a noble cause. Walzer rejects some canonical ways of thinking about the sort of treatment attendant on political actors who have dirtied their hands by breaking a moral code to achieve a political good. The Machiavellian way, according to him, says nothing about the penalty that awaits political actors who commit morally wrong actions. The Weberian way, in turn, tackles the problem of dirty hands exclusively within the confines of the individual conscience; the politician with dirty hands is a "tragic hero" who suffers as a result of his decision, but such self-awareness, although valuable, is insufficient. In contrast to these approaches, Walzer advances one that resembles the doctrines of just assassination and civil disobedience. According to Walzer's approach, political actors who violate moral or legal rules to do what they believe they should do, must at the same time acknowledge their responsibility for the transgression by accepting punishment or doing penance. William Miller argues along similar lines when he presents us with what he calls the moral menial: an individual who performs a vital role for the functioning of a political public order that most people consider immoral, even disgusting. Miller writes: "Moral menials deal with moral dirt, or they have to get morally dirty to do what the polity needs them to do. And despite the fact that we need to attract people to this kind of labor, we still hold them accountable for being so attracted."[50]

The reason to defend some form of sanction or at least a public condemnation of political actors who dirty their hands rests on a principle of caution and prudence. As Walzer puts it, "political action

[50] William Miller, *The Anatomy of Disgust* (Cambridge, MA: Harvard University Press, 1997), 184.

is so uncertain that politicians necessarily take moral as well as political risks, committing crimes that they only think ought to be committed. They override the rules without ever being certain that they have found the best way to the results they hope to achieve, and we don't want them to do that too quickly or too often. So it is important that the moral stakes be very high – which is to say, that the rules be rightly valued."[51]

With this framework as a background, consider Stolpe's case. As a moral menial, he dirtied his hands. He was the architect of the *Kirche im Sozialismus* doctrine, the construction of which could not have been carried out without the work that he performed, or so at least he claims. He was willing to engage the Stasi for reasons that cannot be associated with personal gain or malicious intent; furthermore, the evidence proving he *willingly* worked as an informer was far from conclusive. But no matter how good his intentions or how beneficial the outcome of his actions for society, many politicians and activists held him accountable for those actions. They encourage the practice of public dishonor of moral menials like Stolpe to enshrine an ideal of political action, one where compromises are unacceptable and where violations of the moral code should not be tolerated. If Walzer is right, this reaction might be justified because it protects important moral norms, such as an injunction against lying. This is particularly important in a society like the German one – or at least its local societies in the eastern part of the country. As happened in many other postcommunist societies, in the GDR the surveillance imposed by the state, bred, and indeed fed on, the mutual distrust among citizens.

Now, it is important to observe that not all political and social actors support public identifications. For some of them, it is fully justified that public exposures lambast unofficial collaborators on account of their civic degradation. But as an unintended consequence, public exposures also engender the opposite effect – resistance from groups that are partially sympathetic to collaborators (some of them at least) or who believe that public identifications are not the ideal way to confront them. Shaming interpellations, in other words, sometimes fail.

[51] Walzer, "Political Action," 179–180.

4.5 FAILED INTERPELLATION?

Public honor, Walzer argues, is conferred only on the basis of deserts, as determined by an "objective measure:" "What is called for is an absolute judgment. When the church designates its saints or the state its heroes, questions are asked that have to be answered with a Yes or a No. The miracle did or did not occur; the courageous action was or was not performed."[52] The same goes for public dishonor; it too calls for an absolute judgment. The sin was or was not committed; the degrading action was or was not performed. Part of what the shaming interpellation does is precisely to produce an absolute judgment about whether the actions of unofficial collaborators were degrading or not, and by implication, whether the actions of the rest of the citizenry were courageous or not. But as one might anticipate, producing such judgments is not an easy task. Public authorities can manipulate them "so as to encourage politically or socially useful performances."[53] More important, social disagreement may on occasion frustrate the search for absolute judgments. And the difficulty of producing persuasive and widely accepted standards for public honor or dishonor is precisely a sign of what Jill Locke calls an interpellation failure. Many social and political actors in society challenge the absolute judgment of public honor or dishonor for political action by advancing and defending alternative narratives about the limits and possibilities of civic courage in the GDR. And as we shall see, this challenge is in part due to the fact that many citizens in Germany perceive the shaming interpellation of unofficial collaborators as harboring disrespectful social interactions. What for some counts as unobjectionable public dishonor of IMs, for others is objectionable public disparagement not only of those IMs, but also, to a lesser degree, of other East Germans who relate to the moral predicaments that, they think, unofficial collaborators faced. These conflicting

[52] Walzer, *Spheres of Justice*, 259.

[53] The risk, Walzer argues, is that authorities "think it best to invent a performance and to 'frame' an appropriate performer so as to make sure that they are encouraging exactly what they want to encourage"(Walzer, *Spheres of Justice*, 262).

social understandings of the same practice show how, as Hobbes contended, expressions of respect and disrespect can easily be misinterpreted and are a source of conflict.

Citizens can contest shaming interpellations, and when resistance is considerable enough, interpellations are subject to failure. To illustrate this, Jill Locke offers an account of the disappearance of chain gangs and other forms of public punishments such as forced labor in eighteenth-century France. They were discontinued largely due to the fact that, instead of aggrandizing the power of the monarch and conveying a normative message, which was their intended purpose, they could create a form of solidarity between the convict and passersby and defied the message that was intended to be communicated to audiences, unleashing "a whole set of significations wholly out of the control of the people who put them [these forms of punishment] there."[54] Similar punitive measures such as forced labor could go as far, in the United States, as "subverting the very distinction between vice and virtue,"[55] as the criminal garners empathy from the public. Briefly put, interpellations fail when the authority to punish abject individuals, as well as the legitimacy of the punishment itself, is called into question and when, instead of upholding a model of ideal behavior, interpellations create unexpected bonds of solidarity between culprits and audiences.

Public exposures of unofficial collaborators are not forms of punishment but civic disqualifications. Nevertheless, the unintended consequences they generate are similar to those associated with punishments like chain gangs or public labor. This becomes clear when one considers two facts associated with public identifications. First, the authority of the BStU, in theory a mere provider of information at the service of citizens and other branches of the government, but in practice a promoter of IM exposures, has been disputed on account of its motivations and goals. Second, I mentioned before that public punishments threaten to create a bond of solidarity between the misfeasor and the audience, one that may even lead to the subversion of the moral and even legal parameters that turned the individual into

[54] Locke, "Work, Shame, and the Chain Gang," 293.
[55] Locke, "Work, Shame, and the Chain Gang," 290.

a misfeasor. In an analogous fashion, public identifications of unofficial collaborators have fostered a kind of solidarity between the latter and political and social actors; in turn, bonds of solidarity ultimately motivate these groups to doubt and contest the validity of the moral and political bases for condemning informants. The following lines develop these two contentions.

Some scholars have criticized the Stasi Records Office in rather strong terms.[56] One of them calls the agency an "apparatus of memory control"; complains that it was guided "by a man [Joachim Gauck] who, as a pastor, had a professional stake, and as a former dissident, a personal stake, in seeing the world divided into light and darkness and in classifying its inhabitants as either righteous or sinners"; and insists that it "has done its best to keep these distinctions clean by sheltering the victims and by exposing the perpetrators to public shame."[57] Signs of social and political discontent with the work of the Stasi agency are also common in public opinion. "This agency achieves nothing but propagandistic goals and the disparagement of individuals."[58] That is the animosity with which a reader of the newspaper *Die Welt* expresses her discontent with the work of the bureau in charge of administrating the Stasi archives.

[56] These scholars question the desirability of Stasi Records Office. Claus Offe has been skeptical that strategies of "civic disqualification," of which public exposures are an instance, can render their desired purpose of reconciliation and points out that they lend themselves to misuse (as when they are used as political weapons or as opportunities to blackmail others) or incite acts of revenge; more important, he claims, these strategies violate several rules of principles of the law and rely on files whose accuracy is very dubious. See Offe, "Disqualification, Retribution, Restitution", 17–44.

[57] Inga Markovits, "Selective Memory: How the Law Affects What We Remember and Forget about the Past. The Case of East Germany," *Law & Society Review* 35, no. 3 (2001): 540–2. In the same passages, Markovits casts doubt on the extent to which Gauck's agency is really conducting a job to help victims make peace with their own past and likens the activities of the agency to "the recollection process in which what actually happened in the past is gradually filtered and condensed into a few handy images that fit the self-perception and political interest of those who do the recollecting."

[58] A response to the article D. Von Banse, R. Herzinger, and T. Schmid, "Viele Stasi-Spitzel im Westen noch nicht enttarnt," *Die Welt*, May 24, 2009.

Her language is incisive, especially in its use of the notion of disparagement, which is an illegitimate loss of standing and an act of disrespect. In what sense can the Stasi Records Office be seen as an instrument of disrespect?

The complaint is part and parcel with a broader phenomenon: the belief, widespread mostly in East Germany and amply documented, that with the unification of Germany, West German political values were "imposed" on the whole of the nation, just like the Grundgesetz (Basic Law), the Constitution of the Bundesrepublik, was adopted after the reunification, to become the constitutional order of the whole nation. Some scholars have further argued that East German self-identification took shape as a reaction to what were perceived as "colonialist" stereotypes and narratives encouraged by Western elites seeking to legitimize their predominance in ruling positions in unified Germany, discredit Eastern intelligentsia, and construct an imagined community predicated on a distorted and patronizing view of the GDR and its citizens.[59] Indeed, immediately after unification, East Germans "began defiantly to defend their identity."[60] They did so not only by cultivating a rather uncanny nostalgia for the past, or *Ostalgie* (Eastalgia), as it has come to be known, but also by supporting public figures that to a greater or lesser extent collaborated with the Stasi and afterward struggled to maintain their public standing in unified Germany. Manfred Stolpe's (IM Sekretär) is one such case; writer Christa Wolf's (IM Margarete) is another. These "indigenous" leaders who had not directly participated at the higher echelons of the communist regime turned out to be appealing to the average East German, so the argument goes, because, like her, they were perceived as fallible individuals who were forced by circumstances to conform

[59] For the view that East Germany was "colonized" see Wolfgang Dümcke and Fritz Vilmar (eds.), *Kolonialisierung der DDR: Kritische Analysen und Alternativen des Einigungsprozesses* (Münster: Agenda Verlag, 1996).

[60] Bernd Faulenbach, "Die Enquete-Kommissionen und die Geschichtsdebatte in Deutschland seit 1989," in *The GDR and its History: Rückblick und Revision. Die DDR im Spiegel der Enquete-Kommissionen* (Amstedam: Rodopi, 2000), 30. See also Paul Cooke, *Representing East Germany since Unification. From Colonization to Nostalgia* (Oxford: Berg, 2005), 8ff.

outwardly with the regime, yet cunning in using the system to achieve positive goals.[61] In other words, according to these views, many citizens in the eastern German states experienced public exposures, and their embedded narrative of courageous citizens and cowardly "others" is patronizing and belittling not only of informers but also of those in their milieu. Put in slightly different terms, perceived colonialist attitudes, which are inherently disrespectful, nurtured a dose of skepticism with regard to public unveilings.

Take again the case of Stolpe as an example of this *perception* (I cannot stress this noun strongly enough) of disrespect. Stolpe's popularity in Brandenburg remained unaltered despite the recriminations against him for his Stasi contacts.[62] A 1994 interview of Brandenburg parliamentarians revealed that with the exception of members of Bündnis 90 (Alliance 90), whose members came to politics from more protest-oriented milieus in East Germany and tended to see the Stolpe issue in absolute terms of guilt and innocence, most parliamentarians believed that the eastern public backed Stolpe because he was regarded as one of their own, embodying the contradictions and ambiguities of their owns pasts. He was perhaps more "representative," they claimed, than civic activists who resisted the *ancien régime* and now sought to purify East German politics in the name of morality. Furthermore, these parliamentarians overwhelmingly supported Stolpe and considered that his East German identity was a defining factor in their support, and the electorate's, for him. He did not perceive himself as a "loser" of unification or as a victim. Rather, he was a self-confident politician who was proud of his Brandenburg roots and eastern identity.[63]

After the conclusion of the parliamentary debate on Stolpe's case, mentioned in the previous chapter, his party, the SPD, received an

[61] For example, Dolores Augustine, "The Impact of Two Reunification-Era Debates on the East German Sense of Identity," 563–578.

[62] According to a poll that appeared in "Sympathien für Stolpe ungebrochen," *Tagesspiegel*, December 4, 1993.

[63] For the interviews and their interpretation see Jennifer A. Yode, *From East Germans to Germans?: The New Postcommunist Elites* (Durham, NC: Duke University Press, 1999), 139, 173.

absolute majority in the Brandenburg elections; by contrast, Bündnis 90 suffered a major defeat and even lost its representation in the local parliament. Jennifer Yoder contends that "the moral crusades of some of [Bündnis 90] leaders, especially where transitional justice is concerned, may have the unintended effect of repelling easterners who prefer to forget the past."[64] This is particularly true in Brandenburg, where Günther Nooke, at the time the Bündnis 90's leader (he later joined the CDU) headed the offensive against Stolpe and was extremely vocal about unveiling unofficial collaborators. In view of all of this, Dolores Augustine might be right in claiming that "the very fact that it was impossible to know for sure which side Stolpe had been on, whether he had been working for the SED or working to subtly undermine it, made him such a powerful symbol because average eastern Germans were not certain themselves where they had stood. The controversy mobilized Easterners in an act of defiance."[65] This act of defiance and the uneasiness about the Bündnis 90's "moral crusade" is not unlike the social resistance toward public labor in prerevolutionary France – they are manifestations of a failed shaming interpellation, where a punitive or quasi-punitive practice is contested and is unsuccessful in conveying its intended normative message.

For social actors who resist the interpellation, Stolpe and Wolf are not abject individuals who lacked the civic courage to resist authorities and who therefore deserve to be put in the pillory, but citizens who made necessary compromises and should be treated in a less condemnatory fashion. The moral compass that casts informing as a barbaric and degrading activity promotes the self-aggrandizing attitudes of some citizens towards others. Thus, instead of creating a civic "we," public unveilings can strengthen a bond among the abject "they," and this is to a large extent owed to the fact that unveilings are frequently perceived not as legitimate recriminations meant to hold some citizens accountable, but as practices based on condescending views of GDR citizens. In short, in this view public exposures distribute dishonor not on the basis of desert but on the basis of contempt.

[64] Yode, *From East Germans to Germans?*, 173.

[65] Augustine, "The Impact of Two Reunification-Era Debates on the East German Sense of Identity," 568.

It matters, then, how public exposures are perceived. To conclude this section, consider Christina Tarnopolsky's insights on public shaming.[66] Shame, Tarnopolsky argues, is the "discomforting and perplexing cognitive recognition of the gaze of another that reveals an inadequacy in the self, or in the 'other' by which one currently measures the self." Far from assessing them in a negative light, Tarnopolsky submits that the discomfort and perplexity created by shame are "potentially salutary" because they are necessary for self-consciousness, self-criticism, and moral and political deliberation. Shaming, in her view, does not necessarily exclude respect by stigmatizing individuals, and then using the stigma to strip them of dignity and deny them political standing. Rather, shaming can work within a political structure of respect. However, for that to happen – and this is her crucial point – shaming must unfold within a political situation in which it is clear that producing the kind of cognitive recognition described before is the goal of the acts of shaming for all parties engaged in democratic deliberation and/or of the structures that enable these deliberations. In other words, the motives behind the shaming must be clear to all parties involved, especially to those who are being shamed.[67] Otherwise, the possibility of the salutary moment is foreclosed, and shaming spirals into embarrassment or humiliation, in a word – disrespect.[68] Admittedly, Tarnopolsky's is an extremely demanding standard. It would be naïve to expect that the motives of

[66] Christina Tarnopolsky, "Prudes, Perverts, and Tyrants. Plato and the Contemporary Politics of Shame," *Political Theory* 32, no. 4 (2004): 476–479.
[67] Tarnopolsky, "Prudes, Perverts, and Tyrants," 480, 485, 486.
[68] In articulating her view of what she calls "respectful shame," Tarnopolsky builds on the basis of Platonic dialogues. In her example, Socrates' interlocutors often feel vexed about the manner of his ironic interaction with them. Many of them believe that he is simply ridiculing them. However, motivating his seemingly impolite manner of "exposing" the nonsense or the contradictions of his interlocutors is Socrates' pursuit of truth. The latter, however, are unaware of this, which causes their sense of vexation, Tarnopolsky concludes. In epistemic or deliberative contexts, the lack of clarity about motives (are you trying to ridicule me or to clarify a philosophical question?) bears relevance for the simple reason that, say, if I am not clear about your intentions, I might simply stop the conversation and leave.

those who promote public exposures are as transparent to other citizens as this standard would have them be. But the closer they come to that ideal of transparency, the less equivocal public exposures will be, and the smaller the likelihood that they will be perceived as being unjustifiably disrespectful.

4.6 CONCLUSION

Let me conclude by suggesting an analogy that at first blush might appear to be far-fetched but that will be fruitful in tying together public exposures to the ideas of civic courage and the ideas of respect and self-respect. The analogy is between the public exposure of unofficial collaborators in Germany and that of homosexuals in the United States. In the latter case, the outing of gays was justified on the basis of an argument about moral and communal responsibility. During the 1980s, so-called gay liberationists in the United States engaged in a series of outings of prominent members of the community, disregarding the latter's claims to privacy. The justification of gay liberationists for doing so was based on the argument that these important figures were turning a blind eye on active discrimination against homosexuals and were keeping their own homosexuality hidden while benefiting from the status quo. By acting in this way, so the rationale went, not only did they turn their backs on the gay community, to which they owed a measure of accountability and allegiance,[69] they also "debased" (i.e. disrespected) themselves.[70]

69 Larry Gross, *Contested Closets. The Politics and Ethics of Outing* (Minneapolis: University of Minnesota Press, 1993). Gross is skeptical about the plausibility of talking about homosexuals as a community. Class and racial identities, he claims, militate against homosexual bonds of commonality. There is no superseding gay identity, according to him. On gay outings see also: David Mayo and Martin Gunderson, "Privacy and the Ethics of Outing," in Timothy Murphy (ed.), *Gay ethics: Controversies in Outing, Civil Rights, and Sexual Science* (Binghamton, NY: Haworth Press, 1994), 47–66; and Mark Chekola, "Outing, Truth-telling, and the Shame of the Closet," in Murphy (ed.), *Gay Ethics*, 67–90.

70 Richard Mohr, *Gay Ideas: Outings and Other Controversies* (Boston: Beacon Press, 1992), 32.

The argument in the case of unofficial collaboration is analogous. Not all informal collaborators were notorious figures within the political community. That lack of notoriety notwithstanding, public discourse often stresses the fact that they presumably overlooked their allegiance to their fellow citizens and that they failed to behave according to the standards accepted by the community, hence the justification to out them, to shame them for their actions. The BStU, through the outings it encourages in civil society, is a government agency that plays the role of censor in Rousseau's social contract: it honors the "virtuous citizen" and shames the barbarian. But barbarians can feel unfairly targeted, patronized, and unjustifiably disrespected.

5 STASI AGENTS AS RESPONSIBLE AGENTS? RESPONSIBILITY AND RESPECT

5.1 THE COMPLEXITY OF RESPONSIBILITY AND THE FINE LINE OF RESPECT

This chapter focuses on the issue of assigning moral and political responsibility for collaboration with the Stasi and on the *ambivalent* implications that such attributions of blame can have in terms of respect.[1] There are grounds for affirming that public exposures promote respect for unofficial collaborators in one sense but undermine it another. To begin with, one should take seriously the difficulty of ascribing moral responsibility for past wrongful action committed in contexts of political oppression. The attributions of responsibility implied in public exposures are oftentimes not sensitive to the circumstances in which IMs acted and ignore the variables that may have pressured them to act in the way they did. In this sense, the language of blame and recrimination of public identifications may be problematic. It implies that even though circumstances under the GDR were, by admission of most social and political actors, rather harsh, citizens were not allowed to show signs of weakness and yield to the pressure that the regime exercised on citizens, on some more

[1] The debate on responsibility has dominated discussion ever since the reunification and has an obvious precedent: the debates around German guilt in the postwar era, with Karl Jaspers and Hannah Arendt among its most prestigious participants. For a recent rendition of the debate see Jennifer M. Kapczynski, *The German Patient. Crisis and Recovery in Postwar Culture* (Ann Arbor: University of Michigan Press, 2008). This chapter approaches the discussion on responsibility from a slightly different, although related, angle.

than on others. If this expectation is unreasonable, it disrespects those who in the end became unofficial collaborators by regarding them as if they were not ordinary agents subject to the frailties of human psychology. The fact that some said "no" does not mean that all *could* say no, not only because not all were subject to similar degrees of pressure or manipulation from the Stasi, but also because even if they were, some were more vulnerable than others. Furthermore, the fact that some IMs said yes out of selfishness and for opportunistic motives does not mean that all were motivated by the same reasons.

This line of reasoning should be pondered seriously. And yet it is not a conclusive argument against public exposures or for understanding how public identifications promote or undercut respect for IMs. This is for two reasons. First, given the variety of types of IMs, who differed from one another in virtue of their motivations for collaborating with the Stasi, the degree of their involvement, their current evaluation of their past behavior, and the context in which their collaboration took place, very fine-grained assessments need to be made if one is to ascribe moral responsibility to particular collaborators. In principle, at least, IM exposures *can* enable precisely such assessments. If properly carried out (and this is, of course, an important conditional), they can make it possible to differentiate between IMs who acted voluntarily, unscrupulously, out of self-interest or motivated by misplaced patriotism, and are unapologetic today about their Stasi past, and those who acted under pressure and went on to do what they had very little choice but to do, for instance, those collaborators who agreed to collaborate out of fear or under duress or who were manipulated or blackmailed into collaboration. IM exposures open up windows of opportunity for publicly discussing the contours and degrees of responsibility of collaborators. In this sense, exposures are an expression of respect for informers.

Second, the case for publicly exposing IMs and holding them responsible is independent of whether or not they collaborated voluntarily. In the view of many political actors (and in this they are in line with recent philosophical discussions on the subject), moral responsibility is not about voluntary control, that is, about whether they could or could not have avoided informing for the Stasi, but about *justifying* their behavior, regardless of what brought it about.

Judgmental activity is the site of moral responsibility. Understanding moral responsibility in this way has an important consequence in terms of respect – if IMs are to be regarded as full-fledged agents and not as a group of dangerous beasts, passive infants, or unfortunate puppets of destiny, they should be held morally responsible, regardless of whether they freely collaborated or not. Anything else would be patronizing treatment, or one that characterizes them as unwilling puppets or as unworthy demons. It would be, in a word, disrespectful.

A third strand of arguments accompanies the previous two that comprise this chapter. It requires us to move from an individual level of analysis to a collective one. Ascribing *individual* responsibility can have a perverse effect on processes of reckoning with the past: It can produce scapegoats out of unofficial collaborators, who are then used for the purposes of what some critics of public exposures have described as forms of "responsibility displacement." Through this mechanism, as some commentators have argued, many East Germans try to extricate themselves from their own active or passive involvement in injustice, minimal as this involvement might have been. In other words, IM exposures relieve some citizens from taking on their own responsibility for injustice, and for this reason such exposures do not achieve the ideal of respect for persons.

To cover all this ground, the chapter proceeds as follows. Section two explains why in a context of political oppression such as the GDR, dwelling on the theme of moral responsibility runs the risk of being a disrespectful pursuit. After examining the case of unofficial collaborators in light of two prerequisites for moral responsibility – the requirement of freedom (moral responsibility can be attributed only with regard to decisions over which one had *voluntary control*) and the epistemic requirement (one is morally responsible if one's actions can be traced back to *culpable* ignorance), this section contends that many IMs can make a credible argument that they are not morally responsible. Section three explores the view that although indeed there may be grounds to support the belief that the exercise of free political agency was severely constrained in the GDR, and that therefore unofficial collaborators had little choice but to collaborate, this does not make the question of individual responsibility disappear.

Here it will be necessary to tease out two conceptions of responsibility at work in debates about IMs, as well as in philosophical discussions, one that was already mentioned and that considers responsibility to be all about a matter of voluntary control, and another one that regards responsibility as an exercise of justification of our actions, attitudes, or beliefs. Finally, section four develops the argument that IM exposures may generate a perverse incentive whereby not all who are to some extent responsible for past injustice are made accountable for their contribution to wrongdoing.

5.2 THE MOST IMPORTANT WEAPON AGAINST THE ENEMY

Although the public exposure of unofficial collaborators is generally accepted and has its constant supporters, it is not without its challengers, as was noted in the previous chapter. In part this is because no consensus exists in German public discourse about whether the political and social circumstances during the communist regime were such that we should ascribe moral responsibility to IMs. Many commentators underscore the role of the "system" in producing and manipulating informers; in turn, such systemic variables and not the personal intentions of informers, are supposed to account for their behavior and therefore render superfluous, even malicious, the question of the moral responsibility of unofficial collaborators.

Contemporary philosophical debates about moral responsibility focus on what have been called the Aristotelian conditions of moral responsibility – the condition of freedom and the epistemic condition.[2] These conditions can be useful in reflecting on these debates, so let me discuss them in some detail.

It is common and unsurprising to find unofficial collaborators who are extremely vocal about the view that under the GDR the conditions for the exercise of free agency were absent, a belief that resonates with much of the public in Germany, especially in the East. After his public

[2] These conditions come from John Martin Fischer, "Recent Work on Moral Responsibility," *Ethics* 110, no. 1 (1999): 93–139.

exposure as an IM, actor Thomas Lawinky explains his collaboration with the Stasi as originating with

> a situation of embarrassment, shame, and disgrace. Of course I could have said that I didn't want to have anything to do with them. But at the age of 21, 22, in a state of shock, a scenario that the Stasi created, you only think about how to get out of it. You're overwhelmed and frightened [. . .] I didn't have much time to think it over whether or not to sell myself to the devil. Furthermore I had one goal in mind: I wanted to get to the West, and I looked for an opportunity to get there – with or without Stasi.[3]

After confessing to his Faustian pact, Lawinky goes on to hum the usual incantation to dispel his guilt ("we all collaborated") and even proposes a new terminology to classify the nature of one's complicity with the GDR regime: "There are victims, perpetrators, victimperpetrators, and perpetratorvictims. We all lived in a system where people had to 'bend,' some more than others. Distinguishing between victims and perpetrators does not lead anywhere, and neither does outing one another." Lawinky portrays himself and all Germans as fearful victims of political circumstances, a fact that in his view is a mitigating or even absolutory factor.

An examination of some of the ways in which the Stasi recruited and controlled its collaborators further suggests that, even if they do not apply to Lawinky himself, his characterization of the situation is not fully misleading, and that *some* IMs bear little if any moral responsibility for their actions. These recruitment and control mechanisms suggest that the decision making of some of those individuals who were eventually enrolled by the Stasi was unduly burdened, and therefore their decision to collaborate in some cases cannot count as *fully* consensual.

The first thing to consider is that the MfS seldom recruited voluntary comers as IMs. This is because the Stasi was suspicious of

[3] Barbara Bollwahn, "Im Bauch bin ich Opfer, im Kopf bin ich Täter," *die tageszeitung*, April 4, 2006. On Lawinky, see also: "Menschen brechen," *die tageszeitung*, February 12, 2007, a note covering a theater piece where Lawinky plays the role of his own *Führungsoffizier*.

such individuals, as they might hide disloyal reasons for collaborating. As was mentioned in Chapter 2, the MfS itself "selected" prospective IMs from among the population after a thorough search. It then applied varied persuasion mechanisms, ranging from brainwashing and mild threats to upfront blackmail and intimidation.[4] It should be noted that the fact that the Stasi sometimes resorted to sheer coercion (through blackmail, for instance) to recruit IMs does not mean that all other cases where it did not use these measures should be understood as voluntary collaboration. Stasi recruitment methods should not be conceptualized on a simplistic binary code, where collaborators were either forced to work for the Stasi or did so on a voluntary basis. The situation was by far more complex, not only because the Stasi could deploy subtle manipulation mechanisms instead of coercion, but also because not all citizens who were approached by the Stasi were equally "equipped," as it were, to reject its propositions.

Based on therapeutic work on unofficial collaborators, the argument has been made that some individuals were constitutively and circumstantially more vulnerable to the song of the Stasi sirens than others.[5] To begin with, the goal of education in the GDR was to encourage people to align and to discourage independent thinking and actions, which usually opposed state ideology and which could be criminalized. This is obviously not an appropriate environment for cultivating autonomy and self-reliance, which necessitate a sense of security, both in the family and in society. Although this is true for every East German pupil, not all of those who were exposed to communist education absorbed it in the same way (some approvingly, some critically), and this is for reasons that escaped their control (e.g., the political orientation of the family).

4 Helmut Müller-Enbergs, "Über Ja-Sager und Nein-Sager – Inoffizielle Mitarbeiter und stille Verweigerer," in Marco Hecht and Gerald Praschl (eds.), *Ich habe 'Nein!' gesagt: überZivilcourage in der DDR* (Berlin: Homilius, 2002), 159.

5 Ingrid Kerz-Rühling and Tomas Plänkers, *Verräter oder Verführte. Eine psychoanalytische Untersuchung Inoffizieller Mitarbeiter der Stasi* (Berlin: Links, 2004), 231–233.

There are, however, more tangible considerations that could strengthen or debilitate the ability of an ordinary citizen to reject the Stasi. For example, according to the same source, members of religious or oppositional groups found it easier to resist recruitment from the Stasi and endure the ensuing pressure from the state. Individuals who had no previous attachment to groups like these were easy prey for the secret police. Furthermore, many unofficial collaborators came from broken households. These IMs were very susceptible to the "seduction" of guidance officers, who often resorted to psychological assistance in recruiting unofficial collaborators and who offered to compensate for the neglect of the family.[6] Finally, some IMs were highly dependent on the state for their livelihood or spent most of their time in state-sponsored environments. They had a relationship of dependence with the state (*staatliche Abhängigkeitsverhältinsse*). For them, conforming to the Stasi did not seem anything out of the ordinary, or even obligatory. For many of the individuals who fell in one or several of these categories, putting wax in their ears so as not to hear the song of the Stasi sirens would have been demanding. Put aside the fact that to some extent all Germans, including dissidents, shared the same educational background; and put aside, too, the fact that some of them were delusional about their ability to have political influence via their collaboration with the Stasi. If the diagnosis sketched is accurate, then their social isolation; their difficult upbringing; and their dependency on the state made some individuals susceptible to becoming entangled with the secret police.

In other words, these differences with regard to degree of social connection, upbringing, and independence vis-à-vis the state can produce instances of what philosophers call moral luck.[7] Those with

[6] As another study based on the Stasi archives puts it, the aim of the Stasi "was to create an unambiguous relationship of dependence" between IMs, and on account of this there was a "systematic bias towards those with unhappy childhoods seeking the parents they never had." See Schmeidel, *Shield and Sword of the Party*, 38.

[7] The seminal source is Bernard Williams, "Moral Luck," in *Moral Luck. Philosophical Papers 1973–1980* (Cambridge: Cambridge University Press, 1981), 20–39; and Thomas Nagel, "Moral Luck," in *Mortal Questions* (New York: Cambridge University Press, 1979), 24–38.

a specific social, familial, and professional background, which they could not choose, were more likely to join the Stasi. Had others been socialized in the same way, would they have been inclined to say no? Furthermore, even if we ignore differences in upbringing and all the other factors mentioned earlier, by virtue of sheer fortune, some individuals can be thrust into situations in which they end up committing wrongful actions; we do not know what others would have done had they been facing the same situation. In the GDR, the Stasi approached some individuals but not others; what would those who were not approached by the secret police had responded, had they been in the shoes of those who were? Admittedly, not being confronted with the opportunity to commit wrongdoing does not deprive one of the standing to engage in moral criticism; however, it should serve as a moderating force, that is, it should refrain us from drawing hasty conclusions about whether people are culpable and to what degree. The existence of moral luck erodes the certainty with which we can make moral judgments about responsibility. This is true in any case, but it is particularly true when these judgments refer to civic behavior under strenuous situations, for example in circumstances of political oppression.

Defenders of outing tend to invoke two empirical arguments to defend their case that unofficial collaborators are, without a doubt, morally responsible. One is that only a marginal percentage of the citizenry participated as IMs (1.5 percent of the population). The second is that more than eight out of ten citizens declined to join the Stasi as unofficial collaborators.[8] These data can be deceptive, though. Neither argument necessarily implies that those very few individuals who were recruited by the Stasi had morally dubious reasons to do so. These two facts – only a very marginal number of citizens accepted to become IMs, and a great proportion of those approached said no – can be interpreted in many ways. One of them, for instance, is that despite their efforts to find suitable candidates, not many of them were so psychologically frail or isolated that they would not resist pressure by the Stasi.

[8] These data come from Karsten Dümmel, "Verweigerung der Mitarbeit," in Dümmel and Schmitz (eds.), *Was war die Stasi?*, 95.

The case of adolescents is perhaps one of the most telling in showing how the Stasi could subtly manipulate individuals to recruit them. Because adolescents are in the process of forming their character, moral and political theories tell us, they are not entirely rational and have not developed the capacities of fully fledged agents. They are therefore more easily manipulated. According to the estimations of the Stasi Records Office, of the 173,000 IMs registered as of 1989, between 6 and 10 percent were under the age of 18. Many of them were 13 or 14 years old at the time when they were recruited. Führungsoffiziere (guidance officers) received explicit instructions as to how these young candidates should be enrolled. According to Stasi guidelines, of particular interest were young individuals who for one reason or another were going through a difficult stage in their lives. They should be the prime targets. The Führungsoffizier was instructed to establish a relationship based on trust, "a particular and deep human relationship."[9] Stasi guidelines discouraged the use of authoritarian pedagogy. By contrast, the Führungsoffizier should approach young prospects with sensibility and tact and take an interest in their needs, their professional interests, and the development of their personalities. The point, according to the guidelines, was to leave a lasting impression on the adolescent so that he created emotional bonds with the Stasi and could therefore be safely relied on: "it is essential to concentrate on such causes and problems, which emotionally touch the IM, which deeply influence his life and on offering help and support, to leave behind a real strong binding effect to the Stasi."[10]

A commentator discussing this particular aspect of the Stasi's modus operandi argues that this recruitment strategy used "human sciences" to abuse citizens. The relationship of trust was, in his view, fraudulently obtained. The strategy of the Stasi vis-à-vis prospective adolescent candidates was successful at least some of the time. In a letter addressed to one of the citizens he spied on, one of these IMs

[9] Hans Bernhard Kaufmann, "Verstörte Gewissen – beschädigte Seelen. Junge Menschen wurden als IM missbraucht," *Horch und Guck* 20, no. 6 (1997): 1–11.

[10] Hans Bernhard Kaufmann, "Verstörte Gewissen," 3.

writes that Führungsoffiziere "were not bad people. They were public officials who were doing their duty for the people and the homeland. They were truly concerned for the well-being of citizens."[11]

Once they had been recruited, IMs were discouraged from engaging in autonomous decision making, as the Stasi riveted the locus of evaluation and judgment on IM supervisors. Stasi officials crafted and constantly revised guidelines for IM and their Führungsoffiziere to prevent informers from evaluating the information they passed along to their supervisors. The significance of that information was to be determined elsewhere, and informers were to perform as mere conduits, instruments, or operators, simply passing information along. According to guidelines instituted in 1979, for instance, instructions given to informers were to be more concrete and detailed, and the range of independent actions or maneuvering exactly specified. Instructions were to be so detailed so as to eliminate the possibility of "any confusion," in the belief that situations in which it was not entirely clear how to proceed might invite informants to question what they were doing. At the same time, Stasi supervisors circulated misinformation to these informers so as to obscure their actual objectives. Stories were to be fabricated and given to informers more often so that they would "never know the exact goal of the supervising officer."[12] Put briefly, the Stasi sought to disguise their objectives, while also seeking to minimize the ambiguity or lack of clarity that these informants were likely to encounter as they went about their work. The purpose of both strategies was to turn unofficial

[11] Hans Bernhard Kaufmann, "Verstörte Gewissen," 4. For an account of how *Führungsoffiziere* sought to gain the trust of female IMs, and the gender implications of this, see Alison Lewis, "En-Gendering Remembrance: Memory, Gender and Informers for the Stasi," *New German Critique* 86 (2002): 103–134.

[12] Joan Hackeling, "To whom, and for whom, must I respond? Negotiating responsibility during the last years of East German state socialism,"*Geografiska Annaler* 84, no. 1 (2002): 28–29. Hackeling's information on the Stasi comes from Müller-Enbergs (ed.), *Inoffizielle Mitarbeiter des Ministeriums für Staatssicherheit: Richtlinien und Durchführungsbestimmungen* (Berlin: Links, 1996), 51, 123, 125, 327–328.

collaborators into cogs in the machine,[13] to reduce their margins for autonomous decision making.

By way of contrast, compare these strategies for reducing the decision-making autonomy of IMs to the admonitions of a Lutheran pastor about the proper exercise of responsibility under the communist regime.[14] In a sermon he delivered to a group of young men about to begin their military service in 1982, he admonished them about their unconditional moral autonomy in the following terms: “Do you allow your personality to conform to circumstances due to stress, exhaustion, drill, structures of authority? Some people, as soon as they put on a uniform, become other people entirely, and do things for which they would be ashamed in civilian life.” In a different sermon, addressed this time to a group of students contemplating conscientious objection, the pastor suggested they ask themselves: “How far can I go? Where is the end? Do I know my own limits or is my conscience infinitely malleable?” This is the sort of deliberation an autonomous and rational agent engages in to be the author of her own life, based on her own conception of what is best. The pastor is more Kantian than Kant: He will not even endorse Kant’s distinction between the public and private uses of reason, according to which, to put it bluntly, a person might use her reason to address “the entire public” unless she is enmeshed in relations of command and obedience, in which case she must be restricted in her use of reason.[15]

Given the foregoing considerations, it comes as no surprise that documents from the Ministry describe IMs as mere instruments, as the “most important weapon” in the fight against the “enemy,” or as the “high road” satisfying the informational needs of the state. And to what end were these weapons to be used? “To the protection of the socialist society from significant disturbances, damages and losses, to the timely prevention of hostile and negative actions as well as to

[13] Joan Hackeling, “To whom, and for whom, must I respond?,” 28–29.

[14] The example and the accompanying discussion is borrowed from Joan Hackeling, “To whom, and for whom, must I respond?,” 28–29.

[15] This is the famous distinction introduced by Kant in “An Answer to the Question: What is Enlightenment?,” in *Practical Philosophy*, trans. and ed. Mary Gregor (Cambridge: Cambridge University Press, 1996), 11–22.

ensure effective anti-damage work." IMs, then, were to be "used" as *tools* of the Stasi, expecting the minimum of autonomous action from them.[16]

To recapitulate, I just described some of the ways in which the Stasi enlisted unofficial collaborators, which candidates were unlikely to be able to resist, and which ones it chose in the end. In bringing all this to the forefront, I want to show why it may be problematic to ascribe *moral* responsibility or fault to IMs – as opposed to mere *causal* responsibility, which can be easily made – without proper caution. Part of the reason is that because the margins of free agency under the GDR were severely constrained through coercion, threats thereof, or subtler mechanisms, citizens who yielded to the Stasi were not even *fully* autonomous in the first place. Acknowledging these constraints does not commit one to endorsing a deterministic account of IM behavior. Many unofficial collaborators could, of course, have acted otherwise. Autonomy is, after all, a matter of degrees. But ascribing moral responsibility to an individual whose autonomous agency has been severely curtailed presupposes a great deal of knowledge about the conditions under which she acted, her motivations, and so on, and this kind of knowledge is not always available.[17]

Let me now turn to the second precondition of moral responsibility – the epistemic one. In disclosing their past and making sense of it, some collaborators use an extensive battery of excuses, some of which resonate with certain groups in East Germany. I already pointed out some of them in Lawinky's case: "I was confused, I did it because at the moment I thought it was the right thing to do;" "Fear had gotten the best of me, and I needed to leave Germany at any cost." There were others: "At the time that I did it,

[16] Helmut Müller-Enbergs, "Der 'Inoffizielle Mitarbeiter:' Anatomie eines Spitzels," 17.

[17] I am echoing here Jürgen Habermas's suggestion that the succession of the two German "dictatorships" (that is, the Nazi and the communist regimes) created a "panoptic state, which not only directly subverted public life [. . .] but also its foundation, civil society and the private sphere," and produced "the structural dispossession of citizens who were robbed of their social and legal autonomy." Jürgen Habermas, "Burdens of the Double Past," *Dissent* 41, no. 4 (1994): 514–515.

I did not know I was causing harm to others." "How could I know how the information I provided to the Stasi was going to be used?" These self-exculpations, of which I note only some paradigmatic forms to spare the reader an extensive catalog, often parade in public discourse as objections against the ascription of moral responsibility to IMs. Such exculpations appeal to what one might call the *epistemic* grounds of moral responsibility. For someone to be held responsible for wrongdoing, it must be clear that the person in question knew that her actions were wrong. If she has a credible story about why she could not have possibly known that she was acting wrongly, then she is not blameworthy. As we will see in this section, some unofficial collaborators can make this case convincingly. Others cannot. In any case, the point of exploring the epistemic bases of moral responsibility is to show the difficulty entailed in ascribing it in contexts such as the GDR.

Common to much exculpation circulating in public discourse is that it relies on what one may call "arguments from ignorance." One type of ignorance is *factual*, as in not knowing that certain circumstances will bring about a wrong action. Falling under this category, the following is perhaps the most common public exculpation: I could not know that the information I passed on to the Stasi while I was an informer would "end up delivering people to the knives," that is, that it might get fellow citizens fired from their jobs, deported, or imprisoned.

The other type of ignorance is moral, as in not knowing that one's action is wrong, or in being unclear about what is right or wrong in the first place. This type of ignorance may arise in any moral deliberation, regardless of the political context. Gideon Rosen argues that the epistemic obligation to distinguish between the right and the wrong course of action may be extremely difficult to discharge: "One can fail to know what one ought to do in some particular case; one can fail to know a general moral rule. One can fail to know that people have certain rights, or that one has certain duties. One can fail to know that a certain act would be cruel or abusive, and so on."[18] The epistemic

[18] Gideon Rosen, "Culpability and Moral Ignorance," *Proceedings of the Aristotelian Society*, 103, no. 1 (2003): 64.

route might be long and winding, and an agent could get lost in the labyrinth. Even if the road is not one that invites confusion, indeterminacy pervades moral deliberation, Rosen continues: "It may be that an agent who has flouted no procedural norm in arriving at the wrong answer could easily have arrived at the right one if his deliberation had taken a slightly different course."[19]

What I just described are the epistemic difficulties that *anyone* deliberating about what she ought to do might face regardless of her political or social circumstances. When we factor those circumstances in, moral deliberation gets even more intricate. Rosen argues that it is extremely difficult (and in his view supererogatory, not obligatory) for individuals to "rethink the uncontroversial normative principles that form the framework for social life." He goes on to argue: "One is obliged to reflect on hard cases, in response to serious criticism, in response to known diversity of opinion and in response to perceived tension in one's moral view. But when what one takes to be a transparently correct moral verdict meets with no such friction, one is neither negligent nor reckless in failing to subject that verdict to special scrutiny."[20]

The question is whether under a "framework for social life," such as the one prevailing in the GDR, moral injunctions against denunciating fellow citizens were uncontroversial. Could informing have struck some citizens as being the right thing to do given the *circumstances?* At the very least in the early years of the GDR, a positive answer is plausible in a nation whose succeeding political regimes (the Nazi regime and Communist rule) made extensive use of informers for a span of roughly five decades. Notwithstanding the fact that denunciations in the GDR were more institutionalized, regulated, and routinized than in Nazi Germany, where they flowed freely from below,[21] the fact is that, although some German citizens were

[19] Rosen, "Culpability and Moral Ignorance," 70.

[20] Rosen, "Culpability and Moral Ignorance," 65.

[21] Robert Gellately, "Denunciations in Twentieth-Century Germany: Aspects of Self-Policing in the Third Reich and the German Democratic Republic," *The Journal of Modern History* 68, no. 4 (1996): 931–967. See also Herbert Reinke, "Policing Politics in Germany from Weimar to the Stasi," in Mark Mozower

enthusiastic informers on purely self-interested and opportunistic grounds, others had arguably been socialized in a polity that made informing a politically acceptable action.[22]

Many IMs may have collaborated with the Stasi because they were led to believe that their actions were acceptable for and even required of committed socialist citizens. The relevant question then becomes how justified IMs were in holding those false beliefs, that is, whether they were culpable for holding them. I argue that in many cases collaborators were strongly justified in holding their (false) beliefs, given the role of the state in creating and disseminating them. In turn, these beliefs created a social environment in which the likelihood that informers would misunderstand or misapply moral principles was extremely high.

Several authors have stressed the extent to which social context has an impact on the process of interpreting and applying moral principles.[23] Pauer-Studer and Velleman, elaborating on some of the insights of Arendt's *Eichmann in Jerusalem*, also emphasize the contribution of social context to moral reasoning. The central idea these authors develop is that morality may become distorted "at the level of its social articulation," as they put it. According to them, the social environment provides what they call, following Barbara Herman, rules of moral salience, a minimal kind of moral knowledge that is needed to pick out the "morally questionable" features in light of which actions need to be examined to determine whether they are permissible (say, through the categorical imperative procedure). These rules may allow individuals to mischaracterize their situation and consequently to misinterpret and misapply the guidelines of their conventional morality. Even if fundamental

(ed.) *The Politics of Policing in the Twentieth Century* (Oxford: Berghahn, 1997), 91–106.

22 Note also that in the postwar period only very few Gestapo informers were actually sentenced for denunciating other citizens.

23 Barbara Herman, *The Practice of Moral Judgment* (Cambridge, MA: Harvard University Press, 1993); Gideon Rosen, "Culpability and Ignorance," 2004; Mika LaVaque-Manty, "Kant's Children," *Social Theory and Practice* 32, no. 3 (2006): 365–388; Herlinde Pauer-Studer and David J. Velleman, "Distortions of Normativity," *Ethical Theory and Moral Practice* 14, no. 3 (2011): 329–356.

principles remain intact in their abstract form, they still have to be given a socially relevant interpretation, and they have to be applied by agents with socially inculcated habits of moral perception. This explains why ordinary people might not be deterred by morality: moral principles are filtered through socially conditioned interpretations and perceptions that give events a distorted normative significance. Pauer-Studer and Velleman offer the example of a physician involved in murdering Jews during the Second World War, who ideologically reinterpreted a moral concept such as respect by situating it in the context of inimical racial relations; this physician thus concluded that "fellow countrymen" (*Volksgenossen)* and their enemies (*Volksfeinde)* show respect for each other by having the courage of their mutual enmity; other medical doctors prioritized workplace codes of conduct rather than moral principles, thus normalizing murderous attitudes.

In East Germany, many factors were in place to distort ordinary moral reasoning, that is, to transform the way citizens understood the scope and the nature of their moral obligations; how they were supposed to discharge them; and which ones they should prioritize when two of them came into conflict, as when personal moral duties competed with purported civic duties. Thus, state officials offered unofficial collaborators many resources to inject positive values into their activities and offered a "(cold) wartime" narrative that included a problem frame – there are enemies among us – and a solution frame – inform authorities about them. For instance, informers were given what one might call *civic reassurance*–they were led to believe that their actions were a necessary measure fighting the enemies of communism. Consider the language and the ceremony that characterized recruitment as an IM; this language injected a sense of civic duty into Stasi informal collaboration. It is a noteworthy fact that, on being recruited, prospective informers were asked to sign a letter of commitment or duty ("*Verpflichtungserklärung*"). The letter was less a legal document than a sort of civic oath or pledge. According to a standard format of the letter, the IM who signed it was encouraged to see herself as a tool "against all attacks of the enemy and for the sustaining of peace." Aside from demanding the utmost secrecy about her task (not even family members were to learn about the IM's "duty:" civic bonds supersede familial ones in the context of the task assigned to the informer) the letter usually read something along these lines: "I commit to give the Ministry of State Security voluntary support and to share all information, that suggest an enemy action, with the known agents of the Ministry."[24] Informing, then, was portrayed as a patriotic activity to defend and to be honored by the state. In light of this civic narrative, it is not an exaggeration to argue that some IMs might have honestly believed that their actions were not wrong, all things considered. Obviously, all of this does not rule out that some of IMs did collaborate for the Stasi out of reasons of self-interest. If we liken the IM network to an army, undoubtedly some collaborators were mercenaries, whereas others were voluntary soldiers. Or in Jon Elster's taxonomy, described before, some collaborators could be opportunists, others fanatics and principled actors. The two Schuberts in a previous chapter were probably opportunists. But not all collaborators were like them.

An extreme case of an IM who claims to have believed to be doing the right thing is that of the so-called red pastor, who affirms to have believed "that the Church can only survive if it strives actively towards the fulfillment of the goals of socialist society."[25] In consonance with that belief, the red pastor did not hesitate to inform on those citizens who failed to work toward such a goal. Or take the case of Olympic athlete Ingo Steuer, which I will be commenting on more extensively in another chapter. After his outing, Steuer offered clarifications of the following sort about his involvement with the Stasi as an IM: "At the moment in which I did it, I did it in full consciousness [. . .] But not because I intended to cause any harm to anyone, but because I found it to be the right thing to do."[26] Or "I am so ashamed that I had cooperated with the Stasi. At that time I was not at all clear

[24] Helmut Müller-Enbergs, "Der 'InoffizielleMitarbeiter:' Anatomie eines Spitzels," *Damals: das aktuelle Geschichtsmagazin* 25, no. 6 (1993): 17.

[25] Michael Ploenus, "Der Fall des 'roten Franz' von Kapellendorf," *Gerbergasse 184* (2006): 16.

[26] "Die Schuld des Ingo Steuer hilft Offenheit, dem Eislauftrainer zu verzeihen?," *3 Sat*, June 5, 2008.

about what I was doing."[27] Steuer insinuates that the epistemic barriers erected by the Stasi prevented him from discerning what the right course of action was.

The existence of this "toxic" belief-environment speaks against a tacit assumption of the public shaming of IM – that it is acceptable to make moral judgments about informers based on the same standards that would be used to judge individuals who committed wrongdoing in ordinary circumstances. Under ordinary circumstances, moral theories and interpersonal reactions operate vis-à-vis wrongdoing on the basis of an "idealized epistemic standard."[28] This standard presupposes widely shared social norms that assign moral obligations, and it provides a sense of the costs of discharging these obligations, as well as the burdens of moral deliberation. A good example of this standard is the figure of the "reasonable person," so common in American common law, especially in the law of torts. The reasonable person is an abstraction, a representative of the normal standard of community behavior. It embodies "the general level of moral judgment of the community, what it feels ought ordinarily to be done."[29] Such an idealized epistemic standard for ordinary circumstances is not apt to morally judge IMs. The social norms that their actions transgressed (e.g., do not betray the trust of fellow citizens) cannot be said to have had wide acceptance, if only because the state created, disseminated, and sustained false beliefs that many unofficial collaborators and other citizens accepted nonculpably; in turn, these false beliefs justified their maintaining a dose of skepticism about the validity of such norms.

An objection might be raised at this point. Even conceding that contingent social factors mediate between abstract moral principles and their use in concrete situations, and that such social factors may distort normativity, as I claim could have been the case for many

[27] Timo Frasch, "Ingo Steuer: 'Schandfleck' in meinem Leben," *Frankfurter Allgemeine Zeitung*, March 20, 2006.

[28] Christopher Kutz, *Complicity, Ethics and Law for a Collective Age* (New York: Cambridge University Press, 2000), 208.

[29] Robert Post, *Constitutional Domains: Democracy, Community, Management* (Cambridge, MA: Harvard University Press, 1995), 53.

unofficial collaborators, it does not follow from this that those who failed to interpret moral principles correctly are not morally culpable. For example, Thomas Hill Jr. distinguishes between first- and second-order responsibility to argue that when collaborators for an oppressive regime are in the grips of a social belief that makes it hard to critically assess the wrongness of their collaboration, they may be released from their first-order responsibility: their duty to not collaborate with such a regime (say, one that encourages citizens to spy on one another). But Hill Jr. argues for the existence of a second-order responsibility: the duty to cultivate the mind and the disposition that will allow us to understand and implement our primary responsibility to oppose, eliminate, or not collaborate with an oppressive regime. More specifically, second-order responsibility is one of deliberation and is prior to and, to some extent, independent of circumstances. It is the responsibility "to make ourselves ready of mind and will to see what we must do and to follow through on our best judgment," and it involves a duty of due care in moral deliberation, a duty of moral self-scrutiny, and a duty to develop moral virtue.[30] Thus, in East Germany, candidates to becoming unofficial collaborators should have made the precommitment not to collaborate with the secret police and tie themselves to the mast so as not to heed the proposals of the Stasi.

By postulating a set of context-independent duties or virtues, views like this one fail to acknowledge the social ethics of belief-formation. They underestimate the difficulty that, in contexts where normativity has been distorted, many individuals may have in rejecting false beliefs, particularly when they arise from a source that they consider to be reliable. Individuals are epistemically dependent beings: They rely on social practices and institutions to provide beliefs that will guide their behavior. Some individuals have cognitive resources that dispose them to permanently examine and eventually reject false beliefs. But it is doubtful whether the average person has this ability regardless of the specific context she finds herself embedded in. The ability to scrutinize and eventually reject false beliefs can and should, of course, be cultivated. Developing this

[30] Thomas E. Hill, Jr., "Moral Responsibilities of Bystanders," *Journal of Social Philosophy* 41, no. 1 (2010): 28–39.

ability presupposes *inter alia* the existence of a plurality of sources of beliefs, made accessible through something resembling a public sphere, where beliefs compete for acceptance.[31] It also presupposes a state that encourages the acquisition of those duties of due care in moral deliberation, moral self-scrutiny, of development of moral virtue. Such things were absent in the GDR.

Let me draw a parallel between the infamous case of East German border guards, who were prosecuted for some of the shooting incidents that occurred along the Berlin Wall in the years leading to the collapse of the regime, and that of unofficial collaborators. The successful prosecution of many of those border guards relied on an appeal to natural law and the rejection of positivism, with its nonretroactivity principle (*nulla poena sine lege*). The debate between positivist and natural lawyers is a well-rehearsed one, and I need not go into its details. The point I want to underscore here is that the judge who convicted one of the guards contended, closely following the standard natural law argument, that no one had "a right to ignore his conscience when it comes to killing people on behalf of the power structure." The reliance on these arguments can only be successful by postulating the existence of a transparent and uncontroversial moral code (and objective measure) and by imputing to the accused individual the knowledge that his actions were contrary to this code and, therefore, plainly wrong, even if sanctioned by positive law.[32] This is

[31] On this, see Allen Buchanan's work on social moral epistemology, "Judging the Past: The Case of the Human Radiation Experiments," *The Hastings Center Report* 26, no. 3 (1996):25–30; "Social Moral Epistemology," *Social Philosophy and Policy* 19, no. 2 (2002): 126–152; "Political Liberalism and Social Epistemology," *Philosophy and Public Affairs* 32, no. 2 (2004): 95–130; "Social Moral Epistemology and the Tasks of Ethics," N. Ann Davis, Richard Keshen and Jeff McMahan, *Ethics and Humanity: Themes from the Philosophy of Jonathan Glover* (New York: Oxford University Press, 2010): 105–125.

[32] Kif Augustine Adams, "What is Just?: The Rule of Law and Natural Law in the Trials of Former East German Border Guards," in Neil J. Kritz, (ed.), *Transitional Justice: How Emerging Democracies Reckon with Former Regimes* (Washington, DC: United States Institute of Peace, 1995), v. 2, 172. Although as just seen, the prosecution against guards ultimately rests on a natural law argument, there was some ambiguity as to whether under East

the doctrine of "manifest illegality" – the idea that some orders are so contrary to minimal standards of morality that they should appear to any soldier as ostensibly inappropriate and therefore impermissible. Yet, as Mark Osiel has forcibly argued, in many contexts, manifest illegality is not so manifest as some commentators would lead one to believe.[33] For example, soldiers are oftentimes not learned in moral theory, are explicitly discouraged from engaging in spontaneous thinking in many situations, and are heavily indoctrinated. Additional factors can prevent soldiers from displaying critical thinking with respect to superior orders. In a similar fashion, for all of the reasons mentioned before, the wrongfulness of the actions of unofficial collaborators may not have been manifestly obvious to many of them.

With this discussion as a background, let me now turn back to the theme of respect. In many cases, at least, treating IMs just as ordinary thieves or embezzlers is wrong-headed. Attributions of moral responsibility must take into account the conditions of possibility for the meaningful exercise of such responsible agency. It would be disrespectful to hold someone responsible for having failed to discharge extremely demanding moral obligations or for having succumbed to overwhelming social pressure. It is precisely for these reasons that if carried through without due consideration, IM exposures may be disrespectful practices. They disrespect collaborators if they underestimate the difficulty that saying no to the Stasi entailed for some individuals and therefore conclude that the motivations to join the secret police as an informer were transparently malicious. The fact that some citizens were willing and able to reject the Stasi

German law, guards had committed a crime. No such ambiguity exists in the case of informers: they committed no legal crime because there was clearly no law against informing in the books (actually informing was encouraged and even rewarded by the state). Therefore, an even stronger case needs to be made that informers knew they were doing something wrong.

33 For an examination of the doctrine of "manifest illegality," see, from Mark Osiel, *Obeying Orders* (New Brunswick, NJ: Transaction Publishers, 2009), 71–89; and *Mass Atrocity, Ordinary Evil, and Hannah Arendt* (New Haven, CT: Yale University Press, 2001), ch. 3.

does not mean that all could or thought they should. Not only would IMs have been disrespected in the past, having been treated by the communist regime merely as means and not ends-in-themselves, to put it in Kantian terms (recall that Kant objects to spying on the grounds that it amounts to treating persons as mere means and not as ends, or as he puts it, to making use "only of others' dishonesty").[34] They would also be disrespected in the present for being attributed responsibility that they do not deserve, or put less strongly, for being attributed *more* responsibility than they deserve.

The conclusion to drive home from the foregoing remarks is not that we can never know whether an agent is morally responsible for her wrongdoing and that, therefore, ascriptions of moral responsibility are *never* fully warranted in any case. This would be too strong a conclusion. Rather, the point is that *if* epistemic burdens really were hard to discharge in the GDR, then legitimate ascriptions of moral responsibility need to be made very cautiously. And perhaps caution has been found lacking in many of the outings that have taken place after the fall of the Wall.

5.3 FORFEITING ONE'S SOUL: THE RECALCITRANCE OF PERSONAL INTENTIONS

The case made in the previous section against ascribing moral responsibility to many unofficial collaborators is, however, not a conclusive one against public exposures. The preceding line of reasoning does not imply that the public identification of IMs should *never* take place. Rather, the implication is that public identifications should be carried out in a very careful manner, taking mitigating factors into account. There are at least two reasons why, despite the difficulty of ascribing moral responsibility to unofficial collaborators, public exposures are still warranted. For one, such identification can be useful in assessing degrees of culpability because some unofficial collaborators were more culpable than others. For another, as will be

[34] Kant, in "Toward Perpetual Peace," in *Practical Philosophy*, 311–51.

seen here, responsibility may be independent of the element so heavily emphasized in the previous section: voluntary control.

The first reason why public exposures are justified is that they can be helpful in clarifying whether or not, and to what degree, moral responsibility can be ascribed to IMs in specific cases. That is, they can clarify the extent of involvement of this or that unofficial collaborator. For example, those who reported on a fellow citizen's taste for Western music (let alone those who underreported or plainly lied on their reports) are obviously less culpable (or not culpable at all) than those who reported on someone who was attempting to flee the GDR. Furthermore, as was mentioned in Chapter 2 and elsewhere, there were many kinds of IMs in the GDR. Some merely provided logistical support; for instance, they put their houses at the Stasi's disposal as places for its officials to arrange meetings with other IMs or, if they were medical doctors, they prescribed vacations to a person under the Stasi's surveillance in these cases unofficial collaborators were completely ignorant of detailed information about the operation that Stasi officials were carrying out, even if they were vaguely aware that the Stasi was up to anything. In contrast, other IMs – a very limited number of them – were in the line of combat, as it were, or as the bureaucratic job description put it, in contact with the enemy. They were well trained, and they infiltrated, sabotaged and helped dismantle dissident groups, and delivered information to the Stasi for the prosecution and imprisonment of individuals; they were not order takers who limited themselves to reporting, but rather more engaged collaborators who could even contribute to psychologically upset individuals; they knew enough about the operations in which they were involved.[35] Finally, the most common kind of unofficial collaborator had to familiarize him- or herself with the opinions of the citizenry, in the best of cases, or with the activities of specific "unreliable" citizens, in the worst of cases, and report on them to a guidance officer. In the latter case, these reports could somewhere down the line have serious consequences for the citizens in question, such as preventing an escape from the GDR, imprisonment, and so on. The specifics of each case remained unknown to the collaborator,

[35] Müller-Enbergs, "Die Inoffiziellen Mitarbeiter," 32–35; Schmeidel, 35.

although as in the first case, it was common knowledge that the Stasi's intentions were suspicious, to put it mildly.

These differences should be reflected in our judgment about the degree of moral responsibility that can be ascribed to unofficial collaborators. To the degree that public exposures contribute to making these assessments, they can be said to be respectful of wrongdoers. Public exposure can help attribute IMs no less and no more moral responsibility than they deserve. One should note, though, that it is unclear whether publicity is a good companion to inquiries into the nature of the collaboration with oppressive regimes of ordinary citizens in societies in transition from dictatorship to democracy. But here I will put that question to rest and assume at least such publicity is compatible with precise assessments of moral responsibility.

The second reason why public exposures are legitimate, despite the difficulties involved in ascribing moral responsibility, is more philosophical. This reason centers on the view that, even if unofficial collaboration was not voluntary, unofficial collaborators nevertheless remain responsible. This view hinges on an understanding of responsibility that merits a detailed discussion. I shall unpack this view in the rest of the section.

Let us go back to Lawinky's account of the reasons for his collaboration. They represent the kind of exculpatory narrative that many citizens and moral entrepreneurs reject. These critics rile against the idea of putting so much emphasis on "the circumstances," and instead insist on the importance of the *moral integrity* of the citizens who collaborated with the Stasi. As was mentioned in the previous chapter, the initial presumption in public discourse tends to be that collaboration is a sign of moral weakness and that IMs are shameless and cowardly individuals who are prone to lying. Reproducing or creating this paradigm of collaboration, the media eagerly goes after evidence showing how this or that particular IM received a stipend, a medal, or a trip to the Soviet Union in return for his services, or how this or that particular IM produced abundant and detailed reports on colleagues, neighbors, family, or even patients.[36] Photographs of

[36] Some physicians reported on their patients. Wolf Schmidt, "Fragen Sie Ihren Arzt und Spitzel," *die tageszeitung*, November 21, 2007. According to the

unofficial collaborators with sinister looks may even accompany the public framing of collaboration as morally flawed.[37] The tenor of public discourse in relation to IMs is no doubt influenced by journalistic sensationalism: the grimmer the type of IM, the more appealing the article.

Consistent with the idea that character matters more than or as much as circumstances, many participants in the debate cast doubt on the belief that unofficial collaborators really had no margin of choice as to whether they collaborated with the Stasi. For example, Helmut Müller-Enbergs, the Stasi bureau expert on IMs, discounts the significance of the threats that the Stasi made to prospective candidates. He claims that although Stasi acts reveal that most citizens were in fact fearful about what would ensue if they declined an offer to collaborate with the secret police, some did. Confrontational rejections of the sort: "I will not work for the red Gestapo" were seldom, but more diplomatic ones were common.[38] In most cases, those who refused to work for the Stasi did not suffer any consequences, although, to be sure, there were instances of IM recruitment through blackmail, where this case might be harder to make. In other words, in this a posteriori diagnosis, the negative incentives used by the secret police were surmountable, it is claimed. On this view, even if individual behavior was overwhelmingly shaped by structural considerations, it is still an open question how particular individuals negotiated those structures.[39]

study reviewed by *taz,* up to 5 percent of physicians in the GDR were informers.

[37] This perception quite often takes absurd and ludicrous turns. A recent emission of the highly popular sitcom *Tatort* broadcasted an episode about the Stasi and its IMs, who in the show were "active" and in the business of informing on innocent citizens in the year 2010. See Kathrin Buchner, "Schneewittchen und die Stasi-Schergen," *Stern,* May 31, 2010.

[38] Helmut Müller-Enbergs, "Über Ja-Sager und Nein-Sager – InoffizielleMitarbeiter und stille Verweigerer," 2002, 159.

[39] The insistence of paying attention to the moral integrity of citizens regardless of the circumstances under which they acted has some philosophical pedigree. Harry Frankfurt famously argues that the presence of circumstances that prevent the actor from acting otherwise does not rule out the possibility that

Along the same lines, Joachim Gauck, who had been a pastor before becoming head of the Stasi archives, authored one of the very first public testimonies about the importance of the archival legacy of the Stasi.[40] The work documents some of the ways in which the secret police enrolled its unofficial collaborators and some of the reasons why a number of citizens turned down the offer to inform on other citizens. On the former point, he clarifies that money was never an important variable in accounting for the collaboration with the secret police. On the latter point, and more important for the present purposes, he constantly underscores the idea that it was always possible for citizens to decline an invitation to work for the organization and, in so doing, he appeals to a Biblical reference. He argues that prospective candidates could appeal to their attachment to a strong ethical code (physicians and devout believers are his examples) in order to excuse themselves. In the archives he finds a written rejection of a man who adduces his Christian conviction in order to turn down an offer by the Stasi: "For what will it profit a man if he gains the whole world and forfeits his soul?" (Matthew 16: 26).[41] This anonymous hero, after moral deliberation and self-scrutiny, refused to "forfeit his soul." In contrast, Lawinky is not a reader of the Gospel. He was willing to sign a Faustian pact and sell his soul for a travel pass to West Germany. In Gauck's view Lawinky is, after all, morally responsible.

the actual motivation to perform the action was independent of such circumstance. Frankfurt contends that, even if in a particular case, the circumstances prevailed, we still do not know whether the person would not have performed in the way she did regardless of them. For example, with the case of the Stasi in mind, it is not enough to say that a threat (the circumstantial factor) was present in carrying out the action. What needs to be said is that the threat actually accounts for having performed that action, which incidentally is a hard thing to prove. The possibility (the doubt) remains that she would have acted in the same way regardless of the circumstances. She might be morally responsible after all, even if the circumstances "made" her do what she did. In his classic article "The Principle of Alternate Possibilities," *Journal of Philosophy* 66, no. 3 (1969): 828–39.

40 Joachim Gauck, *Die Stasi-Akten. Das unheimliche Erbe der DDR* (Hamburg: Rowohlt, 1991).

41 Gauck, *Die Stasi-Akten*, 59.

This, again, harks back to the idea of epistemic virtues previously discussed: IMs are culpable of not cultivating a set of virtues that predisposed them against collaboration with the Stasi.

Furthermore, according to views like Gauck's, some members of German society, on account of their professions, had a stronger obligation to remain impervious to Stasi pressure, and their failure can only mean cowardliness. Referring to the outing of writer Fritz Rudolf Fries (IM "Pedro Hagen") a commentator argues: "Perhaps everyone has a right to cowardliness, but as a writer, particularly in Germany, he will be judged more severely, because of the moral responsibility of the 'master of the word.'"[42] By contrast, take the example of Angela Merkel. In an interview given in the midst of her campaign for reelection, which she won, the German Chancellor made a public revelation probably with an eye on electoral profit. At the end of the seventies, as she was applying for a job at a university in the GDR, a Stasi official attempted to recruit her as an informant for the secret police. She declined the offer. With a candor attuned to campaigning times, she explained that in anticipation of such an eventuality, she had even devised a strategy to reject such a proposition without upsetting the MfS: "I am not a suitable candidate for a job whose main requirement is secrecy and discretion," she told the Stasi official, "because I cannot keep my mouth shut, and would immediately confess the truth to friends and relatives."[43] If the Chancellor successfully refused to collaborate, could others not do the same?

What is the point of putting so much emphasis on the moral character of collaborators even if, as was shown in the previous section, it may be too harsh and even unfair to do so? To address this question, what is needed is an account of the notion of responsibility that is more capacious than the one used so far in this chapter. Up to

[42] Manfred Jaeger, "Fritz Rudolf Fries – IM 'Pedro Hagen'," *Deutschland Archiv* 29, no. 4 (1996): 348.

[43] "Stasi wollte Angela Merkel anwerben,"*Der Spiegel*, May 19, 2009. I portray Merkel's revelation as being motivated by her desire to seek electoral gain. I should clarify that, by the same token, many IMs with political ambitions could "out" themselves for similar strategic reasons.

this point it has been argued that an agent is morally responsible only insofar as she has the capacity to *choose* ends freely and act accordingly, that is, only to the extent that she had the opportunity to avoid infringing the standard for the violation of which she is held responsible. This is what Gary Watson calls the accountability aspect of responsibility.[44] According to this volitionist perspective, as it is called, you can only be held responsible for wrongdoing, and be accountable for it, if you deliberately and knowingly pursued the wrongful act in question. Alternatively, instead of focusing on specific actions one could concentrate on the attitudes or disposition that gave rise to them. In this case, your attitudes are culpable if it would have been reasonable to expect that you revised them but you did not; you culpably deploy epistemic vices, such as laziness or dishonesty. In any case, voluntary control or choice is the basic condition of moral responsibility. In this line of reasoning, and with regard to the case under examination, an unofficial collaborator would be responsible only if he knew that his actions were wrong, and that neither the socialist goals of the nation nor any other reason justified them, but carried them out nonetheless.

Now let us concede for the sake of argument that IMs did *not* commit wrongdoing knowingly and willingly, and let us further grant the point that they are *not* responsible in the accountability sense. This presupposition does not end the matter, for responsibility has yet another "face," which Watson calls attributability. It is this alternative aspect of responsibility that interests us here. According to so-called attributionists, all that is needed for ascribing responsibility to an actor is that her actions are imputable to her; that these actions, in a very loose sense, "belong" to her; that they reflect her attitudes and

[44] Gary Watson, "Two Faces of Responsibility," *Philosophical Topics* 24, no. 2 (1996): 227–48. Particularly forceful about the idea that this is the only appropriate understanding of moral responsibility is Neil Levy, "The Good, the Bad, and the Blameworthy," *Journal of Ethics and Social Philosophy* 1, no. 2 (2005): 2–16; Neil Levy, "Culpable Ignorance and Moral Responsibility: A Reply to FitzPatrick," *Ethics* 119, no. 4 (2009): 729–41; Neil Levy and Michael McKenna, "Recent Work on Free Will and Moral Responsibility," *Philosophy Compass* 4, no. 1 (2009): 96–133.

beliefs. The act is attributable to an agent if it expresses who she is, not how she came to be such a person. Here, voluntary control is not the basic condition of moral responsibility but rational judgment. Attributionists like Angela Smith put it in the following way: "To say that an agent is morally responsible for something, in this view, is to say that that thing reflects her rational judgment in a way that makes it appropriate, in principle, to ask her to defend it or justify it."[45]

While attributionists and volitionist debate over which of the two, choice or rational judgment, is the appropriate precondition of moral responsibility, others argue that both conceptions of responsibility are embodied in our moral practice. In fact, they claim that the coexistence of these two aspects of responsibility is what sustains the ambivalence that we feel when, for example, we consider a criminal who is him or herself a victim of an abusive childhood. On the one hand, "his conduct is attributable to him as an exercise of his 'moral capacities.' It expresses and constitutes his practical identity, what he stands for, what he has made of his life as he found it."[46] On the other hand, "Facts about his formative years give rise to the thought that the individual has already suffered too much and that we too would probably have been morally ruined by such a childhood."[47] This is precisely the ambivalence that many citizens in Germany may feel toward unofficial collaborators who came from broken households and were subtly manipulated by their guidance officers.

At any rate, the attributionist account has a clear implication from the point of view of respect. I quote Smith at some length to clarify this: "if I assess an (otherwise normal) adult human being as 'cruel' I am not merely attributing a trait to him for which he may or may not be responsible (as when I say a dog has a 'vicious disposition'). I am (in part) making a demand of him, a demand that he justify the objectionable judgments his actions and attitudes express concerning the moral status of others. This demand by its very nature implies responsibility, for it is directed at his judgmental activity, activity for

[45] Angela M. Smith, "Control, Responsibility, and Moral Assessment," *Philosophical Studies* 138, no. 3 (2008): 369.

[46] Watson, "Two Faces of Responsibility," 240.

[47] Watson, "Two Faces of Responsibility," 240.

which we must regard him as responsible if we are to regard him as a moral agent in any sense. To say that a person's judgmental activity is bad but that he is not responsible for it is, in effect, to say that he is not to be regarded as someone to be reasoned with, but merely as someone to be understood, treated, managed, or controlled. It is to regard a person as we would regard a vicious dog or a bratty toddler, someone to be avoided and/or trained, if possible, but not someone with whom it is possible to enter into a relationship of mutual respect and recognition."[48]

Put in different terms, the idea that all people should be regarded as justificatory beings (as agents and addressees of justifications with regard to practices and institutions that affect them) is, as Rainer Forst argues, the best possible way to philosophically reconstruct the Kantian categorical imperative to respect other persons as "ends in themselves." In holding collaborators accountable, we treat them as ends in themselves, as free persons capable of offering justifications; in short, as fully-fledged agents. This is a sign of respect for them.[49]

To illustrate the two reasons I offered in this section to show why public exposures might be acceptable after all – they can contribute to making fine-grained ascriptions of moral responsibility and they treat agents as justificatory beings – consider the case of IM Schubert, discussed in Chapter 2. For the present purposes, the most interesting part of the controversy around his public exposure is an open letter written by a group of Stasi victims, asking him to stop his litigation against Käbisch and instead come out before the public. The letter puts the question of responsibility in the forefront: "*Take on the responsibility* – the letter says – like we had to do. [. . .] We hope that you succeed at taking responsibility for your actions at the time [during the GDR regime]. Only those who learn to think about their past responsibly win liberty for future life."[50]

[48] Smith, "Control, Responsibility, and Moral Assessment," 388.

[49] Rainer Forst, *The Right to Justification: Elements of a Constructivist Theory of Justice* (New York: Columbia University Press, 2012), 2. Along similar lines, see George Sher, *Desert* (Princeton, NJ: Princeton University Press, 1985), 75.

[50] Emphasis added. The letter is entitled: "Erinnern kann nicht gerichtlich verboten werden. Zur Ausstellung, Christliches Handeln in der DDR' im

I already described how Schubert betrayed the trust of pastor Käbisch and his circle in the church of Reichenbach as well as that of other citizens, a disrespectful action in and of itself. The repercussions of his actions were significant, as some citizens were imprisoned as a result of his collaboration. This is what the citizens in the open letter mentioned earlier hold him responsible for, and they demand a justification for his actions, regardless of what provoked them. Furthermore, the outing of Schubert allows the general public to consider the case of a particularly engaged IM, one who was particularly active in denouncing individuals, providing incriminating evidence against them, and harassing individuals, etc., and who therefore bears more responsibility than others who had a fleeting or more superficial involvement with the Stasi. The exposure gives Schubert himself the opportunity to make a case for his exculpation. This particular collaborator might not be able to provide a redeeming account of his actions. But other IMs could do that. And as a result of this practice of justification, a debate about the responsibility of collaborators is established. If instead of such a debate there were global and sweeping attributions of innocence or culpability, the result would be ascribing responsibility to the blameless and sparing the culpable from such ascriptions. The sort of collective deliberation triggered by outings may never fully determine whether or not specific unofficial collaborators are morally responsible for collaborating with the Stasi. Nonetheless, it will produce more nuanced and respectful moral judgments; and as important, this deliberation presupposes that citizens should be treated as agents who can give reasons for their actions.

5.4 DISPLACING RESPONSIBILITY: WHY *WUT* IS NOT *MUT*

Based on the argument of the previous section, it should be clear that the practice of exposing unofficial collaborators walks a very fine line

Rathaus Reichenbach." The letter can be found at www.spiegel.de/politik/deutschland/brief-im-wortlaut-stelle-dich-der-vergangenheit-genau-wie-wir-es-tun-mussten-a-546173.html.

between building respect for citizens and undermining the very same value. In this section I consider yet another concern about public exposures: When individualizing culpability in the way that they do, they may be shedding most of the light on one character in the dramatis personae of post-Stasi coming to terms with the past, thereby leaving in relative obscurity other characters who bear some kind of responsibility for keeping the denunciatory system alive. This section describes these other forms of responsibility whose existence is not openly confronted. Furthermore, in view of the disproportionate attention paid to IMs at the expense of other responsible agents, this section also revisits the idea of collective responsibility attribution and explores whether and how it could promote respectful treatment of persons.

To put in succinctly, ascribing individual moral responsibility can produce, in cases such as the one that concerns us here, a moral responsibility deficit. Singling out unofficial collaborators by publicly exposing them oversimplifies the repertoire of responsibilities for political action and attitudes that made the activities of IMs possible in the first place. Other types of contributions to, and other varieties of complicity with, the Stasi, are left outside the scope of moral scrutiny in German public discourse as a consequence of the narrow focus on the public shaming of IMs.

To illustrate the latter point, consider how such discourse extols "courageous" East German citizens who "said no" in the face of attempts of recruitment from the Stasi. One example of this is *Ich habe Nein gesagt. Zivilcourage in der DDR [I said No. Civic Courage in the GDR]*, a book addressed to a wide readership that collects exemplary stories about citizens who refused to work for the Stasi. It includes a preface where prominent politician and former New Forum member Wolfgang Thierse praises the courage of those who led the "right life" in the "false system." "Self-determined thinking, as well as courageous and responsible action, were also among the possible options under the complicated conditions of everyday life under the GDR."[51] Thierse celebrates those who, despite the

[51] Hech and Praschl, eds. *Ich habe 'Nein!' gesagt: über Zivilcourage in der DDR* (Berlin: Homilius, 2002), 13–14.

"psychological pressure," and of the uncertain consequences of their decision, rejected the offer to become denunciators. Notice that in Thierse's praise of the righteous citizen, a connection is made between courage and responsibility. Here some citizens are responsible for praiseworthy acts, not blameworthy ones. Note further that the sort of responsibility at stake in the courageous action of the noncollaborator, as is commonly defended in Germany, is not a political one, in the sense of presupposing some degree of collective and public action. Rather, it is something close to conscientious refusal. This is a point that warrants closer examination because it sets the stage for the argument I want to advance about collective responsibility.

Iris Young makes a distinction between two different understandings of responsibility, one that she calls moral, and the other political.[52] The first one, in Young's reconstruction of Arendt's work, is private, religiously held, and focused on the self. It is the responsibility of the person who would refuse to collaborate with the Stasi. In writing about Nazi Germany, Arendt discusses a real scenario, roughly analogous to the one faced by informers during the communist regime, in which two young men who were about to be drafted into the infamous *Waffen-SS*, an armed organ of the Nazi Party, refused to sign the induction papers at the last minute because they knew enough about the mission of this particular branch. These two men, Arendt says, "practically speaking, did nothing." They are free of guilt. They engaged in actions that were praiseworthy from a moral point of view. "Their ability to tell right from wrong had remained intact, and they never suffered a 'crisis of conscience' [. . .] they were neither heroes nor saints, and they remained completely silent."[53] This last remark suggests, in Young's reading of Arendt, that their actions, to the extent that they were not public, were not political

[52] Here I rely heavily on Iris Young's reading of Arendt in *Responsibility for Justice* (New York: Oxford University Press, 2010), ch. 3, where she teases out an alternative Arendtian understanding of political responsibility drawing on *Eichmann in Jerusalem* and Arendt's short essay, "Organized Guilt and Universal Responsibility."

[53] Hannah Arendt, *Eichmann in Jerusalem*, 103–104.

either. Many citizens tried to distance their actions from complicity with Nazism or positively made efforts to help those in danger, but they did so on their own, privately, without making much of an issue of it. Their actions are acts of moral refusal, not political resistance, Arendt concludes.

In contrast to this kind of responsibility, political responsibility is, according to Young, public, secular, and based on the conditions of the world. It is a more specific and active understanding of responsibility than mere membership of a collectivity.[54] On this understanding, we bear political responsibility not simply by virtue of membership in a community but depending on more concrete social relationships and actions. Legal guilt or active commission should not be presupposed to ascribe political responsibility, to this reading.[55] Political responsibility falls, in Arendt's view as explained by Iris Young, on "those who dwell within the social system that enables the crimes and supplies that system with at least *passive* support. In this case, their *passivity* produces a political vacuum. The attitudes and behavior of the majority of people is so privatized that little organized public space exists in which actors can appear to others with their judgment of events, let alone join in collective action to transform them."[56]

[54] Young, *Responsibility for Justice*, ch. 3.

[55] Arendt's ideas are along the lines of those of Karl Jaspers in *Die Schuldfrage* (München: Piper, 1965). Jaspers made a famous distinction between moral guilt that is based on what one does and moral guilt that is based on who one is. He argued that the latter, which he calls "metaphysical guilt," could be distributed to all members of a community who stand by while their fellows do harm, e.g., murder Jews. In this context, being morally blameworthy of harm is largely a matter of belonging to an "evil" community without asserting one's own moral powers over the community to cleanse it of such evil. According to Jaspers, "[t]here exists a solidarity among men as human beings that makes each as responsible for every wrong and every injustice in the world, especially for crimes committed in his presence or with his knowledge. If I fail to do whatever I can do to prevent them, I too am guilty." Jaspers, as should become clear from the foregoing quotes, rejected collective categories and emphasized the role of the individual in the process of *Aufarbeitung* (an argument that was shared by most of his contemporaries). Instead of collective responsibility, he advanced the notion of shared responsibility (*kollektive Haftung*).

[56] Young, *Responsibility for Justice*, 86.

Put differently, citizens bear the responsibility for having "evacuated any space of popular organization and critical accountability, leaving isolated and ineffectual the few of their fellow members who were inclined to think and criticize."[57]

Iris Young's interpretations of Arendtian responsibility might overstate Arendt's case for open political action and its importance under totalitarian conditions, while overlooking the relevance of strategic passivity as a form of responsible action. Nonetheless, the distinction between moral and political responsibility is helpful in showing that public identifications put emphasis on the first kind of responsibility – IMs' unwillingness to engage in conscientious refusal – and subject it to strict moral evaluation. In contrast, they subject the second kind of responsibility – the polity's unwillingness to organize a public space and orchestrate collective action (or to act in concert, as Arendt would phrase it) – to a more lenient moral standard, or fail to put it under moral scrutiny altogether. This is a problem because the rest of society, excluding dissidents who openly or covertly struggled against the system, had a contributory role in wrongdoing, even if they did not themselves inform on other citizens. Admittedly, under a regime that aspires to maintain strict control over society, coordinated political action is difficult to undertake; such coordinated action is very likely to face numerous and considerable collective action problems. But alternatives to upfront and violent rebellion were available. The fact that some people did not openly speak against the regime and were extremely secretive about their criticism of the system is a way of supporting this system. One can imagine a situation in which most citizens systematically and openly criticized the system; in such a situation Stasi authorities would have been overwhelmed by the amount of "critical" information, rendering the work of IMs extremely difficult and virtually useless.

The implication of the foregoing discussion is that it is possible to invoke what one might call civic passivity as grounds for attributing a type of responsibility to citizens who did not join the Stasi but nonetheless indirectly *contributed* to its existence. This is a case of

[57] Young, *Responsibility for Justice*, 87.

noncomplicit contribution in the sense that it produced wrongdoing even if not deliberately. It might be less morally troublesome than the complicity of unofficial collaborators, but it merits confrontation nevertheless.

Besides noncomplicit contributors to the existence of the denunciatory system, a considerable number of citizens (how many is impossible to know) made a more direct and complicit contribution to the Stasi; that is, strictly speaking, IMs were only one group of collaborators among others. To classify these complicit contributors, one can think in terms of concentric circles of complicity, where those in the innermost circles bear a higher degree of moral responsibility than those in the outer circles. High-level public officials of the communist party and the Stasi would fall into the innermost circle. To follow the language that Lepora and Goodin use to describe different kinds of complicity,[58] these public officials were the *principals* of wrongdoing (call it political oppression) because they crafted the "plan" (call it comprehensive surveillance of the citizenry) that was *constitutive* of the main wrongdoing. To that end, they sought to create a network of informers, the latter being *contributory agents* – not principals – with a *causal* – not constitutive – role in wrongdoing; most of them delivered information that the Stasi could later use to control citizenry. For their causal contribution, informers are located in the next ring of the circle of complicity. But one should hasten to underscore that unofficial collaborators are not alone in this circle. They have at least two other groups of companions. The first one is formed by individuals who are sometimes referred to in Stasi documents as collaborative operational partners (*Partner des operativen Zusammenwirkens*) but more frequently as contact persons (*Kontaktpersonen*). These could be factory bosses, police officers, teachers, and so on. The Stasi relied on the occasional cooperation of such people, who otherwise had no exchanges with the Stasi. In other words, as Gary Bruce argues, "the repressive apparatus of the Stasi cannot be measured solely on the basis of its official workers and

[58] On the various kinds of contribution to wrongdoing see Chiara Lepora and Robert Goodin, *On Complicity and Compromise* (Oxford: Oxford University Press, 2013), 31–58.

informants."[59] As Bruce further suggests, this has consequences on how we think about complicity in the GDR. I quote him at some length:

> In a country that had become far too accustomed to using abbreviations as a shorthand for villainy – SS (Schutzstaffel – protection squads), SA (Sturmabteilung – storm troops), KZ (Konzentrationslager – concentration camp) – a new abbreviation began making the rounds: IM, the abbreviation for "unofficial co-worker" of the Stasi. The letters entered into everyday conversations, often uttered in disgust. Although our understanding of informants is now more complex, at the time IM became synonymous with the person whom Dante deemed the worst of traitors – the individual who betrayed friends and family. It is time that KP (Kontaktpersonen) assumed its place beside IM and accordingly to revise our view of the Stasi as a strictly proactive secret police to one of a secret police that frequently reacted to spontaneous tips from those in privileged positions in East Germany as well as from its informants.[60]

A weakness of the Stasi Files Law of 1991 is that it lustrated full-time Stasi employees and registered informants but failed to address the issue of contact persons. A former Stasi officer interviewed by Bruce rightly complained about this "unfair" aspect of the law. As he put it, while he was banned from employment in the public sector after 1989 and was even vilified in the streets because he had been a full-time Stasi officer, his contact in the local police, who telephoned him around five times per day with information about "threatening" individuals, remained in his post in unified Germany.[61]

The second companion of the IM next to the contact person was the irregular contact. Irregular contacts were personal friends or casual acquaintances of Stasi officers. As a public official for the secret police celebrates, "he never lost contact with the masses" and proudly recalls that citizens on the street would commonly let him know about what was happening in town. The information received through these

[59] Gary Bruce, *The Firm. The Inside Story of the Stasi* (New York: Oxford University Press, 2010), 126.

[60] Bruce, *The Firm*, 138. [61] Bruce, *The Firm*, 127

informal networks could later be used for official purposes.[62] Again, just as contact persons, for the purposes of public accountability these informal contacts are left "off the hook," as it were. They are never pressured to take responsibility for their complicity with the Stasi. They are, along with contact persons, an example of the responsibility deficit in the GDR.

Other kinds of complicity aside from collaboration (of IMs, contact persons, and irregular collaborators) include conniving or condoning. Agents who were complicit in these ways witnessed wrongdoing and approvingly overlooked it (conniving) or pardoned it (condoning); when suspecting that other citizens were IMs, they made sure not to interfere with their activities. For this type of complicity, these agents are situated in subsequent rings; they are less morally culpable perhaps, but also culpable if IMs are.

One might dispute the idea that collaborators in the inner ring bear more responsibility than those outside it. For one, unlike Stasi official employees and communist leaders, who made no attempt to hide their roles, IMs carried out their work in secret. For another, and related to this, informers deeply penetrated the lives of the citizenry. Ordinary citizens would disclose secrets to an IM that they would be careful to withhold from a Stasi officer. For these two reasons, so the argument would go, IMs were justifiably singled out by postcommunist transitional justice policies. My reply to this objection is that Stasi officers did not hide their roles, but rather concealed every detail about their actions to the public; they were secretive about their targets and plans. Furthermore, it would be a mistake to claim that unofficial collaborators knew more about the secrets of the nations than Stasi officers; the latter ended up learning about those secrets via their informers, with the aggravating element that they could then use that information to harm citizens.

I take pains to flesh out these layers of complicity simply to suggest that the public exposure of unofficial collaborators targets only one ring of complicity, leaving other rings unjustifiably unexamined. Oddly, the central circle of complicity seems to receive even less

[62] Bruce, *The Firm*, 126.

attention than that of unofficial collaborators, despite the fact that the former includes high-level public officials of the communist party and the Stasi (i.e., the principals of wrongdoing), who are fully culpable and should therefore be the main focus of public attention. Something similar goes for other rings of complicity – they fall outside the scope of moral examination that outings presumably trigger. Even the ring that does fall within the scope of examination is only partially scrutinized, as contact persons and irregular contacts are commonly ignored. Put briefly, the focus on unofficial collaborators discourages a comprehensive examination of the phenomenon of complicity, regardless of the degrees and kinds of moral culpability in each ring.

Some of these ideas about responsibility can already be found in the sermons and essays of German theologian Friedrich Schorlemmer. Like Joachim Gauck, Schorlemmer initially defended the idea of using the Stasi archives for the purpose of historical clarification. But unlike Gauck, he seems to have been more keenly aware of their potential perils. This is why he always recommended that they be used with the utmost caution.[63] He later grew skeptical that the benefits of opening the files would outweigh the costs in terms of achieving reconciliation, and even came to sympathize with the idea of "burning the archives."[64] His reason for recommending caution in the use of Stasi files was that they could be used to produce scapegoats. Along these lines, Schorlemmer described the public exposure of many IMs as a "projection mechanism" by which some East German citizens tried to extricate themselves from their own active or passive involvement. He described this phenomenon with terms such as guilt displacement (*Schuldverschiebung*) or exculpation (*Entlastung*).[65] Without downplaying the oppressive character of the Stasi, he also noted the tendency of some citizens to exaggerate their plight during the GDR, especially on the eve of its collapse, thereby

[63] Friedrich Schorlemmer, *Versöhnung in der Wahrheit. Nachschläge und Vorschläge eines Ostdeutschen* (Berlin: Knaur, 1992), 227.

[64] A position that led his erstwhile friends and allies to break with him on account of his "immorality." See Wolf Biermann, "Des Satans Spießgesellen," *Der Spiegel*, December 12, 1993.

[65] Schorlemmer, *Versöhnung in der Wahrheit*, 186–187.

justifying their lack of courage in resisting the regime. As he pithily put it, "*Was früher an Mut fehlte, kommt jetzt als Wut.*" (What was once lacking in courage now comes as anger). Furthermore, in thinking about the appropriate or "civilized" way – as he put it – of coming to terms with the past, he defended the idea of a tribunal that would "evaluate" instead of "judging." In his words: "Evaluating involves determining the different degrees of participation or guilt [. . .] I am still not sure whether guilt should be personalized or whether one should not rather speak of functions [. . .] My main goal is to reveal structures, backgrounds, ideological justifications, psychological mechanisms through which power was working."[66] Publicly identifying specific individuals was certainly compatible with such a goal, but in his viewpoint unlikely to encourage it.

Schorlemmer's assessment, particularly his emphasis on the problems associated with displacing responsibility, can be read in the spirit of defending the idea of collective responsibility. Indeed, ascriptions of collective moral responsibility could bring to light a richer and more textured account of the full range of responsibilities for the harm that the Stasi brought on East German society. But whereas Schorlemmer's preferred view would be to discourage public identifications altogether, his view might be problematic for the reasons indicated earlier. A more moderate solution to the problem of collaboration would be to find mechanisms that assign blame both at the individual and the collective levels. Schorlemmer's proposal for a tribunal that evaluates functions without judging individuals lacks specificity but is on the right track. One thing is certain, though: public exposures should be premised on a less simplistic narrative about degrees of collaboration. The current predominant narrative is that there were two types of citizens under the GDR; those who said yes to the Stasi – its public officials and Inoffizieller Mitarbeiter – and those who said no. Doing away with this gross oversimplification, promoted vehemently by some public press and media outlets, and even some public officials, would be a good place to start.

[66] A. Schwarz and G. Spörl, "Es geht nicht um Siegerjustiz," *Der Spiegel*, September 23, 1991.

In any case, the relevance of Schorlemmer's argument resides for us in the implication that his view has about the idea of respect. By bringing more persons into the circle of moral agents, that is, by expanding the number of individuals who should be attributed moral responsibility for their contribution to the actions carried out by the Stasi, collective attributions of responsibility build respect for persons. Addressing a responsibility deficit is also addressing a respect deficit.

Furthermore, collective attribution of responsibility can have a "developmental" effect, which public exposure might preclude due, among other things, to its potential of stigmatizing. Philip Pettit and Christian List have argued for such a developmental understanding of collective responsibility. They make reference to the effects that take place in loose groupings when the latter are held responsible for any wrongdoing taking place in them – the school group where there are incidents of bullying; the loose professional association where some of its members misbehave; the neighborhood where those who live in it indulge in certain socially exclusionary acts, say of a racist character. Petit and List write: "It may not be strictly appropriate to hold such a loose grouping responsible, since some of the conditions necessary for fitness to be held responsible are missing. But *holding it responsible may actually prompt the grouping to incorporate and organize against the condemned behavior.*"[67] In contrast, public exposures fail to produce this developmental potential. A morally responsible collectivity may seek to individualize culpability to produce "scapegoats" and thus avoid examination about how different degrees of culpability should be distributed within the collectivity. After finding blame in a very narrow set of individuals, such collectivity can turn the page, as it were, and fail to organize against the condemned behavior.[68]

[67] Christian List and Philip Pettit, *Group Agency. The Possibility, Design, and Status of Corporate Agents* (Princeton, NJ: Princeton University Press, 2011), 169. Emphasis added.

[68] See Bernhard Schlink, *Vergangenheitsschuld*, 47. See also, in a different context, Jelena Subotic, "Expanding the Scope of Post-Conflict Justice: Individual, State and Societal Responsibility for Mass Atrocity," *Journal of Peace Research* 48, no. 2 (2011): 157–169.

Ascriptions of collective moral responsibility entail risks, of course. In fact they are the usual targets of trenchant criticism, both academic and nonacademic. For instance, Mark Reiff argues that ascriptions of collective moral responsibility are not only unfair and imprecise, but also self-defeating because they provide incentives for adopting the worst common denominator of conduct. If I am going to be held morally responsible qua member of a collectivity, I might as well behave badly because I will be held responsible for the wrongdoing that others commit anyways.[69] Such a criticism, however, would not apply to the German case. The wrongful action in question – informing on other citizens – could only take place in a system like the GDR, which aspired to have a totalitarian grip on society. Thus, the kind of wrongdoing for which IMs are held responsible could not be repeated under democratic conditions.

Perhaps more relevant to East Germany, another criticism against attributions of collective moral responsibility is that they produce a moral responsibility deficit, captured by the saying "If we're all guilty, then no one is guilty." Admittedly, political actors across Germany and elsewhere have indeed used the notion of collective moral responsibility to exculpate themselves from past wrongdoing, as in the case of Manfred Stolpe, or so at least his critics say.[70]

Before concluding I would like to insist on how holding a collectivity responsible, as opposed to simply blaming a few "barbarians," as Gauck calls them, may contribute to serving forward-looking purposes that are crucially connected with the notion of respect. I take it that something along these lines is what Jürgen Habermas had in mind in his intervention in the so-called Goldhagen debates. Historian Daniel Goldhagen published his controversial *Hitler's Willing Executioners*, whose main thesis is that without the voluntary contribution of ordinary German citizens, the Holocaust would not

[69] Mark Reiff, "Terrorism, Retribution, and Collective Responsibility," *Social Theory and Practice* 34, no. 2 (2008): 240.

[70] See Manfred Stolpe, *Schwieriger Aufbruch* (Hamburg: Goldmann, 1992), 111–142.

have been possible. The reception of the work in Germany was unfavorable among some public opinion circles, but Habermas praised Goldhagen's book because, he claimed, it initiated a long overdue debate about the past, more concretely about "the truly fundamental question [. . .]: the meaning of a retrospective ascription of criminal responsibility, which we undertake in the present for the ends of the *ethical-political* process of understanding among citizens."[71] Put differently, the book triggered "public discourses of self-understanding," the point of which is to determine the values that are to prevail in the present in the political community. These processes, Habermas continued, reveal how German citizens can "respect one another" and how they wish to be "recognized by others."[72] Note that the contribution of Goldhagen's book in stirring this process of self-understanding is that, according to Habermas, it points to the existence of widespread anti-Semitism as a necessary – though obviously not sufficient – condition for the Holocaust. In other words, it underscores the fact that even if the Nazis wielded the murder weapons, a set of widely shared cultural beliefs rendered atrocities against Jews possible. And just as Germany's first process of coming to terms with the past would be extremely limited if it examined the actions of Nazi officials without also paying attention to the collaboration, connivance, or nonculpable contributions of ordinary citizens, so would Germany's second process of coming to terms with the past be deficient if it merely focused on the acts of Stasi officials or its informers without confronting the role of East Germans more generally. But that is precisely the approach to reckoning with the past that IM exposures induce; an approach that, for the reasons mentioned in the chapter, discourages public discourses of self-understanding, and thus fails to contribute to building mutual respect among the citizenry.

[71] In Habermas, "On the Public Use of History," *The Postnational Constellation: Political Essays* (Cambridge, MA: MIT Press, 2001), 27–28.

[72] Habermas, "On the Public Use of History," 28.

5.5 CONCLUSION

Unofficial collaborators were not cogs in the Stasi machinery, to use the language that Hannah Arendt used to evaluate Adolf Eichmann's exculpations before the Israeli Court that judged him. Although systemic incentives and fear for the consequences of their refusal to work for the secret police were undoubtedly strong causal factors shaping their behavior during the GDR, many citizens and activists in Germany argue that IMs still retained agency. And this might be an appropriate way to address unofficial collaborators. Being recognized as capable of being responsible is a sign of respect. Treating a collaborator respectfully implies that we will hold her responsible and accountable for her complicity with the Stasi. Ideally, she would need to come out in public and give reasons why she decided to collaborate or at least acknowledge that she did. But whether she does that or not is inconsequential to the point being made: She should be treated that way, lest we think of her as something less or other than a fully fledged agent. That is the sort of respect she is due.

However, this is not to say that deciding whether responsibility can be ascribed or not is an easy matter. Holding someone responsible is indeed under normal circumstances a respectful action. But holding someone responsible when she did not have the resources, the possibility of behaving like a responsible agent is exactly the opposite: to disrespect her. For example, it disrespects handicapped people to treat them as if they could do what able-bodied people can do if only they wanted to. In such a case, the failure to recognize their limitations is a form of disrespect. Put briefly, ascriptions of responsibility hinge on some basis for recognizing the conditions of possibility for the meaningful exercise of responsible agency. The public exposure of unofficial collaborators and the public debates ensuing them *can* provide such basis for recognition. If, that is, it is carried out in the proper way; and if it is not merely a scapegoating mechanism, thus relieving the community from assuming its responsibility for past wrongdoing.

6 AN APOLOGY FOR PUBLIC APOLOGIES: A MATTER OF RESPECT?

6.1 A LESS RESPECTFUL KIND OF APOLOGY?

It is a commonplace of transitional justice scholarship that in post-conflict societies, public apologies by former wrongdoers are practices that promote respect for victims. An apology, even in the simplest of senses, involves recognition that the victim was not treated appropriately, and that at the very least she deserves redress in the form of an acknowledgment of the wrong done. Notwithstanding the potential of apologies to foster respect, this chapter makes the case for considering an ambivalence in the acts of apologizing that are common to transitional justice situations, and the case of unofficial collaborators is no exception. *Public* apologies might build respect, but they can also circumvent that possibility. This ambivalence, I contend, has not been fully appreciated in the relevant literature, where apologies are regarded by and large as what one scholar calls "performative redress."[1]

Skepticism toward offers of public apologies as a response to political wrongdoing, and more generally toward the cycle of forgiveness (asking for, giving, and accepting apologies), is a common theme in the context of transitional justice.[2] Most of these skeptical perspectives, however, allude only indirectly, if at all, to the ideal of

[1] John Borneman, "Public Apologies as Performative Redress," *SAIS Review of International Affairs* 25, no. 2 (2005): 53–66.

[2] A recent skeptical line of reasoning may be found at Rebecca Saunders, "Questionable Associations: The Role of Forgiveness in Transitional Justice," *The International Journal of Transitional Justice* 5, no. 1 (2011): 119–141.

respect for persons, so central to transitional justice scholarship.[3] Their goal is to flesh out why forgiveness is an inappropriate or insufficient response to injustice. By contrast, I do not argue that this forgiveness cycle is a form of incomplete justice, but rather that, instead of functioning as performative redress and thereby as a respect-building practice, the expectation and the delivery of public apologies may in fact work against the purpose of achieving respect.

Recent scholarship has insisted on acknowledging the different dimensions of forgiveness and apologies – personal, interpersonal, public.[4] It has done so in an effort to carve out a political understanding of these notions. Thus, for instance, according to most authors within this paradigm, ordinarily we speak of forgiveness as a strictly moral action whose motivations, effects, and rationale can be extrapolated to the political realm. Political forgiveness, however, is ultimately and crucially distinct from ordinary (personal and even interpersonal) forgiveness. Political forgiveness is not solipsistic forgiveness, where one individual comes to terms with her own vindictive emotions such as resentment, anger, or hatred. Neither is it

[3] One exception is David Sussman, "Kantian Forgiveness," *Kant-Studien* 96, no. 1 (2005): 85–107.

[4] The list of articles and books is extensive, but some of the major works used in this chapter are the following: Lucy Allais, "Wiping the Slate Clean. The Heart of Forgiveness," *Philosophy and Public Affairs* 36, no. 1 (2008): 33–68; Christopher Bennet, "Is Amnesty an Act of Political Forgiveness?" *Contemporary Political Theory* 2, no. 1 (2003): 67–76; P. E. Digeser, *Political Forgiveness* (Ithaca, NY: Cornell University Press, 2001); Trudy Govier, *Forgiveness and Revenge* (London: Routledge, 2002); Charles Griswold, *Forgiveness: A Philosophical Exploration* (Cambridge: Cambridge University Press, 2007); Jeffrey G. Murphy, *Getting Even: Forgiveness and Its Limits* (Oxford: Oxford University Press, 2003); Andrew Schaap, "Political Grounds for Forgiveness," *Contemporary Political Theory* 2, no. 1 (2003): 77–87; Nick Smith, *I Was Wrong: The Meanings of Apologies* (Cambridge: Cambridge University Press, 2008); Nicholas Tavuchis, *Mea Culpa: A Sociology of Apology and Reconciliation* (Stanford, CA: Stanford University Press, 1991); Glen Pettigrove, "Hannah Arendt and Collective Forgiveness," *Journal of Social Philosophy* 37, no. 4 (2006): 483–500; Danielle Celermajer, *The Sins of the Nation and the Ritual of Apologies* (Cambridge: Cambridge University Press, 2009).

interpersonal forgiveness, where one individual confronts her wrongdoer, and both parties come to terms with their common past in a private setting. Political forgiveness has to do with *publicly* recognizing that harm was done to a group of individuals and *publicly* offering perpetrators the opportunity to have their civic and political status fully restored after having acknowledged their wrongdoings and having been forgiven by their victims.

The public component of public apologies is credited with contributing to construct respect for victims by acknowledging both their right to an apology and their standing to demand that right in the eyes of others. It is also considered a mechanism of membership recertification that shows respect for the perpetrators by providing a means for them to be readmitted into the political community. What is usually neglected, however, is that turning the cycle of forgiveness into a collective performance runs the risk of undercutting the respect-promoting potential usually associated with more private kinds of apology. At an interpersonal level, an apology involves a request from one party to the other. This presupposes some sort of interaction and interlocution, as well as recognition of the status of the would-be forgiver as an agent who can forgive or decide not to forgive; this is the sort of process that truly builds respect. By contrast, public apologies might dispense with such a process. In fact, they might dispense with victims altogether, in the sense that engaging them directly is no longer necessary to fulfill or issue the public apology. In short, the problem arises when the performance of the apology becomes a substitute for the sort of interpersonal interaction on which ordinary forgiveness is predicated and when a monologue takes the place of interlocution or conversation. In other words, the element of publicity that is constitutive of public apologies might negatively affect the quality of the interaction between the victims and the perpetrator.

One of the most salient features of public discourse around IMs is the way it traffics in the language of forgiveness and related terms, such as apologies, repentance, atonement, regret, and so on. I will be arguing, given the language employed in public debates, that IM exposures are practices that seek to elicit public apologies from former Stasi denunciators and forgiveness from their victims and other citizens, practices, in other words, that provide a context in which IMs may apologize in public for their complicity with the Stasi and in which their victims and the polity at large may forgive them for such complicity.

This chapter proceeds as follows. In the second section, I develop the thesis that in the German context, political forgiveness is more about creating or encouraging repentance in unofficial collaborators than it is about eliminating the resentment of victims; repentance in this view restores a moral and political balance among citizens that the activity of informing had previously disrupted. In section three, I develop the claim that what is at stake in IM exposures is the public recognition of citizens who were victims of informers. Furthermore, in section four, I argue that these exposures are forms of membership reaccreditation: Apologies are required if former denunciators are to be included as respected members of the polity. However, in section five, I explain why public apologies have the potential to undercut the purported goal of apologies – namely to reestablish political relations based on the ideal of equal respect among citizens.

6.2 DELIVERANCE FROM RESENTMENT OR DELIVERY OF REPENTANCE?

Political forgiveness is not about what we oftentimes associate ordinary forgiveness with: clearing the offended party from resentment. Instead, it requires a display of repentance, and that is precisely what the discourse and practice of IM exposures in postcommunist Germany seek and elicit: an ostensible, unambiguous display of regret from former unofficial collaborators.

In 1989, a year before the formal dissolution of the communist regime, the GDR's foremost authority, Erich Honecker, was forced to resign in the face of mounting social and political discontent. After his resignation, he and his wife started the pilgrimage of the defenestrated. Their journey began in the residence of Lutheran Pastor Uwe Holmer, where they stayed for ten weeks. Many years later, Pastor Holmer gave the following answer to why he opened the doors of his home to them and why, more generally, he forgave public officials and

"Stasi-people" who did not show any repentance (*Reue*) for their actions. I quote him at length:

> Obviously it is better if the other one repents.... But forgiveness simply means to be delivered from what has become a poison within oneself. How the other one should deal with my forgiveness, I leave that to God's hands. I simply expel that poison, and refuse to remember the past any longer, to torment myself any longer. I know that is hard, particularly for those who experienced such terrible things as political persecution or the families of those who were shot at the Wall. But one becomes a prisoner of its hate if one does not forgive perpetrators.... They [victims] must forgive so that they do not become bitter. Victims who still carry in the heart the bitterness and hate from back then will become sick.[5]

I make reference to Pastor Holmer's understanding of forgiveness to contrast it to the kind of forgiveness that, I argue, underlies the public exposure of IMs. Holmer casts forgiveness as a practice that can be reduced to an act of generosity, inspired by a religious doctrine, and performed for the sake of releasing the potential forgiver from his or her own resentment or from retributive emotions.[6] Forgiveness à la Holmer, then, to the extent that it amounts to a reaction whose main purpose is to purge one from, or mitigate, resentment, is a self-regarding action, an affective, privatized form of forgiveness that can take place away from the public eye and can even be done *sotto voce* – I can forgive you without you (or others) even knowing it. This is not forgiveness in its political sense, but what Michael Oakeshott calls self-enactment, that is, the ability to choose or alter the sentiments on which one acts. Forgiving, in the ordinary sense of the notion, is a form of self-fashioning, not a political act.[7] Furthermore, it is a moral

[5] "Der Mann, bei dem Honi wohnte: 'Ich habe ihm damals schon verziehen,'" *SuperIllu*, December 4, 2009.

[6] For an account that calls into question the idea that ordinary forgiveness actually involves this banishment from resentment, see Lucy Allais, "Wiping the Slate Clean."

[7] I am following P. E. Digeser's, *Political Forgiveness*, 11–35, who references Oakeshott.

virtue: the overcoming, on moral grounds (not out of instrumental reasons: getting a better job, passing as generous), of vindictive passions such as anger, resentment, and hatred.[8] No repentance is asked but freedom from resentment.

Hannah Arendt is one to note (although without duly emphasizing) the limits of viewing forgiveness as the mitigation of vindictiveness and to stress the role of repentance in the practice of political forgiveness. Arendt draws on the Scriptural legacy of Christianity. Jesus, she argues, is the "discoverer of the role of forgiveness in the realm of human affairs," and the political import of his ideas has been "neglected because of their allegedly exclusively religious nature."[9] However, she claims, couched in a religious language, many insights in the New Testament have secular and political validity. Such is the case of the awareness of the necessary role of forgiveness in correcting the inexorable damages occasioned by political action. In one of the several passages Arendt quotes from the New Testament, she highlights the role of repentance: "And if he trespass against thee seven times a day, and seven times in a day turn again to thee, saying, I repent; thou shalt forgive him."[10] Repenting, understood in this context as changing one's mind and "sinning" (offending, transgressing) no more, is a necessary step toward forgiveness.

But why is the prescription of repentance valued over the proscription of resentment? What does the display of regret accomplish that the self-enactment of resentment avoidance does not? The answer is that the expectation of repentance is crucial in thinking about forgiveness relationally, as a practice that opens up the possibility of restoring a moral or political (civic) relationship and asserts the equal worth of the parties involved. Part of the injury of being wronged is the degrading message that you are less worthy than the wrongdoer, or unworthy enough that the wrongdoer may use you merely as a means or as an object in the service of his or her desires and projects. If the wrongdoer sincerely repents, however, he or she joins you in

8 Jeffrey G. Murphy, *Getting Even*, 16.

9 Hannah Arendt, *The Human Condition* (Chicago: University of Chicago Press, 1958), 239.

10 Arendt, *The Human Condition*, 240.

repudiating the degrading message, allowing you to relate to the wrongdoer as an equal.[11]

To illustrate this point, take the following commentary published in the *Bild-Zeitung*, a German newspaper/tabloid that, like most of the German press, engaged the debate about unofficial collaborators and the appropriate way to come to terms with their role in the GDR. The *Bild-Zeitung* weighed in on the discussion by straightforwardly posing the question: "How should we deal with former Stasi denunciators? Isn't it time for reconciliation just yet?" To respond to it, the newspaper summoned the Protestant Bishop from Brandenburg and Berlin, who began his reply by offering something of a parable, the parable of the informer, as it were. I imagine, the Bishop says, that an unknown man (he calls him Günter) comes to my confessionary. He has a great need to speak. He tells me, the Bishop continues, he was an IM; he told on people around him and wrote reports on them. After the reunification, "he said, he had tried to repress/hide his cooperation [with the Stasi]. This was a new era, one simply remained silent and tried to forget. But the past weighed on him more and more. Now Günter wanted to finally get rid of this increasingly heavy burden." Then comes the crux of the story: reconciliation cannot be achieved, the Bishop argues, simply by appeal to perpetrators. Rather, it is the other way around: reconciliation presupposes that the perpetrators have taken the first active steps by contacting those to whom they have caused harm. The Bible, he says, calls these steps "reversal." "The Gospel begins with Jesus' call to repent." Such steps pave the way toward reconciliation, a lesson, he claims, that the evangelical church followed after 1945 in its reappraisal of the Nazi past. The road to reconciliation is a long one, in his view, and we can only start thinking about forgiveness when perpetrators have taken the first steps. "The effects of the repentance of the perpetrator are uncertain. Such repentance runs the risk of not being accepted. But without it there is no reconciliation." He concludes: "If Günter were to actually knock on my door, I would probably advise him to seek contact with those to whom he has wronged. Next he would have to ask for

[11] Murphy, *Getting Even*, 35. See also Linda Radzik, *Making Amends: Atonement in Morality, Law, and Politics* (Oxford: Oxford University Press, 2009), 94.

forgiveness. Whether his apology would be accepted or not is uncertain. But at least the first step would have been taken."[12]

The Bishop, unlike Pastor Holmer, values the importance of repentance. One might be misled by the Bishop's narrative in thinking that the sole point of repentance is to assuage IM Günter's guilt and to allow him to carry out a self-regarding act of contrition. That would be no less an apolitical act than Holmer's reigning in his vindictive passions. But what the Bishop emphasizes over Günter's emotional report and his desire to relieve himself of the burden of guilt is the imperative of taking the initiative to restore a relationship. The Bishop's is an admonition to understand forgiveness as a practice that can only thrive in a relationship between a victim and a perpetrator; otherwise it is unachievable.

The appeal to repentance is not a monopoly of religious figures, as my previous examples might lead one to suspect. Even thoroughly secular political discourse highly values the place of repentance in successfully achieving political forgiveness. Consider the case of an important dissident during the GDR regime, Ulrike Poppe. Dissidents of her kind were very likely to be surrounded by IMs. Monica H., alias Karin Lenz, was one of them. She infiltrated a circle of dissidents in East Berlin and befriended and then informed on several of them. The activists themselves in 1989, however, eventually uncovered Karin Lenz. Instead of following Günter's way of hiding and keeping silent, she was willing to work through her complicity along with the activists she informed on, an exchange that was published as a book and constitutes what a scholar called a successful "model of reconciliation," for "on the part of the perpetrator there is a willingness to tell her story frankly, to admit wrongdoing, to explain motives, to express her shame. On the part of victims, there is also a preparedness to listen, to understand, and eventually to forgive."[13] In a different context, but still addressing the same problem, Poppe

[12] Markus Droege, an Evangelical Bishop from Berlin and Brandenburg. "Was würde Jesus dazu sagen?," *Bild-Zeitung*, November 26, 2009, 17.

[13] Alison Lewis, "En-Gendering Remembrance: Memory, Gender and Informers for the Stasi," *New German Critique* 86, Spring–Summer (2002): 121.

underscores the importance of such repentance: "Some, very few unofficial collaborators have even asked for an informal conversation and apologized to me. Some regretted their activity and showed remorse. Others tried to justify their Stasi activities. For me it is crucial how people today relate to their history."[14]

In sum, I have underscored a crucial element motivating IM exposures: the existence, restoration, and cultivation of a civic relationship. This is part of what is at stake in the demand that unofficial collaborators take the first active steps in the pursuit of forgiveness by contacting their victims and showing repentance. And this display of what another political actor aptly calls "active repentance"[15] is a sign of respect toward them.

6.3 INTERPERSONAL REPENTANCE OR PUBLIC RECOGNITION?

In conceptualizing political forgiveness in the previous section, I argued that the emphasis is put on urging repentance from the perpetrator, not on purging resentment from the victim, as in the case of private forgiveness. Likewise, the accent lies on the malefactor's display of regret, not on his or her personal contrition. These

[14] "Ulrike Poppe: "'Es gab ein richtiges Leben im falschen,' Künftige Stasiunterlagen-Beauftragte," *Der Tagesspiegel*, December 9, 2009, www.tagesspiegel.de/berlin/brandenburg/kuenftige-stasiunterlagen-beauftragte-ulrike-poppe-es-gab-ein-richtiges-leben-im-falschen/1646008.html. According to a study, there are three kinds of former unofficial collaborators according to how they come to terms with their collaboration for the Stasi. The first kind comprises those IMs who at once repress and rationalize their collaboration; these individuals do not genuinely confront their past. The next two categories refer to individuals who do confront it. In the first category, some individuals try to distance themselves from their past actions and regret having committed them, whereas others admit to their collaboration but claim not to regret it. See Gerhard Barkleit and Anette Dunsch, "Inoffizielle Mitarbeiter in der Hochtechnologie," *Deutschland Archive* 2 (1996): 213–221.

[15] "Stasi-Verstrickungen; Platzeck fühlt sich getäuscht und geprellt," *Berliner Morgenpost*, December 4, 2009, www.morgenpost.de/brandenburg/article1218166/Platzeck-fuehlt-sich-getaeuscht-und-geprellt.html

conceptual clarifications, as critical as they are for teasing out the notion of political forgiveness and for clarifying their potential to build respect, are still insufficient for fully explicating it because they remain grounded in interpersonal interactions. The additional layer that needs to be fleshed out is the public dimension of political forgiveness.

It might be tempting to understand IM exposure simply as the victims' and activists' strategy to force unofficial collaborators to contact and apologize to the latter because they will not offer words of apology voluntarily. This, indeed, is part of the explanation. As I mentioned before, scholar Anne Sa'adah offers a similar account in explaining public identification of IMs in the early years of the reunified nation. During that period, she claims, New Forum dissidents worked intensely to put the IM question on the public agenda, not by arguing for legal punishment for former denunciators but by calling for the formation of "tribunals" in which perpetrators and victims would come together and confront one another verbally across a common table. The spirit of these tribunals was summarized by one of its advocates in the following way: "We plead for individual or group conversations with absolute confidentiality. Psychologists, jurists, clergy, together or individually, should be available for these conversations."[16] In the view of activists, Sa'adah argues, such private encounters would have enormous benefits for victims: they would help establish a new hierarchy of power between the parties involved, one based on moral merit. The ideal situation would be that the unofficial collaborator confesses her guilt and her betrayal of trust, apologizes, and finally ratifies a new power relationship, where she would be dependent on the forgiveness of the former victim. Unsurprisingly, however, instances of this model of dialogue and reckoning with the past between informers and their target were infrequent. Against the best hopes and efforts of activists, IMs did not rush into these tribunals to incriminate themselves. For this reason, Sa'adah concludes, activists began to take a more "punitive and exclusionary" direction. Among other things, a newspaper close to the movement

[16] Quoted by Sa'adah, *Germany's Second Chance*, 74.

published the names of informants who had been involved with the Stasi. This publicity, then, was an explicit reaction to the lack of responsiveness from former perpetrators for failing to confront their victims in the "confidential" encounters that the activists tried to stage.[17]

This interpretation might accurately describe some IM exposures as an *ersatz* for the private tribunals of forgiveness, which give victims the means to unveil the identity of and confront their offenders, or as radical measures designed to set a general example to other unofficial collaborators (this is what happens to those who do not respond to the call) and encourage them in the future to take part in confidential (i.e., private) meetings, following the format proposed by New Forum. However, I argue that the exposure of IMs can be interpreted at least partly in terms that are irreducible to private forgiveness. This requires that we take note of the fact that the public nature of IM exposures is relevant in its own right; that is, IM exposures are not public simply because they may help to bring about a private confrontation between victims and wrongdoers, penalizing the latter in case they refuse to participate in them.

Political forgiveness entails two forms of public recognition, albeit of two distinct kinds: that of the victims, which I develop next, and that of perpetrators, which I leave for the next section. The function of public apologies is amply documented in the political forgiveness literature. For example, based on Christopher Bennet's historical example of the South African Truth and Reconciliation Committee, the actions of wrongdoers express "values inimical to any form of society premised on mutual recognition,"[18] and wrongdoers themselves must repudiate them before they can be accepted as partners in a shared democratic enterprise. Bennet asks, "how can victims share a civic space with wrongdoers, when these wrongdoers do not acknowledge that their victims are worthy of an apology?"[19] Without such

[17] Sa'adah, *Germany's Second Chance*, 74.

[18] Bennet, "Is Amnesty an Act of Political Forgiveness?," 69.

[19] Bennet, "Is Amnesty an Act of Political Forgiveness?," 73. See also Schaap, "Political Grounds for Forgiveness," 82.

public repudiation, citizens cannot regard each other as equal partners in the polity. Were a wrongdoing to go without an ensuing apology, the wrongdoer would get away with a false claim to superiority. Charles Griswold offers a similar argument about the balancing effect of political apologies. He claims that the function of such apologies is "to communicate a moral point publicly."[20] Political apologies, Griswold argues, bring "the offender to a level of moral parity with the offended by recognizing the capacity and fact of moral error on the former's part." Through the apology, he further argues, "the offended is due a public expression of that recognition ... political apology is a public act: the offended person's comparative status is reaffirmed by it."[21] Finally, in a similar vein, anthropologist John Borneman argues that political apologies "are a form of performative redress that link the fate of the wrongdoer and the victim in a public event, which seeks to defeat the wrongdoer's claim to mastery over the victim." A public apology, then, amounts to a "retroactive recognition of dignity."[22] It is a symbolic exchange whereby the wrongdoer voluntarily lowers his or her own status as a person.

In my interpretation, IM exposures play a similar role to the one that John Borneman ascribes to the work of many of the commissions set up in the workplace of certain firms after reunification, such as the Commission of Vindication/Rehabilitation or Rehabilitierungskommission. From late 1989 through 1994, these firms took it upon themselves to address, not claims related to material redress (say, obtain monetary retribution, or reclaim property), but rather "moral" injuries that had occurred in those firms during the GDR regime. For instance, in their appearances before the commission, most people simply asked for acknowledgment of having been unfairly fired for their criticism of communist authorities. Some of the most common remedies for these wrongs were formal apologies, the purpose of which were, according to Borneman, "to restore the dignity of victims of the old regime through acts of vindication or rehabilitation." He argues that the relation of the victim to the perpetrator is usually the crux of the process of vindication: "for in order to confirm

[20] Griswold, *Forgiveness*, 142. [21] Griswold, *Forgiveness*, 142.

[22] John Borneman, "Public Apologies as Performative Redress," 2005.

the victim's importance through a procedure of vindication, it is often necessary to lower the unjustly elevated status of the wrongdoer. To reestablish the self-worth and value – the dignity – of the victim requires that an event be staged whereby there is a public repudiation of the message of superiority that initially caused the diminishment in the victim's worth." This "public recognition," he claims, contributes to the "restoration of dignity."[23]

To illustrate these points in the German case, consider the exposure of IM Schubert by Pastor Käbisch, in the exhibition mentioned in Chapter 3, which originated a legal dispute between the two. In the context of the public debate around such a dispute, the local Christian Democratic Union (CDU),[24] sympathetic to Pastor Käbisch's cause, circulated a pamphlet collecting donations for the costs of the trial against Käbisch. These costs were so high, Käbisch claimed, that he could not afford them. Commenting on this and similar cases in which other citizens faced similar suits, former commissioner of the Stasi files, Marianne Birthler, argued that former denunciators used legal demands as a form of intimidation. Käbisch and Birthler's statements echo the widely shared opinion that those who want to expose informers are intentionally made subject to financial and other threats. The perception, more to the point, is that some informers attempt to silence the reckoning with the past through litigation and that this silence perpetuates an asymmetry of power in the midst of civil society, which is the legacy of the communist regime. But Käbisch was vocal about the fact that he was not going to yield to the pressure of IM Schubert and his legal assault. Käbisch acts as if he had, in the words of a prominent German politician, a "right to an apology, to the regret of the perpetrator,"[25] as well as the standing to demand such a right. Käbisch himself said in a public forum that he had received letters from former Stasi officials who wanted "to create fear, like they had always done." But, under the applause

[23] John Borneman, *Settling Accounts: Violence, Justice, and Accountability in Postsocialist Europe* (Princeton, NJ: Princeton University Press, 1997), 113.

[24] "Die Stasi macht wieder mobil – wehret den Anfängen!" Pamphlet, www.moak.de/forum/forum_entry.php?id=1536.

[25] "Reue vor Versöhnung," *die tageszeitung*, November 24, 2009.

of the audience, he made it clear that he would not budge from his resolve to continue his exhibition.[26] On his part, IM Schubert remained unapologetic about his actions. In this he was no different than other unofficial collaborators, Käbisch claimed. By the mid-nineties, he continued, he met about a third of the 62 IMs who had collaborated with the Stasi to his detriment. None of them had a word of regret or apology. By contrast, most of them affirmed, sincerely or not, that they thought that through their collaboration they were helping to avert a third world war and to guarantee world peace.[27]

It is noteworthy that right from the beginning, and throughout the whole process, Käbisch's main intention was to tell his story. First, he organized a public exhibition in the city of Zwickau to expose the ways in which the Stasi besieged him and other members of the Church, and it was this exhibition that triggered the legal conflict mentioned earlier. Later, in the face of what he rightly called intimidating pressure against him and his exhibition, he attended public fora to make his point that he would not yield to such threats of IM. He even created an Internet site to document and publicize the details of his exhibition and of his legal and political defense against Schubert. Käbisch, and his case is by no means the only one among Stasi victims, is addressing and thereby creating a public; he organized, along with others, a social space where his narrative could circulate and appeal to strangers. In this he resembles another victim who said he needed to come to terms with the past, and to that end proceeded to create an Internet site (ddr-ausreise.de) that included a narrative of his experience as a victim of the Stasi.[28] Victims like Käbisch might have been looking for what, as a public commentator puts it, is "largely owed to them: public recognition (*Anerkennung*) and

[26] "Vergeben ja, vergessen nein," www.freiepresse.de/NACHRICHTEN/HINTERGRUND/HINTERGRUND18/1432299.php.

[27] Cathrin Wilhelm, "Was macht eigentlich Pfarrer Käbisch?" *Cicero*, June 2008.

[28] The victim, Schaarschmidt, had been subject to multiple forms of harassment by the Stasi and was later forced to leave East Germany, as a result of which his daughter quit her studies. Unable to cope with the pressure, his wife later committed suicide. Von Wensierski, "Recht Auf Vergessen?," 38–43.

empathy,"[29] or, in the words of a magazine editorial, what is being recognized is "the worth of victims."[30]

The point of examining Käbisch's case closely, as a representative of a broader set of cases, is to shed light on the logic of respect that underlies it. Apologies in the context of IM exposures express victims' attempt to humble former denunciators before a public; they also express the victims' attempt to assert their rights to demand an apology and the prerogative to request a public one. In both cases, then, respect for the victim is at stake, and an apology made in the presence of other citizens is the appropriate mechanism to redress the victim and "restore" his or her respect, downtrodden during the communist regime.

In sum, many scholars point out the importance of public apologies and their relevance for dignity concerns. Their conclusions may be extended to the cases I am discussing here. In particular, the analysis of these scholars clarifies how private apologies of unofficial collaborators could not accomplish the restoration of respect in the same way as public apologies. IM outings are the unwilling exposure of informers to the public but also the voluntary public exposure of the victims who demand recognition. It is on such public recognition that the practices of political forgiveness and respect that concern us at present are predicated.

6.4 FROM EMOTIONAL REPORT TO MEMBERSHIP REACCREDITATION

I mentioned before that, for a victim, forgiving the perpetrator in a political sense is not the same as clearing his or her own heart of resentment. By the same token, from the point of view of the perpetrator, the function of an apology, offered in a political context, is not to report an emotion. In IM Günther's example, mentioned before, this guilt-ridden man went to the confessionary to assuage his guilt; his admission was, to a large extent, a therapeutic act. This sort of

[29] Ines Geipel, "Kontaminierte Gesellschaft," *Welt am Sonntag*, April 31, 2007.
[30] "Kein Schlussstrich," *Focus*, April 30, 2007.

motivation, however, is politically irrelevant. It is not the point of political forgiveness to provide emotional relief to the perpetrator. Political forgiveness, then, involves neither the emotions of the would-be forgiver nor those of the would-be forgiven. Likewise, it cannot be reduced to interpersonal forgiveness. IM exposures are public in the more meaningful sense that they stage a collective encounter or ritual in which wrongdoers offer a public mea culpa. This takes us to the second form of recognition that is at stake in political forgiveness and in IM exposures: the perpetrators' public recognition of their actions and their acknowledgment that such actions contradicted important social and moral codes.

A dialogue from J. M. Coetzee's novel *Disgrace* will help to introduce this point. Facing an accusation of sexual abuse, David Lurie, the novel's main character, is offered an opportunity to resume his job at his university in exchange for "apologizing" to the "complainant" and the university.[31] To his reply that repentance "belongs to another world, to another universe of discourse," the following dialogue between the spokesman of the disciplinary committee and Lurie ensues:

> "You are confusing issues [. . .]. You are not being instructed to repent. What goes on in your soul is dark to us, as members of what you call a secular tribunal if not as fellow human beings. You are being asked to issue a statement."
>
> "I am being asked to issue an apology about which I may not be sincere?"
>
> "The criterion is not whether you are sincere. That is a matter, as I say, for your own conscience. The criterion is whether you are prepared to acknowledge your fault in a public manner and take steps to remedy it."[32]

Notice two things about the dialogue. First, the type of repentance expected from David Lurie cannot take place within the four walls of a university office because its envisioned function is not the personal

[31] Jeffrey G. Murphy uses David Lurie's example, although he uses it for a completely different purpose (namely, to argue for the desirability of sincere repentance) and makes very little use of it. See his *Getting Even: Forgiveness and Its Limits*, 2003, 37.

[32] J. M. Coetzee, *Disgrace* (New York: Penguin, 2000), 58.

transformation of the would-be forgiven, and it is more than the simple the restoration of the relationship between Lurie and his victim. Being divorced from any concern for the mental states or the sentiments of the parties involved and being more than a private encounter between the two of them, Lurie's repentance is an act with social and political dimensions, one wherein a previous wrongdoing and the set of values that speak against it are publicly acknowledged. The publicity of the repentance, and only to a lesser extent its sincerity, is relevant to the committee, which will even accept a coerced apology.[33]

The second point to notice is that what the disciplinary committee is offering goes beyond employment guarantees. The bid is not simply that if the offender apologizes he gets to keep his job, but that he will be readmitted into the university *community.* The apology earns the supplicant a form of social reaccreditation. In sum, the committee is not asking for an emotional report from the culprit rendered in all honesty (although sincerity would indeed be appreciated); instead it demands a signal from Lurie that shows his willingness to reenter the community, whose norms he transgressed. Without such signal, he cannot be fully "rehabilitated" as a member of the polity.

In analogous manner, many social and political actors in Germany expect a gesture from unofficial collaborators that shows that they acknowledge the kind and the extent of the wrongdoing that they caused by cooperating with the Stasi. To address this issue more systematically, it might be useful to rely on a distinction made by Nicholas Tavuchis between apologies and accounts. When I offer an account I distance myself from my actions, I deny the imperatives of responsibility and answerability through an appeal to my impaired self, my diminished capacities, the intervention of external forces, and so on. When I offer an apology, by contrast, I do not detach myself from my deeds; I acknowledge and remember them and add a declaration of regret: "I have no excuse for what I did or said. I am sorry

[33] By coerced apologies I mean those that are "those offered in circumstances where a threat or offer significantly compromises someone's ability to choose not to apologize." Nick Smith, *I Was Wrong: The Meanings of Apologies*, 2008, 151.

and regretful. I care. Forgive me." The distinction between an account and an apology is useful in understanding a crucial function of the latter. As Tavuchis argues, apologies are "symbolic foci of secular remedial rituals that serve to recall and reaffirm allegiance to codes of behavior and belief whose integrity has been tested and challenged by transgression, whether knowingly or unwittingly."[34] Political apology reaffirms the social validity and moral legitimacy of the rules that were transgressed and thereby enables forgiveness. In this sense, although an apology cannot undo the act that provoked it, that act "cannot go unnoticed without compromising the current and future relationship of the parties, the legitimacy of the violated rule, and the wider social web in which the participants are enmeshed." An apology is "a relational symbolic gesture occurring in a complex interpersonal field, with enormous reverberatory potential that encapsulates, recapitulates, and pays homage to a moral order rendered problematic by the very act that calls it forth."[35]

Thus, when the transgressor has broken a moral code, ties of membership to the community risk being severed. An apology dispels this threat. It serves as a mechanism for "reaccrediting membership and stabilizing precarious relations." Here it is useful to return to repentance. I said before that victims expect some form of regret from transgressors if they are to forgive them for their wrongdoings. But the point of demanding regret may not be limited to a simple exchange in a moral economy of forgiveness: You show me repentance, I forgive you. Repentance can have a public dimension: it may be seen as a "shared loss," a consequence of one's actions. It refers to something done (or not done), said (or not said) "that betrays and threatens whatever defines, binds, and is deemed worthy."[36] Regret is both recognition and yearning: recognition that my actions (my breach of trust) brought about my estrangement (the alteration of my place in relation to others) and a plea for the restoration of a prior valued state.

According to Tavuchis, a proper and successful apology is the middle term of a moral syllogism that commences with a call and

[34] Tavuchis, *Mea Culpa*, 13. [35] Tavuchis, *Mea Culpa*, 14.

[36] This string of quotes comes from Tavuchis, *Mea Culpa*, 13, 14, and 20.

ends with forgiveness. The call occurs when the action in question "is semantically and symbolically transformed into apologizable discourse." The call is the beginning of a moral dialectic. We think like members when we can anticipate, recognize, and name that which an apology can heal prior to the call. When we respond to the call after the offense by apologizing, we are seeking reconfirmation of our credentials as members by publicly recalling their unstated grounds. Tavuchis writes,

> Just as the precipitating event is transformed into an occasion for apology by virtue of a call, our participation in the ensuing exchange engages us (and our interlocutor[s]) in serious discourse about the moral requisites of interpersonal, group, or collective membership . . . If the goal of apology is ultimately forgiveness as a prelude to reunion and reconciliation, then we must convince the other of our worthiness.[37]

With some nuances, these theoretical insights capture part of the logic that precipitates the public exposure of IM. This logic begins with a call to turn Stasi denunciation into apologizable discourse, and it ends, ideally, with an apology on the part of the informal collaborators that restores them (or should restore them) to their status as full-fledged members of the polity.

Consider, to illustrate the points just made, the case of Ingo Steuer, an (in)famous ice-skater whose international victories turned him into a local celebrity, but whose involvement with the Stasi made him the target of numerous criticisms. Steuer's involvement with the Stasi was by no means fleeting or disengaged. According to the officials of the Stasi Records Office, which stores and administers the archives of the Stasi, his voluminous Stasi act contains denunciations made by Steuer (handwritten and even recorded ones) of fellow athletes. In one of his reports, for instance, he alerts authorities of his suspicion that a fellow ice-skater might attempt to flee the GDR, in another that a West German radio station is interviewing East German sportsmen behind the back of GDR authorities. Two

[37] Tavuchis, *Mea Culpa*, 28.

additional reports provide private information about some of his colleagues, which the Stasi could later use to blackmail them.

Steuer's exposure took place shortly before the 2006 Olympics Games, which he was supposed to attend as an officially appointed trainer. After his outing, however, he was dropped from the German delegation because German sporting bodies, namely the National Olympic Committee (NOK), like other federal governmental agencies, are not allowed to appoint and compensate monetarily individuals who were involved with the Stasi. Indeed, the strenuous screening process in place in unified Germany was at full work in the public agencies in charge of governing sports affairs in the nation. Steuer, critics claimed, was legally disqualified to become an Olympic trainer due to his involvement with the secret police. In the end, he was able to attend the Games thanks to a temporary injunction issued by a Berlin court, the injunction serving as evidence for those who were unsatisfied with the so-called Stasi-screening process in the world of sports and regarded it as too lenient and arbitrary.

Steuer's exposure as an IM sheds light on the importance of forgiveness as a move to reaccredit membership and is particularly relevant in light of the social expectation, very explicitly stated, that athletes be role models and represent ideal social values.[38] Steuer offered clarifications about his involvement with the Stasi: "At the moment in which I did it, I did it in full conscience.... But not because I intended to cause any harm to any one, but because I found it to be the right thing to do."[39] And the closest he came to an unambiguous display of regret: "I am so ashamed that I had cooperated with the Stasi. At that time I was not at all clear about what I was doing."[40] Accounts (in Tavuchis's sense of the term) of

[38] Herbert Fischer-Solms, "IM Torsten: Der Stasi-Fall des Eislauf-Trainers Ingo Steuer," *Deutschland Archiv* 2 (2006): 197–200.

[39] 'Die Schuld des Ingo Steuer hilft Offenheit, dem Eislauftrainer zu verzeihen?', *3 Sat*, June 5, 2008.

[40] "Ingo Steuer: Schandfleck in meinem Leben," *Frankfurter Allgemeine Zeitung*, April 20, 2006, www.faz.net/aktuell/sport/wintersport/stasi-vergangenheit-ingo-steuer-schandfleck-in-meinem-leben-1302876.html.

this sort did not strike many of the publics invested in Stasi *Aufarbeitung* as genuine acknowledgments of responsibility, let alone as authentic apologies. In their view, Steuer needed to expresses more forcefully his allegiance to the moral code (because, as a public official from the Stasi Records Office puts it, "Ingo Steuer did something that is morally reprehensible") and openly disapprove of his past actions, which contradict them.

A different IM, to leave Steuer's case behind, describes her own outing as equivalent to having been "put in a pillory" and publicly shamed and then adds: "The worst for me was the loss of respect, the feeling that I had no longer any worth, that I did not appear as trustworthy anymore."[41] Or consider a piece of moral entrepreneurship: the book *Die Täter sind unter uns* (*The Perpetrators Are among Us*) by Hubertus Knabe, director of the Berlin-Hohenschönhausen Memorial. In that work, the author comments on the loss of social status of IMs under reunified Germany. He explains what informers miss when they avoid the public eye and remain unaccountable. What they lose, in his words, is "their chance [of] forsaking the morally degrading façade they thrust upon themselves in order to serve the regime." More relevant for the present purposes is that, in this author's words, by remaining anonymous IMs fail to "redeem" themselves by "cleaning their record." He concludes: "Repentance and shame, if being sincere, can be astonishingly disarming and earn you respect and recognition."[42] Repentance and shame are here placeholders for an apology, which underscores the alleged potential for reclaiming respect.

In sum, IM exposures carry the expectation that IMs will offer a public apology. Part of the point of apologizing in this context is not to restore the terms of an interpersonal relationship. The function of the political apology is to encourage the wrongdoer's recognition that he or she behaved in ways that contradict a widely accepted, though controversial, moral and political code.

41 "Kabarettistin Gisela Oechelhaeuser schämt sich für Stasi-Vergangenheit," *Die Welt* July 30, 2002.

42 *Hubertus Knabe, Die Täter sind unter uns: über das Schönreden der SEDDiktatur (Berlin: List, 2008), 167.*

6.5 THE ECONOMY OF FORGIVENESS: THE DEPRECIATION OF RESPECT

I have argued so far that on many accounts the public dimension of apologies enhances the potential for building respect in the context of a post-Stasi Germany. On one account, the public performance itself is a form of redress. On another account, the public performance works as a ritual of membership reaccreditation. On both scores, the publicity of the apologies builds respect for victims. Although indeed this publicity may have promoted political relationships based on the ideal of respect, it may also have a side that discourages such relationships.

To see why this would be the case, consider again Steuer's case. I mentioned before that his exculpations did not strike many of the groups invested in Stasi *Vergangenheitsbewältigung* as constituting an authentic apology. A civil rights activist during the GDR regime and current director of a Stasi museum, who opposed Steuer's appointment as an Olympic trainer, argued the following: "If a reappraisal of the past is to be meaningful, it must be made clear that denunciation in the service of a dictatorship has consequences under a democracy. Prior to forgiveness there must be an admission of guilt. So far, however, Steuer has been fully unapologetic before the public."[43] A public official from the agency in charge of managing the Stasi files leveled his criticism along similar lines: "To this day I have heard no public word of apology from Mr. Steuer, so I find it hard to fully understand his own personal transformation and how his insight has grown."[44]

One could be easily misled about the real purchase of statements such as these, which German public discourse abounds in. Certainly, they reflect in part a concern about taking fake apologies for sincere ones. For the purposes of this chapter, however, the real purchase of

[43] Thomas Purschke, "Gauck setzt sich für Stasi-Spitzel *ein,*" *Die Welt*, May 4, 2007, www.welt.de/welt_print/article849780/Gauck-setzt-sich-fuer-Stasi-Spitzel-ein.html. Also: Gerhard Pfeil, "Vergangenheit on Ice," *Der Spiegel*, April 3, 2008, 155–156.

[44] Purschke, "Gauck setzt sich für Stasi-Spitzel ein."

such statements is elsewhere. The point I wish to emphasize about the reasoning behind the recrimination of Steuer's presumably unrepentant public self is the salient omission of concrete victims. Steuer's victims are not explicitly factored into this equation of political forgiveness.[45] Instead, what is crucial is whether or not Steuer atones in public, whether or not he utters public words of apology.

Two things are particularly striking about this omission of victims. First, their place is taken by prominent public officials, by virtue of their having been dissidents under the communist regime, or by virtue of being in charge of "managing" the memory of the past (as bureaucrats of the Stasi files agency, museum directors, or moral entrepreneurs, for example), take the role of *apology brokers*. Such brokers demand repenting attitudes from IMs, as if they had been entrusted by society to do so. Second, and more important, the absence of victims not only increases the likelihood that apologies might be insincere (they are the result of public pressure and not of a genuine desire of perpetrators to atone), but also weakens what, in philosophical terms, has come to be known as the victim's prerogative. In rough terms, the victim's prerogative posits that the victim of a wrongdoing is entitled to set the terms for forgiving the wrongdoer. Because victims have privileged epistemic access to the damage caused by the wrongdoing that needs to be repaired, they are entitled to lay the conditions for successful reconciliation. Some restrictions apply, of course, such as not demanding that wrongdoers engage in degrading or unjust acts. Nonetheless, according to the prerogative it would be inappropriate for others to determine when and how a victim will come to terms with those who harmed her.[46]

In some cases, a public apology is exactly what a victim demands, but that need not always be the case. In fact, public apologies may remove the prerogative of setting the conditions for forgiving

[45] See also, to illustrate, Thomas Purschke, "Bemerkenswerte Stasi-Personalie," *Gerbergasse* 18, no. 4 (2003): 5. A former representative from the New Forum, and currently a public official involved with the management of Stasi affairs, complains that while in service only ten IMs have come to him. Why would anyone need to approach *him*?

[46] Linda Radzik, *Making Amends*, 111–152.

perpetrators off the hands of victims. Ernesto Verdeja identifies a version of this problem in thinking about official or state apologies. I noted before that IM exposures are, for the most part, socially orchestrated practices. Nevertheless, Verdeja's analysis of state apologies illuminates a problematic aspect of the sort of public apology that is expected from IMs. As Verdeja rightly claims, state apologies produce "illocutionary pitfalls," to use a philosophical term – what the state does in offering an apology is actually to issue an apology rather than to ask for it. The difference is not trivial. In the first instance (issuing an apology) the action annuls, at least in part, the importance of the reaction of the would-be forgiver. The would-be forgiven's act of issuing the apology is what really matters. In other words, state apologies are not subject to rejection. They are unilateral through and through.[47]

As in the case of state apologies, when an IM (or any wrongdoer in postconflict scenarios) issue a public apology, the risk is that what comes to matter in the eyes of the polity is the public performance by the repentant wrongdoer. It suffices that the wrongdoer utters public words of apology, whereas the uptake – the acceptance or rejection of such words on the side of the would-be forgiver – loses importance; the would-be forgiver is thereby erased from the horizon of forgiveness. But the fact that the victim vanishes in this way undercuts part of the apology's purpose, which is not only that the wrongdoer shows repentance for past actions, but also that the wrongdoer affirms the equal respect between them. Apologies should entail some sort of "respect negotiation," – a complex form of interaction, not a one-sided declaration, whereby victims set reasonable conditions for forgiving. Apologies, in other words, have an element of coming together to engage in an economy of forgiveness[48] – in return for the atonement of perpetrators, victims offer forgiveness, and the exchange affirms respect. But in a context such

[47] Ernesto Verdeja, "Official Apologies in the Aftermath of Political Violence," *Metaphilosophy* 41, no. 4 (2010): 563–581.

[48] This understanding of forgiveness is contrary to Jacques Derrida's, who maintains that an act of forgiveness must be fully unconditional. An excellent study of Derrida's views on forgiveness is Janna Thompson, "Is Apology a

as the German (and possibly that of other nations coming to terms with their communist past as well), "victimless" apologies gain currency, in the sense that the victims' entitlement to set the terms for forgiveness is diluted. Instead, a group of brokers who demand apologies emerges, and economy of political forgiveness is thereby altered. Public apologies, thus, depreciate the value of respect.[49]

6.6 CONCLUSION

In this chapter I argued for an interpretation of IM exposures as acts that organize social practices of political forgiveness. By triggering a cycle of forgiveness, in which public apologies are asked for, given, and accepted, these exposures have the potential to promote relationships based on the idea of equal respect among citizens. At the same time, however, the insistence of some political actors that IMs offer public words of apology carries the risk that the performative or declarative aspect takes precedence over the interactive or process-based one. The actual purpose of the apology, which, as I claimed before, is expressing respect for the victim, might be lost in the public performance of an IM. If respect was supposed to serve as one justification for demanding the apology, in that it made a perpetrator seek the victim's forgiveness, then the public apology seems to provide the former with a way out of this search. In other words, public apologies might be a way of striving toward forgiveness at a very low price, and that depreciates respect for victims. That political apologies might turn out to be "too cheap" to really contribute to reconciliation does not mean that we should do away with them. They might have some benefits even when they are

Sorry Affair? Derrida and the Moral Force of the Impossible," *The Philosophical Forum* 41, no. 3 (2010): 259–274.

49 On the view that public apologies offer a "cheap" way "for perpetrators and their descendants to assuage their guilt," see Elazar Barkan and Alexander Karn, "Group Apology as an Ethical Imperative," in Barkan and Karn (eds.), *Taking Wrongs Seriously: Apologies and Reconciliation* (Stanford, CA: Stanford University Press, 2006), 6.

insincere.[50] For instance, they may trigger public debates about the kinds of values that a polity wishes to endorse. But we should never think of public apologies as perfect substitutes of private apologies, which governments can also encourage.

[50] On this, see Mathias Thaler, "Just Pretending: Political Apologies for Historical Injustice and Vice's Tribute to Virtue," *Critical Review of International Social and Political Philosophy* 15, no. 3 (2012): 259–278.

7 THE POLITICS OF RECONCILIATION: OFFERING RESPECT?

7.1 INTRODUCTION: THE KAISER'S APOLOGY

In the previous chapter I touched on the subject of public apologies, and how they are widely regarded in the polity as a prerequisite for membership reaccreditation of collaborators. This chapter looks at the other side of this issue. It asks whether atoning IMs who offer public apologies for their past complicity with the Stasi are (and should be) politically forgiven and thereby credited as fully fledged members of the polity, that is, as political agents with unrestrictive access to the whole set of rights attached to the status of citizenship. I argue in favor of the conclusion that, with regard to collaborators, there is a divorce between the promise of political forgiveness or reconciliation (I use the terms interchangeably) and its genuine "supply." I should emphasize that the conception of reconciliation I have in mind is rather minimal. It refers to the ability of reacquiring one's standing as a moral and political agent once one has duly apologized for the wrongdoing one has committed, as long as the wrongdoing in question is not too severe. Colloquial expressions such as "new beginnings," "fresh starts," or "second chances" capture this idea and are common in German public discourse. Public apologies and reconciliation are supposed to go in tandem for IMs; the former presumably makes the latter possible. In fact, however, the prospects of postapology reconciliation are slim. Rhetorically, political and social actors make the case for striving toward political forgiveness, but in practice many of them drag their feet. This inconsistency generates what I call a respect asymmetry. Former victims and the polity at large demand public repentance from IMs. As we saw in the previous chapter, with all due caveats, such repentance can be conceptualized as an expression of respect for past victims and the present society. However, even after former victims and a considerable segment of the polity are in a position of adopting a reconciliatory disposition toward IMs, they choose not to do it. The decision to withhold a reconciliatory attitude, I argue, is disrespectful because it prevents collaborators from exercising their agency to its fullest extent by curtailing their participation in politics.

The chapter pays particular attention to the public exposure of Kerstin Kaiser, currently a prominent politician from Die Linke, as well as the public debate accompanying her exposure. Kaiser's is a useful case for exploring the considerations that guide this chapter. As will be seen later on, at the time when she became entangled with the Stasi she was eighteen and still at school, that is, she had barely crossed what for many is the threshold of full rational agency; furthermore, she accepted to work as an IM out of (misplaced) patriotism, or so she claims, and at a time when the Stasi was not at the height of its disrepute; later, after the collapse of the GDR, she profusely apologized, in private and in public, for her deeds, and she pledged allegiance to the new democratic regime. She thus seemed to be an ideal candidate for a new beginning.[1] Despite all this, she was pressured into abandoning her aspiration to participate in state-level government as a minister in view of her involvement with the Stasi. This is the motivation in selecting her case, as well as the more strategic reason that her case was widely covered in the media. Not all cases of Stasi collaboration are like Kaiser's, of course. But for those that are, interesting questions can be asked about reconciliation and respect.

The chapter unfolds as follows. Section two sketches the political background in Kaiser's case and illustrates the tenor of public discussion about reconciliation with collaborators. Sections three and four

[1] This chapter addresses the case of former collaborators like Kaiser who are now fully devoted democrats. For an argument as to why even antidemocrats should be allowed to participate in politics, see Alexander Kirshner, *A Theory of Militant Democracy. The Ethics of Combating Political Extremism* (New Haven, CT: Yale University Press, 2014).

provide a theoretical framework suggesting that reconciliation should not be regarded as an absolute prerogative of victims but as a *prima facie* obligation because it offers collaborators the opportunity of a new beginning. This second chance can foster their moral and political agency and thereby build respect for them. Section five examines Kaiser's apology and argues that though it met the standards of a fully fledged apology, it was not "accepted" by important segments of the political community. This shows that reconciliation or closure about the past involves two acts of self-disclosure – that of the wrongdoer as well as that of direct and indirect victims, who must offer robust reasons if they are to reject reconciliation with collaborators.

7.2 A RITUALIZED *VERGANGENHEITSBEWÄLTIGUNG*?

Many politicians from the state of Brandenburg have been publicly exposed as unofficial collaborators since the early days of unified Germany.[2] Manfred Stolpe, whose case was discussed in earlier chapters, is just one example. Nonetheless, contemporary commentators maliciously refer to Brandenburg as "little GDR." This is because, according to some commentators, many of those who were complicit with the communist regime were allowed to continue their careers there, unmolested. Whereas in other former East German states such as Sachsen or Thüringen, local parliaments (Landtage) are closed to individuals who were involved with the Stasi, in Brandenburg this is not the case.[3] Kerstin Kaiser is one of those tainted politicians who was elected to the local congress despite her involvement with the Stasi. However, her past as an unofficial collaborator was not without consequences, as it imposed limits on her participation in politics; thus, in 1994 her own party persuaded her to renounce her seat at the national parliament, the Bundestag, because she had remained

[2] Helmut Müller-Enbergs, "Brandenburgs Bürgerbewegung und das Erbe der Staatssicherheit," *Horch und Guck* 32, no. 4 (2000): 1–9.

[3] Martin Lutz und Uwe Müller, "Stasi-Spitzel drängen für Linke in die Parlamente," *Die Welt*, September 24, 2009.

silent over (but not denied) her entanglement with the Stasi.[4] Later, Kaiser was one of the IMs involved in a controversy around the so-called red-red coalition in Brandenburg. Following state elections in Brandenburg in 2009, Governor Matthias Platzeck, of the Sozialdemokratische Partei Deutschlands or Social Democratic Party of Germany (SPD), entered into a governing coalition with Die Linke, a political move that many voices deemed inappropriate, given the party's communist genealogy. The political maneuver came under fire when some of the politicians appointed by the Die Linke to integrate the ruling coalition, Kaiser among them, were exposed as Stasi collaborators. As a result, she gave up on obtaining a Ministry position.

A brief sketch of the political background against which Kaiser's case unfolded is in order. As was mentioned in Chapter 2, in the aftermath of reunification, the country enforced an aggressive screening policy for removing former Stasi members, including its informers, from public office. The process of vetting for Stasi activity was carried out unsystematically, without any uniform standard of application, and with a force and direction that might have been excessive. It was not until several years into reunification, when the courts (federal, administrative, labor) were thrust into the process, that the grounds for dismissal were progressively refined and narrowed. Over the years, the tendency in the courts' decisions was to set the standard of disqualification for public service to those cases in which Stasi involvement led to serious proven violation of human rights.[5]

The explicit motivation for most of these disqualifications was to cut through what Anne Sa'adah calls the "thick film of

[4] The fact that Kaiser was disqualified, de facto if not de jure, from holding public office, at least at the higher echelons, raises interesting concerns from the point of view of democratic theory that I cannot fully address here. Kaiser herself complains about the discrediting of democratic processes as a result of Stasi screenings. "Stasi-Verstrickungen; Platzeck fühlt sich getäuscht und geprellt," *Berliner Morgenpost*, December 4, 2009.

[5] A. James McAdams, *Judging the Past in Unified Germany* (Cambridge: Cambridge University Press, 2001), chapter 3; Christiane Wilke, "The Shield, the Sword, and the Party: Vetting the East German Public Sector," in Alexander Mayer-Rieckh and Pablo de Greiff, eds. *Justice and Prevention: Vetting Public Employees in Transitional Societies* (New York: SSRC, 2007).

distrust"[6] that the Stasi produced through its actions, and that covered public service in particular. Joachim Gauck, the current president of the German Republic and the first director of the Stasi Records Office, epitomized this view by arguing that if "after more than fifty-five years of Nazi and communist dictatorship citizens were going to trust elected officials under the new democratic system, it was important that those officials be trustworthy." He added that the purpose of barring IMs from public office was "to respond to the East German people's minimal demand that persons who had conspired with the regime, unbeknown to their fellow citizens, should be deemed unsuitable for public positions of trust."[7] Bear in mind this appeal to trust, for it will be relevant later on in the chapter.

Along with the exclusion of "Stasi-positive" individuals from public office came the expectation that they would make amends, showing their repentance and offering public apologies. Some did, some did not. This raises a puzzle: if they do publicly repent and apologize, do (should) they then get the opportunity to fully participate in the new regime, that is, the possibility of the vaunted "new beginning" that reconciliation is supposed to offer? Does (should) an atoning denunciator, through his public apology, (re)gain his status as a fully participating citizen, which would allow him not only to elect his representatives but also to be eligible to hold public office, and to participate in politics without significant restrictions? Whether they do or do not is important in terms of respect for persons.

The tendency in German public discourse is to associate public apologies and reconciliation, or at least some forms thereof. Many public voices hold that citizens have a kind of civic duty to reconcile themselves politically with former denunciators. The language is

[6] Anne Sa'adah, *Germany's Second Chance: Trust, Justice, and Democratization* (Cambridge: Cambridge University Press, 1998), 68.

[7] Quoted by McAdams, *Judging the Past in Unified Germany,* 2001, 58–9. The argument of trust is in fact one justification of why members of the Stasi, and not members from the ruling party during the GDR, the SED, had not been (and should not be) disqualified from occupying positions within the government. The latter did not betray, as did the former, the public confidence because their allegiance to the SED was not a secret, as involvement with the Stasi was.

explicitly normative. Provided that there is on the part of former Stasi collaborators a public acknowledgment of their past political missteps, as well as an unambiguous reprobation of those missteps, informers *should* be "reincorporated" into society. A former dissident in the GDR, unsympathetic both to the past action of IMs and to their present silence, claims in this spirit that the latter have a "right to error and to return" (*Recht auf Irrtum und auf Umkehr*).[8] If this informal right is not an empty formulation and is supposed to be somehow exercised, it must mean that collaborators should be given a "second chance." Take as an additional illustration the plea (as well as the public response to it) made by the bishop of the Protestant Church in Central Germany, Ilse Junkermann, in which she called for a "differentiated coming to terms with the past" (*differenzierten Aufarbeitung*) and argued that even if many among the ranks of the Church had suffered at the hands of unofficial collaborators and Stasi officials during the communist regime, "those people who were close to the regime should not be locked in drawers." She further clarified that reconciliation with Stasi denunciators is a task that belongs "in front of and not behind the church." This plea for reconciliation, endorsed by the synod of her church, was met with deep skepticism. The Union of Victims of Stalinism, a Berlin-based organization that supports victims of the communist regime, criticized the bishop's offer for "blank reconciliation," characterizing it as a slap in the face for victims of the Stasi – that is, as a sign of disrespect. The Union furthermore argued that reconciliation "could only succeed if the perpetrators from the regime showed repentance."[9]

Criticism of this sort was also leveled against Brandenburg Governor Matthias Platzeck (SPD) for advancing a similar argument for reconciliation with former IMs.[10] In an essay entitled "Taking

[8] "Wie sollen wir es mit der Stasi halten, Frau Poppe?" *SuperIllu*, December 16, 2009.

[9] "Reue vor Versöhnung," *die tageszeitung*, November 24, 2009.

[10] It bears mention at this point that Brandenburg has had a moderate "destasification" policy, in comparison to other Eastern Länder. McAdams, *Judging the Past in Unified Germany*, 5–6, 73.

Reconciliation Seriously,"[11] he infuriated readers and politicians alike by making reference to the reconciliatory gesture of Kurt Schumacher, the SPD's first postwar leader who had been willing to meet and engage with former members of the Nazi *Waffen-SS*, of which he had been a victim himself. The example of Schumacher, Platzeck claimed, should be taken as the standard to follow in regard to the question of how to deal with Stasi collaborators.

In drawing this historical parallel, Platzeck was treading on controversial territory. As was argued in Chapter 2, Nazi-*Aufarbeitung* is a highly contested subject in German historiography and public opinion, but there is far-reaching agreement around the idea that after a somewhat mild effort to confront the Nazi past in the aftermath of the war (at least in the West Germany), Chancellor Konrad Adenauer's so-called *Vergangenheitspolitik* encouraged the termination of that process through strong doses of amnesia and amnesty, instead of endorsing a more thorough investigation of and, where necessary, legal prosecution for past crimes.[12] In opposition to this consensus about the failure of Germany's postwar regimes to give a comprehensive and immediate treatment to a problematic past, Platzeck's historical analogy and his call for the "integration" of IMs was likely to be looked on with suspicion, as a step in the direction of Adenhauer's policies. Platzeck was taken to be offering a kind of reconciliation based on oblivion, on wiping the slate clean without any need for collaborators to publicly apologize. This perception was fueled by the fact that in his essay on reconciliation, none of the notions related to forgiveness and apologies (*Verzeihung*, *Vergebung*, *Entschuldigung*, etc.) are even mentioned. When Platzeck prescribes reconciliation, repentance is nowhere to be found in the list of conditions leading to it. The essay considers mainly what society must do to "integrate" former collaborators, at least those who did not commit criminal acts, but no particular action is asked of them. Instead the emphasis is put on the need to give collaborators the

[11] "Versöhnung ernst nehmen", *Der Spiegel*, November 2, 2009.

[12] On the contrast between Konrad Adenhauer and Kurt Schumacher with regard to their approach on the Nazi past, see Jeffrey Herf, "The Emergence and Legacies of Divided Memory."

opportunity for new beginnings: "If we draw the right lessons from history, [reconciliation] turns less on a ritualized *Vergangenheitsbewältigung* than on our willingness to encourage active new beginnings."[13] It took very little for Platzeck, in view of the criticisms he faced, to reconsider the importance of apologies and repentance and to claim that, indeed, it was apposite to the process of reconciliation "that one admits to one's own erratic behavior and displays active repentance."[14]

It might very well be the case that in recalling the integration of former members of the Waffen-SS in postwar Germany, Platzeck was attempting to construct a façade of magnanimity around his maneuvers to build a parliamentary coalition, presenting them as acts in favor of reconciliation and against political exclusion (*Ausgrenzung*). This possibility notwithstanding, it is telling that the nerve of the criticism against both his reconciliatory pleas, and Junkermann's,[15] is that they sell reconciliation for too little. Public atonement is left for a later day. By contrast, their critics insist that an apology, particularly a public one, is a necessary if not sufficient condition for reconciliation.

The preceding discussion should have made it clear that for many social and political actors in Germany, reconciliation is not just any progression of steps that ultimately leads to some sort of pragmatic agreement to settle the past, or to construct a temporary *modus vivendi*, where citizens are no longer at each other's throats. Such a process cannot be undertaken simply by attempting to forget the past.

[13] "Versöhnung ernst nehmen", *Der Spiegel*, December 2, 2009.

[14] "Stasi-Verstrickungen; Platzeck fuehlt sich getäuscht und geprellt," *Die Welt*, December 4, 2009.

[15] To the question of whether Platzeck "was right" in his demand for reconciliation, the majority (72%) of over a thousand readers of the online edition of Die Welt said no, whereas only a minority supported this demand (28%). "Platzeck fordert Versöhnung mit Erben der SED," *Die Welt*, October 31, 2009. This is consistent with a different survey conducted in 2008, where people were asked whether politicians who had worked for the Stasi should resign: 56% thought they should, 35% thought that they should not, and 9% did not know. See http://de.statista.com/statistik/daten/studie/793/umfrage/ruecktritt-von-politiker-wegen-stasi-vergangenheit/.

Opposition to forgetfulness as a route to reconciliation has been vocal and relentless in Germany.[16]

Platzeck's statements should not be read as an attempt to trivialize *Vergangenheitsbewältigung*. His statements suggest that a perpetual ban from public office is neither an appropriate measure for coming to terms with the past nor a proportionate penalty for IMs; rather, such a ban is simply a "ritual" in the pejorative sense of that term: a knee-jerk reaction divorced from any moral claim. Platzcek further implies, as will be seen more clearly later, that reconciliation is a matter of respect – it is owed to IMs, provided they apologize in public. Offering reconciliation for little in return would be disrespectful to victims, as the Union of Victims of Stalinism complains; but offering no reconciliation at all would be disrespectful to atoning perpetrators. The next two sections develop a philosophical foundation for these claims.

7.3 SUPEREROGATION OR OBLIGATION?

There is tension between two philosophical approaches to reconciliation. Succinctly put, one sees it as entirely optional and supererogatory; the other regards it as something close to an obligation. If reconciliation is optional, then repentant wrongdoers could be denied the opportunity of a second chance, which simply means that they might not reacquire their full standing as full political and moral agents. In contrast, if reconciliation is obligatory, then repentant wrongdoers are owed a second chance. The latter approach seems to be more consistent with the idea of respect for persons, as this section will argue.

There is an extensive literature in transitional justice scholarship discussing the normative relevance of apologies in postconflict societies. As was discussed in the previous chapter, such literature rightly regards apologies of wrongdoers to victims as something that is owed

[16] See, for example, the book by Uwe Müller and Grit Hartmann, *Vorwärts und Vergessen! Kader, Spitzel und Komplizen: Das gefährliche Erbe der SED-Diktatur* (Berlin: Rowohlt, 2009).

to the latter as a matter of respect. But do victims thereby acquire any obligations toward wrongdoers?

Consider first a possible obligation of forgiveness. By and large, scholars agree that although perpetrators have a duty to apologize to victims, victims do *not* have a correlative duty to forgive perpetrators: forgiveness, many authors claim, is an act of supererogatory generosity and forbearance whereby victims forswear to act on their justified resentment against their wrongdoers.[17] To the extent that resentment can be, provisionally at least, a legitimate response of victims to harmful actions against them, too forgiving an attitude can be an act of *self*-disrespect on their part. More important, victims of wrongdoing often experience lasting psychological harm that can even include trauma. Holding the view that they must nonetheless forgive wrongdoers is to disregard this fact and is not only disrespectful but could also be damaging to victims.

The German case illustrates why it would be harmful and degrading to force victims to forgive wrongdoers. As was mentioned in Chapter 2, the SED and the Stasi seldom resorted to cold-blooded murder in dealing with dissidents, as was the case in places that are mentioned frequently in transitional justice literature like Argentina and South Africa. Nonetheless, one should not underestimate the harm that the communist regime and its secret police caused to victims. For example, measures like *Zersetzung* (disruption), explained in Chapter 2, might not have had lethal consequences for its targets but it could have severe mental effects on them. These include posttraumatic stress disorders such as the inability to relate to friends and partners, a permanent feeling of fatigue, unreasonable fear of being in enclosed spaces, sleep problems, constant nightmares, inability to concentrate or work, depression, mood swings, personality changes, or psychosomatic high blood-pressure.[18] Recovery from these disorders might require that victims *not* forgive wrongdoers, at least temporarily. If we respect individuals as moral and political

[17] See, for instance, Espen Gamlund, "Supererogatory Forgiveness," *Inquiry* 53, no. 6 (2010): 540–564.

[18] Siegmar Faust, "Die Folgen für die Betroffenen – bis heute," in Dümmel and Schmitz, *Was war die Stasi*, 57–58.

agents, we must accept that they are the best judges of their interests and what it takes to honor them; an obligation of victims to forgive would be contrary to this precept. I will say more about this when I touch on the idea of the victim's prerogative later.

Interestingly, if, as is rightly argued, victims do not have an obligation to forgive their wrongdoers, then, as Marguerite Le Caze puts it, forgiveness and apology are asymmetrical.[19] Le Caze claims that apologies for wrongdoing are a perfect duty, that is, they are obligatory, whereas forgiveness is an imperfect duty – it is discretionary. The asymmetry stems from the fact that wrongdoers owe victims an apology as a matter of respect (for the victims), whereas in contrast, the willingness of victims to forgive repentant wrongdoers does not rest on a claim to respect (for the wrongdoers). Instead, forgiveness is based on "love," on a kind of sympathy for the other. Le Caze makes these arguments in her discussion of Jacques Derrida's (2001) influential argument that *pure* or *genuine* forgiveness is unconditional – it should not involve an exchange whereby the perpetrator repents to erase his guilt and offers an apology *in return for* forgiveness. Derrida writes: "The word most often abused is 'forgive.' Because it always has to do with negotiations more or less acknowledged, with calculated transactions."[20] Le Caze argues that this understanding of forgiveness has the problematic implication of suggesting that victims should forgive without demanding or receiving an apology; that because forgiveness should be unconditional, then apologies are irrelevant and dispensable. Le Caze puts it as follows: "If the obligation to forgive is based on respect alone, then victims have a responsibility to forgive those who have wronged them, whether or not they apologize or atone."[21] Or again: "Forgiveness is not based on respect for others or rather respect alone is not enough to make forgiveness a duty. If the duty to forgive was based on respect then

[19] Marguerite Le Caze, "The Asymmetry between Apology and Forgiveness." *Contemporary Political Theory* 5, no. 4 (2006): 447–468.

[20] Jacques Derrida, *On Cosmopolitanism and Forgiveness* (London: Routledge, 2001), 39.

[21] Le Caze, "The Asymmetry between Apology and Forgiveness," 456.

it would be a universal responsibility and not dependent on repentance or apology."[22] This, Le Caze believes, is unacceptable.

The foregoing arguments about the nonobligatory character of forgiveness are persuasive. There cannot be a duty to forgiveness. These considerations, however, do not extend to the case of reconciliation, understood as a political concept. Linda Radzik holds this view.[23] Her account starts by making reference to the victim and her community's willingness to offer reconciliation to an offender who has made a sincere and proportional atonement. This constitutes the so-called victim's prerogative. Radzik argues that such a prerogative entails that the wrongdoer would need the cooperation of the victim to atone. The offender cannot do it by herself. There are no objective criteria that the wrongdoer might fulfill to atone for her misdeed and consider herself "redeemed" regardless of the participation (or lack thereof) of her victim. In this point of view, it is really up to the latter whether the wrongdoer can atone or not.

Radzik makes a qualified case for the victim's prerogative. Among other arguments supporting her endorsement of this principle, she considers the idea that because victims have privileged epistemic access to the damage caused by the wrongdoing that needs to be repaired, they are entitled to set down the conditions for successful reconciliation. She offers an example to make her case. Imagine A ridicules two of her colleagues at work, B and C, but later acknowledges her fault and sincerely apologizes to them in private. B might accept the private apology, but C might ask for a public apology instead. According to Radzik, both B and C would be justified in asking for different types of apologies. Whereas B cares about being respected and esteemed by A and takes the private apology as sufficient proof that A does value her as a person and as a colleague, C cares more about the harm A did to her standing vis-à-vis other colleagues; she therefore believes she deserves a public apology, which for her entails the appropriate expression of respect. Radzik concludes that B and C, as the victims, get to judge which aspects of the wrong

[22] Le Caze, "The Asymmetry between Apology and Forgiveness," 456.

[23] Linda Radzik, *Making Amends: Atonement in Morality, Law, and Politics* (Oxford: Oxford University Press, 2009), 111–152.

are significant to them, and which forms of redress signal respect to them. An important clarification about the prerogative is its fading character: the further away one moves from the party directly wronged, the less sense it makes to think through forgiveness or reconciliation in terms of the prerogative.[24]

Although sympathetic to it, Radzik also expresses some reservations about the victim's prerogative. The potential danger with the victim's prerogative is not difficult to fathom. If we presuppose that reconciliation requires some sort of atonement from wrongdoers, but atonement can only take place with the participation of both the wrongdoer and the victim, then the former is at the mercy of the latter, and therefore reconciliation is uncertain and contingent on the wishes of former victims. In view of these considerations, Radzik notes that the authority to impose the conditions for reconciliation should be limited. For instance, she claims, victims have authority to dictate the terms of reconciliation, but such authority should be subject to some form of justice, broadly understood. Thus, to note one such restriction, victims should not impose conditions that are degrading of the wrongdoer. To mention another restriction,

[24] To illustrate the fading quality of the victim's prerogative, consider the following example. X is a person who is injured in a bus bombing perpetrated by a terrorist. It makes sense, from a normative point of view, to say that she is entitled to demand an apology, and, moreover, that within certain limits she should be able to set the conditions for forgiving the terrorist. It can also make sense to entitle her parents to demand for an apology and to set the conditions for forgiving the perpetrator, though daughter and parents might not be forgiving the same thing (the extent of X's physical pain is obviously greater than that of her parent's, but the degree of their emotional anguish might have well been greater than hers). It would be more problematic, however, to speak of X's neighbors forgiving the bus bomber for X's injuries, and even more problematic to speak of people whom X has never met forgiving the bomber. Thus, the entitlement to "grant" forgiveness, and to set the conditions thereof, fades as we move away from the victim. There is, put differently, a limited radius in which it makes sense to speak of forgiveness. This means that if forgiveness is going to be posited as a precondition for political reconciliation (reconciliation with a terrorist group, in this example), it might be appropriate to exclude a potentially significant part of the polity from the process. Nir Eisikovits, "Transitional Justice," *Stanford Encyclopedia of Philosophy*, 2009.

the atonement imposed on the wrongdoer should be proportional to her wrongdoing.

The import of Radzik's caveat about an unqualified victim's prerogative is that, stretched beyond reasonable boundaries, the prerogative casts reconciliation as an optional matter, a conclusion to which she objects. Radzik claims that there are some modest, *prima facie* duties that victims have to reconcile with wrongdoers. The reason has to do with the relationship between reconciliation and what I call, following Colleen Murphy, political trust: When a victim reconciles with a wrongdoer she accepts that the latter is once again trustworthy in the political domain. By political trust, all that is meant here is that *former* wrongdoers, the trustees, are presumed to be capable of accepting and living by basic norms for social interaction, and that they can discharge the responsibilities attached to their civic roles. They can be presumed to lack ill will in present circumstances.[25] Without a minimal degree of trust, individuals cannot regain their status as agents and have a fresh start.

In sum, we have seen how reconciliation offers the possibility of a new beginning, and how it is a prima facie obligation. The next section explains at greater length what is at stake in giving collaborators a second chance in terms of the idea of respect for persons.

7.4 OF SUSPENSION AND RELEASE: WITHOUT RECONCILIATION?

One way of understanding reconciliation is to say that its aspiration is that citizens *suspend* their judgment about certain meanings of past actions and thus *release* perpetrators from the moorings of the past, from fixed identities that foreclose the possibility of moral improvement and hinder the reestablishment and cultivation of future relationships. Briefly, without the suspension of moral and political judgment and without release from past deeds, agents would not be able to command respect because their moral and

[25] Colleen Murphy, *A Moral Theory of Reconciliation* (Cambridge: Cambridge University Press, 2010), 81.

political agency would be unjustifiably hampered. I now turn to elaborate on these points.

Let us begin by thinking about how the absence of reconciliation undermines moral agency. Failing to reconcile with an atoning and apologizing wrongdoer amounts to keeping an "indestructible ledger" that records her moral failures and forever affects her moral standing. This runs counter to the notion of a genuinely fresh choice and the related concept of an agent's moral progress. As Jean Harvey argues, "It is not true that once a thief, always a thief. Without the possibility of fresh choices and moral progress, the commitment to a life of moral endeavour makes little conceptual sense."[26] When the agent is denied the possibility of improvement, she is not being treated as a moral agent capable of making her own choices; hence the disrespect. "For a victim to fail to morally reconcile in response to a thorough-going atonement [. . .] would be to fail to show proper respect for the wrongdoer. It would be to deny his status as a moral agent."[27] If the failure to hold agents responsible for their actions is a sign of disrespect, as was argued in Chapter 5, so is the tendency to blame them permanently, to deny agents release from such actions.[28]

Destroying the ledger of moral failures is, of course, not without its risks. It requires something along the lines of what David Sussman calls, borrowing from Soren Kierkegaard, the "teleological suspension of the ethical."[29] In fleshing out Kant's views on the subject, Sussman argues that when a supplicant apologizes, what she does is to ask us to understand our relationship to her not only in terms of what has happened between us in the past, but also in terms of the

[26] Quoted by Radzik, *Making Amends: Atonement in Morality, Law, and Politics,* 2009, 131. This is a variation on a Kantian theme. In the *Metaphysical Principles of Virtue,* Kant discusses the way in which reproach of vice should *not* be expressed. He says it must never "burst out in complete contempt or deny the wrongdoer all moral worth, because on that hypothesis he could never be improved either."

[27] Radzik, *Making Amends,* 2009, 131.

[28] In a similar vein, Trudy Govier argues: "We have an obligation to allow each other fresh starts, provided the wrongdoing is not too serious." See her *Forgiveness and Revenge* (London: Routledge, 2002), 44.

[29] David Sussman, "Kantian Forgiveness," *Kant-Studien* 96, no. 1 (2005): 104.

relationship we might now set ourselves to realizing. As Sussman puts it: "The supplicant bids us to see him through the lens of the person he intends to and might become, if only we do so consider him and receive him back to ourselves. In a sense, the supplicant asks us to trust him enough to reestablish a relationship through which he may become worthy of that very trust, although nothing about him as he is now morally necessitates such an attitude."[30] Reconciliation is forward-looking, and it requires, to a certain extent, a leap of faith on the part of those who wish to display a reconciliatory attitude.[31]

Consider now how a set of attitudes and institutions that discourage reconciliation affect political agency. Colleen Murphy has forcefully argued that the kind of political trust that is part and parcel of reconciliation has noninstrumental moral value; that is, political trust is valuable not only because it promotes reconciliation; it is valuable in itself. The value of political trust stems from the fact that when we trust our fellow citizens and officials as a default position, as Murphy calls it, we make a presumption about fellow citizens and officials, namely that, as was mentioned before, they are capable of honoring basic norms for social interaction as well as discharging their responsibilities as citizens or public officials. Specifically, citizens are presumed to be capable of governing their own lives, whereas officials are presumed to be capable of acting effectively on behalf of their community and of possessing knowledge about appropriate and inappropriate behavior for someone in their position. As Murphy writes, "Adopting trust as a default position in political relationships is an important way of acknowledging the effective agency of citizens and officials."[32] Furthermore, default political trust presumes basic decency and commitment to fair play. I quote Murphy again: "To demand that citizens or officials prove their decency or commitment to fair play, or to presume that they are incompetent, worthy of

30 Sussman, "Kantian Forgiveness," 104.

31 In taking this leap of faith, victims should assume that there are reliable guarantees of nonrepetition of the structural conditions that allowed perpetrators to commit wrongdoing.

32 Murphy, *A Moral Theory of Reconciliation*, 81.

suspicion, or harboring ill will, is normally fundamentally disrespectful, insulting, and calls out for justification."[33]

The underlying idea in Colleen Murphy's view is that when we fail to reconcile with a political actor who has done wrong, we deny her the possibility of removing the identity of the perpetual enemy and wrongdoer. We disrespect her by rejecting the possibility that she becomes an *equal* comember of the polity. Hannah Arendt is the classic representative of this view. She claims that the most important benefit of political forgiveness – a term into which she subsumes the idea of reconciliation – is that it releases political actors from the permanent reiteration of vengeance and creates the possibility for a new start. Political forgiveness, Arendt argues, is necessary "in order to make it possible for life to go on by constantly releasing men from what they have done unknowingly."[34] As an Arendt scholar argues, the word releasing in the previous sentence is crucial because it "implies being unbound from the past in order to go on."[35]

Arendt is very clear and explicit that failure to offer the possibility of a new beginning boils down to a lack of respect. She makes this point by analogizing respect to love under most of its forms (as *eros, caritas, fraternitas, compassio*). Love, she says, is the relationship that most readily enables political forgiveness. Its closeness, intimacy, and in general, its emotional attachments make it possible for individuals under its influence to forgive each other more easily. But the political theorist in Arendt is quick to note that love is an antipolitical force because it destroys what she calls the in-between that is constitutive of politics. The substitute for love "in the realm of public affairs," the "force" that strengthens, instead of undermines, mutuality and togetherness, is respect. Arendt defines respect, "not unlike the Aristotelian philia politike," as a kind of friendship without intimacy or closeness, a "regard for the person from the distance which the space of the world puts between us." The type of friendship that

[33] Murphy, *A Moral Theory of Reconciliation*, 82.

[34] Hannah Arendt, *The Human Condition* (Chicago: University of Chicago Press, 1958), quoted by Elisabeth Young-Bruehl, *Why Arendt Matters* (New Haven, CT: Yale University Press, 2006), 100.

[35] Young-Bruehl, *Why Arendt Matters*, 2006, 100.

Arendt has in mind is an analogia publicae or proto-public sphere, a close "resemblance or image to the public activity of citizens, characteristics of which can consist in spontaneity, discussion, speech, common deliberation, persuasion, cooperation, or absence of hierarchy."[36] Briefly put, just as lovers should forgive one another on account of the love they have for each other, citizens should – to the extent that it is psychologically possible – forgive each other on account of the respect that they have for one another. The point of analogizing love to respect is to claim that just as an unforgiving lover would be a contradiction in terms – as the unwillingness to forgive would undercut the claim to love, – so in the public realm the disrespectful citizen, that is, the political actor unwilling to forgive a fellow citizen, would betray a lack of respect.[37]

If at the moral level, reconciliation involves the teleological suspension of the ethical, at the political register it involves the suspension or annulment of the friend/enemy distinction. Andrew Schaap[38] argues that when citizens politically forgive other citizens, what is implied is a suspension of judgment. Not the judgment of the wrongness of the act, but the judgment that the transgression confirms the other as one's enemy in the present. And this, he further argues, is a form of respect because the suspension of judgment is ventured "for the sake of establishing a new relation based on mutual recognition of each other as cobuilders of a common world." Arendtian forgiveness, then, presupposes the idea of respect for the other as the cobuilder of a common world. This form of respect differs from the Kantian notion of respect in that whereas the latter applies to individuals as autonomous beings who share the universal capacity for reason, the former applies to individuals as political beings who share a particular world as their common end.

[36] Shin Chiba, "Hannah Arendt on Love and the Political: Love, Friendship, and Citizenship," *The Review of Politics* 57, no. 3 (1995): 520.

[37] In *Eichmann in Jerusalem*, Arendt discusses the notion of the unforgivable, especially in relation to the Holocaust.

[38] Andrew Schaap, "Political Grounds for Forgiveness," *Contemporary Political Forgiveness* 2 (2003): 82.

In sum, then, obstructing reconciliation, in the sense of rejecting others as full moral and political agents and of refusing to trust them politically, amounts to denying them the possibility of moral improvement and of considering them equal comembers of the polity. The enormity of a crime might justify such response. But whether this response should extend to acts that are neither criminal nor enormous, which is the kind of misdeeds that IMs committed, is doubtful.

7.5 AN UNREQUITED APOLOGY: ONE CLOSURE TAKES TWO SELF-DISCLOSURES

With the framework put in place in the previous sections, I shall now turn to the case of Kerstin Kaiser. The view to be defended is that in light of the insights developed in the previous sections, in Kaiser's case the ideal of reconciliation was not fulfilled. This, in turn, means that the value of respect for persons was not honored.

In the midst of the public controversy around her designation as a candidate for the cabinet, Kaiser offered a public apology for her involvement with the Stasi. Kaiser's apology is noteworthy on at least two scores. On one hand, Die Linke, her party, and its immediate predecessor, the Partei des Demokratischen Sozialismus or Party of Democratic Socialism (PDS), have a record of disavowing the undemocratic acts of the communist regime, while at the same time refusing to offer public apologies for the violations of human rights perpetrated by the Stasi. A memorable instance of such discursive legerdemain was its refusal to offer a public apology of the construction of the Wall in the context of its fortieth commemoration. Gabriele Zimmer, back then the PDS chairperson, today a politician from the unapologetic Die Linke, argued that she shared "the view that nothing is clarified with rituals of apology. Coming to terms with the past is not about atonement (*Abbitte*)."[39] Another prominent PDS member, Michael Benjamin, argued in 1999 that the erection of the wall had been a "legally (*völkerrechtlich*) permissible and appropriate

[39] Philip Grassmann, "Die PDS wird sich für Mauerbau nicht entschuldigen," *Süddeutsche Zeitung*, June 15, 2001.

action at that time."[40] Peter Porsch, yet another distinguished PDS representative – today in Die Linke – went as far as to say that "in 1961 the Wall brought peace to Europe and the world. It would help nobody if we apologized for the Wall."[41]

On the other hand, Kaiser's case is all the more interesting because she was not publicly exposed by her victims, by a sensationalist tabloid, or by a more respectable newspaper or magazine searching to enrich public debate, which as we saw in previous chapters are the most common avenues for publicly exposing collaborators. Her behavior contrasts to that of Renate Adolphe, a fellow Die Linke representative in the Brandenburg legislature, who like Kaiser was unveiled as an IM, but who unlike Kaiser, originally failed to inform her party and the legislature that she had collaborated for the Stasi, only doing so when the evidence against her was on the table. In contrast to Adolphe, Kaiser engaged in a voluntary act of self-disclosure. In fact, at the time when the episode under examination was unfolding, her involvement with the Stasi should not have come as a surprise to anyone. Over the years, she had repeatedly acknowledged her past engagements with the secret police, and in 1994 she had even renounced a seat in the Bundestag for the same reason she was now declining to participate in Brandenburg's governing coalition fifteen years later.

I now turn to examining in some depth Kaiser's "clarification," as she calls it, of her past collaboration with the Stasi.[42] Commentators have made an issue of the fact that she uses the word *clarification*

[40] "PDS-Politiker lobt Mauerbau," *Bild-Zeitung*, January 24, 1999

[41] *Tageszeitung*, June 14, 2001. For an analysis of Die Linke's historical revisionism, see Gerd Langguth, "Plädoyer für eine Entzauberung der Linkspartei," *Der Spiegel*, September 25, 2009; See also a report prepared by the CDU, "Nicht auf dem Boden der Verfassung! Eine Analyse und Dokumentation zur Partei Die Linke," 2008, 29. Available at www.epenportal.de/core/files/spezial/cdu-fraktion-hessen/analyse_partei_die_linke.pdf.

[42] "Zu meiner politischen Vergangenheit. Erklärung zur Zusammenarbeit mit dem MfS." Accessible at: www.kerstin-kaiser.eu/persoenlich/meine_vergangenheit/. All references to Kaiser's public apology come from this source.

instead of the word *apology* to characterize her statement. But this might be a matter of semantics. The latter contains many of the elements of what Nick Smith calls a categorical apology, which I now turn to examine.[43] She begins by offering a factual record of the events salient to her wrongdoing. The point is to underscore the context in which it happened and to offer full access to all the facts relevant to judging the transgressions. Thus, Kaiser admits that in 1979 as an eighteen-year-old pupil, two Stasi officers recruited her at school in the presence of its director and of the teachers at the former's office. Because she was about to study abroad in Leningrad (today Saint Petersburg), her assignment consisted of informing on twelve fellow students who would travel along.[44] Stasi officers told Kaiser (IM Katrin) that they were worried that the secret service of "capitalist" nations would try to approach East Germans studying abroad, so an eye had to be kept on them. She was doing a service to her country, she believed back then, "But I did not draw the necessary consequences from today's perspective." She asks, "Why didn't I have – as an eighteen year old girl – any doubts about the legitimacy of the requests of the Stasi officers and about the rightness of my decision? Who was I back then that I had no doubt whatsoever?" She offers a tentative response: "Evil existed elsewhere for me." In Pinochet's *coup d'Etat*, in occupied Vietnam, elsewhere in the capitalist world, but not in the GDR.

As can be seen, the public apology is not without mitigating elements. These are not exculpatory excuses, but additional

[43] I am following a standard proposed by Nick Smith, *I Was Wrong: The Meanings of Apologies* (Cambridge: Cambridge University Press, 2008), 140–142.

[44] Her reports contained mostly bland accusations. Of one student she reported that (s)he watched Western television at home. Of another that (s)he was arrogant. Another talked with friends about others behind their backs. Another wore tight clothes, which she found offensive. Another used a T-shirt with American advertisements.... Other reports were more sensitive: of one colleague she says that he is sexually needy, of another that he is not politically reliable. These are far from being harmless statements, but they are not highly incriminating either, as was the case, for example, of IMs who snitched on people attempting to leave the GDR.

considerations that Kaiser introduces to mitigate the gravity of her offense by putting her actions in an institutional and ideological context where they appear to be legitimate and by displacing some of the responsibility for those actions toward the state. As we saw in Chapter 4, these considerations are not to be easily dispensed as unfounded excuses;[45] the institutional and ideological background to which Kaiser makes reference could genuinely distort normativity. Kaiser produces further mitigating factors. I quote her at length:

> Looking back today with all of what I have learned these past years, with all of the knowledge that I have acquired, it is hard to imagine that my decision at that time did not appear wrong to me. I believed in the state in which I lived and I was thankful for this state. These were obvious reasons for my behavior. [. . .] The fact that I was only eighteen years old at the time does not excuse the fact that it was a mistake, but it is one of many reasons why I made this mistake. [. . .] I can say that I never wanted to denounce anyone. Never. And from today's perspective I have to say that the moment in which one has already declared himself ready to have conversations with a secret intelligence service, this intention is no longer of any use. It is no longer up to you whether you denounce someone or not, simply because you have no control over what will be done with the information you have given. The best intentions can have the worst results because the intelligence service decides the outcomes, not the informant.

Further on in her "clarification," Kaiser begins to make her way toward a less ambiguous apology. First, she clearly acknowledges her "mistake," as she calls it, and admits blame. Second, she openly declares that she had already apologized in a private setting to her "victims" (she had already taken "the first steps"). This action, according to what I have argued before, amounts to recognition of her "victims" as respect-worthy interlocutors. I quote her again at length:

> From the very start I did not want to hide myself. From 1992–1994 I could speak with nearly all of my classmates that were affected by my actions. I found out that I had luckily not harmed

[45] On the distinction between mitigating and exculpatory excuses see Govier, *Forgiveness and Revenge,* 2002.

> anyone. Critical discussions and insights about "our earlier life," but also forgiveness and trust defined our meetings and conversations [. . .] Before 1989 I had already spoken with close friends, previous classmates and my family about the contact with the Stasi in Leningrad. That was difficult and uncomfortable. It was clear to me that this cooperation had been a mistake. I had realized that to give opinions about the life and the political reliability of classmates was in this case not only personal and political presumptuousness, but was also a step too far.

Kaiser uses the German word *Anmaßung* (presumptuousness), a notion that carries both the notion of usurpation and arrogance. With this, Kaiser acknowledges not only that she committed an objectionable action, but also that she behaved in a way that positioned her in an unduly and illegitimately elevated political status. By offering an apology, she voluntarily lowers her standing to the place where it belongs, which is one of the functions of apologies.

Kaiser then proceeds to articulate an even more robust public apology. In a statement with Arendtian undertones, she says that she cannot be forgiven in isolation, and she makes a straightforward argument for publicity as the most appropriate vehicle for forgiveness:

> It became clear to me at this point that I wanted cooperation in politics like the cooperation found in private life; cooperation that respected the rights and opinions of the individual, because a self-made, fulfilled life is impossible in a family or in a society filled with concealment, distrust, bullying and surveillance or a society where everyone simply "turns a blind eye" to wrongdoing. [. . .] This was also why "suppression and forgetting" was not an option for me.

Next, comes her public – the apology is available on her website – and categorical display of repentance, where she advances yet another notion reminiscent of Arendtian political thought–responsibility as the ability to say no.

> What I did wrong will torment me for the rest of my life. Torment me because with today's point of view I can say, "It would have been possible to say no, to not have given in." No, I cannot say whether it would have led to different consequences or what these consequences would have been, but the option would have been

> there and that is an important realization for everything that I do today. Just as important as the realization that there may be many reasons to make a mistake, but all of these reasons do not change the fact that it is a mistake and that you have to stand by this mistake if you want to be involved in politics and plan to solicit the trust of others.

Finally, her bid to reform and to forbear from reoffending, a particularly important promise from a politician who has held public office in the past, wishes to continue to do so, and therefore values credibility as one of the most important assets:

> I want to, I can, I must do things differently today. I do not want to accept it when people are shut out and made helpless by the ruling power. If I ever come across something I do not agree with I must criticize it openly and search for alternative ways. My personal dealings throughout the day up to every vote in parliament have a social and political dimension to them and only I am answerable for these dealings.

Briefly put, Kaiser publicly and thoroughly apologized for her collaboration with the Stasi. However, her atonement did not do away with the unfavorable public judgment cast on her and does not seem to have paved the way for reconciliation. She remained a "Stasi-pig," as a graffitist marked on one of her political campaign ads. Many voices chose to disregard her apology and instead highlighted Kaiser's initial silence over her involvement with the secret police, which amounted to a "loss of credibility,"[46] as a national newspaper put it, even though the news about such involvement had belonged in the public domain for over fifteen years already. According to the weekly newspaper *Die Zeit*, Platzeck is said to have complained to those in his closer circle that collaborators were hardly ever allowed to resume an unimpeded political career. He made his point by way of a questionable comparison: some murderers, he pondered, may be set free after fifteen years, moderate criminal offenses are erased from the records, but "the Stasi-stain" of IM remains. Kaiser herself complained "that

[46] "Stasi-Verstrickungen; Platzeck fühlt sich getäuscht und geprellt," *Die Welt*, April 12, 2009.

always the same standard can be set against me, that one part of my biography is singled out and remains all-powerful." Even *Die Zeit*, reporting on these statements, had to concede that as far as may be judged, Kaiser "had accomplished a full reversal (*Umkehr*), externally and internally."[47]

There were some exceptions to the overwhelming skepticism with which Kaiser's apology was received. Some voices valued Kaiser's gesture, contrasting it with the unapologetic behavior of other IMs, such as those examined in Chapter 3, who mobilize legal resources to remain anonymous and thereby spare themselves the trouble of offering an apology. With these IMs, a commentator writes, he would not wish to be reconciled.[48] But these were not the dominant voices.[49] At the end of the day, Kaiser declined participating in the governing coalition.

One reason why Kaiser's apology was incapable of fully cleansing the Stasi stain of distrust might be that her apology was publicly perceived as an instance of what Nick Smith calls a purely instrumental apology, that is, apologizing with the sole goal in mind of furthering one's interests, in Kaiser's case, her political prospects beyond the local level. As Smith himself suggests, a demand for forgiveness that follows the "apology-script" too closely is commonly suspected as lacking authenticity.[50] A suspicion of that sort may be inferred from

47 Tina Hildebrandt, "Die Grenzen der Schuld," *Die Zeit*, November 12, 2009.

48 Richard Schröder, "Versöhnung – mit wem?," *Der Spiegel*, November 9, 2009. This author writes: "I thought it was a noble gesture that Kerstin waived a ministerial position because she knows that for many in the SPD it would be a problem. That speaks highly of her. I would not have asked that from her. But there is a very different kind of IM, who uses all possible judicial means in order to prevent their names from being named, and who even intimidate their victims [. . .]. With those I would not reconcile myself in the future. Their behavior is contemptible."

49 For a good example of how Kaiser's case was addressed in the national media, see Iris Marx und Benedict Maria Mülder, "Pro und Contra: Dürfen ehemalige Stasi-IM Minister werden?" prepared for the newsbroadcast *Klartext*. Available at: www.rbb-online.de/klartext/ueber_den_tag_hinaus/diktaturen/pro_und_contra__duerfen.html.

50 Nick Smith, *I Was Wrong,* 145.

what a newspaper editorial covering Kaiser's story calls the "sorry pattern" (*Entschuldigungsmuster*).[51] This might or might not be the case, but by the same token, one could argue that the public outcry for Kaiser's attempt to participate in Brandenburg's government might simply reflect the reluctance of political elites to accept Kaiser's apology on equally strategic grounds as hers might have been. If her apology could be seen solely as a façade for appearing as an upright civil servant in the eyes of the public, its rejection could also have been part of a scheme orchestrated by other politicians to endanger the prospects of a parliamentary coalition. The lack of a reconciliatory disposition may be no less instrumental than an instrumental apology.

Let us assume, however, that Kaiser's apology was honest. Can Kaiser's exposure and the ensuing impediment to freely take on executive functions of the highest level be said to be appropriate? Christian Wilke rightly observes that when commentators relate past misconduct and present suitability, they rely on "an underlying conception of the possibilities and limits of personal transformation in times of political change."[52] If these possibilities are deemed to be considerable, past misconduct is only partially relevant for present suitability. By contrast, if the limits to personal transformation are judged to be significant, then past misconduct is conclusive evidence of the lack of present suitability.[53] Both views rest on empirical claims about the likelihood that former wrongdoers can undergo a personal makeover. But the latter view is also grounded on a variation on the idea of the indestructible ledger of moral failure and of the perpetual enemy, developed earlier. This position is untenable unless there is conclusive evidence to show that former perpetrators have not mended their ways. In Kaiser's case, boycotting her political participation is a way of refusing to give credence to her personal project of improving morally, as well as presupposing that she bears ill will toward fellow citizens and that under a different regime she cannot honor basic norms of social interaction, even though her record as a

[51] "Die Grenzen der Schuld," *Die Zeit*, November 12, 2009.

[52] Wilke, "The Shield, the Sword, and the Party," 369.

[53] Bernhard Schlink, *Vergangenheitsschd* (Frankfurt am Main: Suhrkamp, 2002), 81.

public official in unified Germany is not sullied. She is suitable for politics only in little-GDR, Brandenburg, where she is a democratically elected representative, and even in Brandenburg, she is not fit in the eyes of her critics to take on executive functions. This unjustifiably encumbers her moral and political agency and is therefore disrespectful.

We can put these ideas in different words. According to P. E. Digeser, the self-disclosure of a perpetrator alone does not lead to a closure of his or her wrongdoing and the opportunity for a new beginning; this type of closure also takes the self-disclosure of those who are in a position to offer reconciliation, that is, their willingness to abide by the *public* norms that organize the practice of reconciliation.[54] In a nutshell, reconciliation is, for victims just as much as it is for perpetrators, an act of self-disclosure.[55] The sense of the latter term is not Arendtian. Instead, Digeser borrows from Michael Oakeshott, who understands self-disclosure as "choosing an action in pursuit of a desired end according to a set of publicly recognized norms and practices."[56] In the case of reconciliation, its success as a course of action depends on whether one lives up to the public rules that govern its practice. This would require, for instance, that the repentant perpetrator of an offense (say, informing on someone else) no longer be treated as someone who behaved wrongly.[57] To put it colloquially, the repentant perpetrator should be spared further reproaches, and she should be treated, if possible, as she was treated prior to her wrongdoing, or as close as possible to that. Otherwise

[54] "Consequently political forgiveness can only make sense if we believe that the public relationship between the parties is worthy of respect and repair." P. E. Digeser, *Political Forgiveness*, 2001, 28.

[55] P. E. Digeser, "Forgiveness and Politics: Dirty Hands and Imperfect Procedures," *Political Theory* 26, no. 5 (1998): 705.

[56] Digeser, "Forgiveness and Politics," 703.

[57] Digeser explains this intuitive idea as follows: "If A forgives B for missing the meeting that B promised to attend, and A then mentions this failure every time they come together, or uses this absence to disparage B publicly, then B can probably call into question whether A had actually forgiven him. If A had truly forgiven B, then he would treat B as he had prior to the wrong." Digeser, "Forgiveness and Politics," 704.

reconciliation is an empty word. In the case of Kaiser, self-disclosure across the board is missing.

7.6 CONCLUSION

Reconciliation in German public discourse is often framed as the reward for IMs who openly acknowledge their repentance and publicly apologize for their past actions. Public apologies, according to this point of view, can bring about the restoration of political relationships. If part of the point of reconciling with an IM is conferring to her full status as a political agent, it follows that she should not be barred from holding elected positions in government. However, this chapter argued that as it actually turns out in contemporary Germany, the prospects for reconciliation following a public apology are uncertain.

There is a problem with the fact that Kaiser was politically disqualified in the manner described in this section. It is certainly *not* the demand that Kaiser atones and apologizes. There are cogent philosophical grounds to argue that it was her obligation to do so. But just as there are legitimate grounds for demanding her atonement and apologies, so too there is a legitimate expectation on her part that because she did not commit any kind of atrocious crime, she would be politically forgiven after she had atoned and apologized. Unofficial collaborators like Kaiser were not high-level perpetrators. There are good reasons why strict lustration policies disqualifying the latter from holding public office are acceptable. After all, these leaders proved that they were capable of designing and putting in place a system that did not respect basic human interests, and so banning them from public office and remaining skeptical about their trustworthiness may ultimately be justified on deterrence-based grounds. But should unofficial collaborators, who did not create or enforce this system, be disqualified too? In cases like theirs, offering reconciliation for little in return is disrespectful to victims, but offering no reconciliation *at all* is disrespectful to informers.

I should underscore that the point of this chapter is not to cast Kaiser as a victim. To put it bluntly, despite the restrictions she has faced in the political arena, she has done well for herself in unified

Germany, becoming a salient member of an important political party, even if only at the local level. But her relative success does not erase the fact that there is more than a grain of truth in her complaint that her Stasi involvement remains all-powerful and defining of her relationship to other citizens in the present. If her complaint is true, this should raise concerns from the point of view of the value of respect for persons. If collaborators repent in public and offer an apology, Kaiser asks, do they not deserve a second chance, on account of the respect that is owed to them as fellow citizens?

8 CONCLUSION

Thou all-spying knave, of all deeds of shame

Many nations have struggled to confront their violent pasts, and political and social actors in such nations have deployed strategies that are similar to public identifications of unofficial collaborators to contribute to this goal. An example is the public denunciation known as the *escrache* or scratching of collaborators of the military dictatorship in Argentina, where activists alert neighbors of a given district that a person suspected of having participated in "genocide" is living among them (*Genocida en el barrio*). As in the German case, *escrache* is a concrete mechanism that activists in Argentine society deemed suitable for coming to terms with the past actions of those who collaborated in the period of military rule. The existence of these mechanisms of civic accountability in societies like Argentina or Germany suggests that the public exposure of former perpetrators plays a crucial role in transitional justice and is therefore worth examining. This book is a contribution to this goal.

I shall conclude by evoking an episode from Greek tragedy that can help me encapsulate the spirit of this book. In Sophocles' *Ajax*, the hero of the tragedy is enraged because Achilles' armor has been awarded to Odysseus and not to him. Ajax believes he has a better claim to the armor because his courage and skills in the battlefield eclipsed those of Odysseus; that Odysseus's abilities have less to do with physical prowess than with cunning is a matter that Ajax is too obfuscated to consider. Ajax concludes that he has been dishonored (i.e., disrespected), and he is therefore infuriated. After slaughtering a flock of sheep, which in his delirium and under Athena's spell he takes to be the group of Achean leaders who deprived him of the cherished armor, he curses (an absent) Odysseus in the following fashion:

> Thou all-spying knave, of all deeds of shame
> The prompt, easy tool, Odysseus the wise!
> Villain, of all the camp the most foul and vile!
> Huge laughter doubtless shakes thee now for sheer delight.[1]

The natural tendency for the reader will be to sympathize with and concentrate on Ajax's suffering, as he has been the victim of Odysseus's deceitful tongue. Were it not for the fact that Odysseus too is a hero in Homer's epics, our sympathy with the plight of Ajax would be total. So in judging the situation, one will have the inclination to focus on the affront done to Ajax, on how he might have really deserved Achilles' armor after all, on how someone (his peers, the gods) should have heard and addressed his grievance, and on how the harm done to him should be redressed.

Those reactions, which are morally appealing and are grounded on the notion of respect for victims, will not take us too far in terms of exploring and understanding a more comprehensive notion of respect. Instead, one can resist the inclination to focus *only* on the harm done to Ajax, the victim, and instead to see things from the perspective of a character whose moral quality is rather dubious. Odysseus is a flawed character – he lies to people if need be, he deceives his own men and whatever Cyclopes he comes across to get his way, and he is unfaithful even to those he loves.[2] He is a "tool of mischief," as another translation of the passage just quoted puts it, because he commits "deeds of shame" and is a "foul and vile" individual. Despite all this, or perhaps precisely because of it, his actions have something crucial to tell us about the idea of respect. In this vein, this book argues that the case of unofficial collaborators, those petty, modern Odysseus types – flawed characters who committed "shameful" political deeds by serving the Stasi as tools of

[1] Sophocles, *Ajax*, trans. R. C. Trevelyan, The Internet Classics Archive, http://classics.mit.edu//Sophocles/ajax.html.

[2] On Odysseus's morality, see Don Herzog, *Cunning* (Princeton: Princeton University Press, 2007), ch. 1.

mischief – shows us something important about many dimension of the notion of respect and how it is valued or disregarded in a concrete transitional justice setting.

Let me recapitulate very succinctly the main arguments of the book and restate one goal it did *not* pursue. The book identifies and examines various claims to respect, as well as their normative purchase, present in political discourse about IM exposures. There might be alternative ways to construe public unveilings in ways that underscore other dimensions of the idea of respect for persons; the ones I offered seemed to me to be the most salient. One prominent and more compelling justification for publicly identifying unofficial collaborators is, of course, respect for victims – their right to know who contributed to their political oppression. But the practice raises the opposing claim to respect on the part of erstwhile collaborators that exposures are forms of public shaming that affect their ability to flourish in unified Germany. This is why they appeal to their reputational rights, as well as to a supposed "right" to throw a mantle of oblivion over their past misdeeds. In the final analysis, however, even if the latter claim has a sound basis, it is outweighed by the claim of victims to knowing the truth about past injustice committed against them with the help of informers. After all, IMs weakened their claim to respect by collaborating with the Stasi, thus disrespecting victims.

Now, informers not only expressed disrespect toward their victims by betraying their trust and reporting on their actions to the secret police. They also disrespected themselves because unofficial collaboration is an act of servility toward public authorities: By lacking in civic courage, unofficial collaborators left themselves open to public dishonor. This does not mean that public identifications, at their best, are merely rituals of public scorn for the sake of "getting even" with collaborators. Public exposures build respect for informers by regarding them as accountable agents who can be asked for, and give, justifications for their past actions. Of course, public exposures can be subverted if they do not represent genuine demands for justification but unsubstantiated recriminations, which ignore considerations that mitigate the moral blame of some informers. Public exposures can also be subverted if they are turned into scapegoat mechanisms that seek to individualize guilt to obscure and leave unexamined the complicity with and contribution to Stasi wrongdoing of other segments of the population aside from informers. Nonetheless, when carried out for the right reasons, the premise of public identifications is the value of respect for persons.

Public identifications promote apologies of informers to victims of the Stasi regime. This builds respect in various ways. From the perspective of collaborators, it gives them the opportunity to reacquire the respect that they lost through their actions. From the perspective of victims, the apology acknowledges the harm done to them and retroactively recognizes their dignity. In this regard, one important qualification is worth underlining. Apologies can be of many different sorts, and some of them are of lesser value from the point of view of respect than others. Public apologies in particular can be problematic if instead of initiating a meaningful relationship of (potential) forgiveness between the victim and the collaborator, they offer the latter the opportunity not to confront the former and instead respond to the demands of intermediaries between the two parties that would ideally be involved. Public apologies can also be sterile from the point of view of respect if they do not contribute to cultivating an environment in which all citizens, including former collaborators, are regarded as full-fledged political agents.

These are the main lines of argumentation I developed in the book. I shall conclude by reminding the reader that its primary goal was not to develop a clear-cut and systematic normative case for or against public exposures. My position toward them was cautious but not uncritical. I started from the assumption that the practice, which is by and large a social enterprise as opposed to a state-sponsored one (even if the complicity, and sometimes the up-front instigation, of political elites is one of their ingredients), arose and evolved as the best possible mechanism that civil society actors could conceive of to confront the past and address a demand for justice on the part of victims. Thus, I regarded public unveilings of informers as a practice reflecting legitimate social interests and therefore, all things considered, as an acceptable one. However, this does not mean that in my view public exposures do not have problematic implications on some fronts. Likewise, it does not mean that we should simply ignore and dismiss the claims to respect of unofficial collaborators; or think that the kind of public apologies that exposures seek to encourage are flawless in terms of the value of respect; or furthermore, that the practice cannot be "improved" on, in the sense of relying on a more sophisticated and nuanced view of unofficial collaboration (and as a matter of fact, over the course of the years public exposures did become more "refined" in this way). As I mentioned in the introduction, this book was more concerned with charting a map of respect than it was with adjudicating between competing claims to respect in contexts of transitional justice. Societies in transition face problems so complex that oftentimes there is no single course of action to address them that does not raise concerns from the point of view of respect for persons.

Perhaps a good way to capture the moral complexity, if not ambivalence, of public exposures is to say that they are a form of imperfect justice. Aviezer Tucker's analysis of what he calls "rough justice" can be helpful in making this argument. He argues that the enforcement and administration of any system of justice requires resources, which are commonly scarce and therefore constrain the possibilities of realization of such a system. In consequence, he contends, normative choices along three dimensions of materially possible forms of justice are unavoidable. The first of these dimensions is accuracy, which refers to the degree of agreement between possible and desired result of some principles of justice: If the principle of justice is that criminals should be convicted and innocents should be acquitted, accuracy is measured by the margins of error of the legal system; if all criminals are convicted and all innocents are acquitted, then principles of justice can be realized in a fully accurate way. The second dimension of materially possible justice is scope, which refers to how broadly principles of justice apply; should they apply to a section of society, to the whole of it, or globally? Finally, the last dimension is depth, which refers to how costly and transformative the desired forms of justice are with regard to existing social norms within a specific scope. All possible forms of justice, then, must fall into these three dimensions, and according to Tucker, in the real-world increases in one dimension may come at the expense of decreases in one or two of the other dimensions. Justice is rough when it must make these compromises.[3]

Tucker considers lustration as an example of rough justice. Generally speaking, new postcommunist regimes lacked resources for conducting trials of employees and collaborators of the secret police. In view of this, exclusion from public service of former secret police agents or its collaborators, regardless of the degree of their involvement with that body, seemed like an affordable measure. But in doing this, and perhaps on the assumption that justice delayed is justice denied, these regimes sacrificed accuracy to scope of justice.[4] In other words, they used a blunt instrument to mete out retribution, and as a result not everyone got individual consideration, and not all got their just deserts. Another way of conceptualizing this concern is that lustration blames groups instead of individuals, which poses a problem for liberalism's commitment to moral individualism.[5]

In Germany's case, lustration policies were no different in sacrificing accuracy of justice to scope, although maybe to a lesser degree than in other postcommunist nations. Recall some of the points I made in the introduction and throughout the book: Early screenings were made somewhat unevenly across the board; they were deemed to be unjust by many individuals who were their targets; and they might have quarantined many former employees who did not commit any crime. In the spirit of letting no guilty politician or bureaucrat off the hook, a bludgeon was used rather than a scalpel. Later on, the Stasi Records Office and some courts introduced some moderation into the process, thus trying to alter the reigning balance that privileged scope to accuracy.

Relatively recent amendments to the law of the Stasi archives are an excellent illustration of how sacrificing the accuracy of justice to its scope is a trade-off that remains popular with politicians and political

[3] Aviezer Tucker, "Scarce Justice: The Accuracy, Scope, and Depth of Justice," *Politics, Philosophy, and Economics* 11, no. 1 (2012): 76–78.

[4] Tucker, "Scarce Justice," 87–88.

[5] Yvone Chiu, "Liberal Lustration," *Journal of Political Philosophy* 19, no. 4 (2011): 440–464. Chiu defends the view that lustration is compatible with liberal principles.

parties in Germany today. In the previous version of the law, screening for Stasi involvement was supposed to conclude in December of 2011. However, with the amendment the expiration date was extended to December of 2019. This amendment, promoted by the current commissioner of the Stasi Records Office, Roland Jahn, who like his predecessors had been a dissident during the GDR, generated no small degree of controversy. A commentator portrayed the amendment as an inhumane and justice-blind form of "German purification" and complained that it contradicted a fundamental principle of a state governed by the rule of law (*Rechtsstaat*), namely the precept that there is a maximum time span within which behavior that was contrary to the law can be prosecuted and criminally punished. The purposes of this statute of limitations, as it is called, are several, but one is to provide legal certainty and another to address the concern that after a long period of time has elapsed, criminal investigations face increasing difficulties; in both cases, the goal is to protect the defendant. This commentator further argued that although the legal criminal framework establishes a period of prescription of five or ten years for several offenses, including membership in a terrorist organization, when it comes to involvement with the Stasi as a public official or as an unofficial collaborator, the period of prescription is much longer, even though such collaboration is not considered a crime.[6]

Extending on Tucker's framework, one could argue that public exposures of unofficial collaborators are a variety of rough, nonlegal justice (with a dose of scapegoating?), even if they are not a form of criminal punishment, in their attempt to increase the scope of justice at the expense of its accuracy. Like lustration, public exposures seek to hold unofficial collaborators coresponsible for injustices committed during the previous regime. Public exposures do it for the purposes of civic disqualification; lustrations do it to ban these people from holding public office. In other words, the latter refer to

[6] Michael Kleine-Cosack, "Geschichtsblind und inhuman-eine deutsche Reinigung," *Frankfurter Allgemeine Zeitung*, November 21, 2011. For another skeptic view on the amendment, see Jasper von Altenbockum, "Deutsche Eisberge," *Frankfurter Allgemeine Zeitung*, September 30, 2011.

suitability as a public official; the former to suitability as a citizen. Tucker mentions the case of postcommunist governments that published or leaked lists of secret police informers. He claims that "as in the case of pedophiles, this is a case of very rough justice because the published lists did not mention how each name came to be on the list, whether the person was an ideological fanatic, a malicious informer, a ruthless careerist, a victim of secret police blackmail, or a person who became an informer under torture."[7] All were given the same treatment. This is exactly what happened in the case I mentioned earlier in the book, in which civil society actors in Halle published a rough list of unofficial collaborators and used it to publicly shame alleged informers. The episode of the list of informers in Halle, one might think, is an anecdote. However, it reflects a trend that even the most enthusiastic defenders of public identification acknowledged and lamented at some point – the sensationalist manner in which the media exposed many IMs, without in-depth consideration of the particular circumstances of each case.[8] Certainly, this happened more often in the early days of IM outings, when vindictive emotions were at their peak and when the Stasi archives remained rather disorganized. As these emotions cooled off, and, just like happened in the case of lustration, as the Stasi Records Office stepped in to offer richer and more systematized information to the public, debates about unofficial collaborators gained in detail and nuance, and the "quality" of public identifications improved.

Just as lustrations entail, from the point of view of a *Rechtsstaat*, weakened legal protection for "Stasi-positive" individuals, so public exposures stand in tension with some of the ideals behind the guarantee of due process. Consider one of the most pressing demands that motivate public identifications of unofficial collaborators, as well as other measures of transitional justice: the right to truth and historical clarification; unveiling the identity of collaborators to unveil the truth about past injustice. In Germany and in many other places (South Africa being the archetypical case), this is usually taken to mean that collaborators must come forth and openly acknowledge their

[7] Tucker, "Scarce Justice," 90.

[8] Joachim Gauck "Dealing with a Stasi Past," *Daedalus* 123, no. 1 (1994): 281.

involvement with the secret police; they cannot remain silent, but, quite the contrary, they should offer reasons for their collaboration and repentance when interpellated. This demand, as we saw in previous chapters, is grounded on the idea of respect for victims or on consideration of public interest. More deeply, it rests on the compelling idea that citizens have a moral duty to be accountable to one another for their conduct. From the perspective of transitional justice, then, the contrived silence of collaborators undermines the aspiration for truth of societies emerging from a violent past. And yet the right to silence is one of the requirements of due process, which are a fundamental part of legal justice. One could simply argue that public exposures are not criminal punishment, and that therefore unofficial collaborators are not legally entitled to guarantees of due process, such as the right to silence. But if one believes that IM outings are a form of weak retributive justice or that they are accountability mechanisms that should approximate adequate legal schemes of justice, then the more confessional approach of transitional justice measures should generate some concerns.

Again, in my view, all these caveats about public exposures do not amount to an indictment of the practice. They simply show that public unveilings are a nonideal mechanism for achieving (imperfect) justice. Ideally, their promoters should work toward smoothing the roughness of public exposures. Reducing the clashes between accuracy and scope can be done, for instance, by making sure that the distinctions between different kinds of unofficial collaborators (opportunist, conformist, good-faith, or lesser-evil informers) do not get lost in the midst of sensationalism, witch-hunting or simply intellectual laziness.

BIBLIOGRAPHY

NEWSPAPER ARTICLES, MEDIA SOURCES, AND RELATED REFERENCES

Barkleit, Gerhard and Anette Dunsch. "Inoffizielle Mitarbeiter in der Hochtechnologie." *Deutschland Archive* 2 (1996): 213–221.

Beyer, Achim. "Märtyrermasche der Täter. IM 'Schubert' bemüht den Rechtsstaat." *Freiheit und Recht. Vierteljahresschrift für streitbare Demokratie und Widerstand gegen Diktatur*, August 2008, 1–2, pp. 8–9. online version, available at: www.bwv-bayern.org/component/content/article/3-suchergebnis/27-maertyrermasche-der-taeter.html.

Biermann, Wolf. "Des Satans Spießgesellen." *Der Spiegel*, December 12, 1993, www.spiegel.de/spiegel/print/d-13682656.html.

Bohley, Bärbel. "Wir wollten Gerechtigkeit und bekamen den Rechtstaat. Bilanz zwölf Jahre danach." In *Recht und Gerechtigkeit XIII. Bautzen-Forum der Friedrich-Ebert-Stiftung*. Leipzig, 2002.

Bollwahn, Barbara. "Im Bauch bin ich Opfer, im Kopf bin ich Täter." *die tageszeitung*, April 4, 2006, www.taz.de/1/archiv/?dig=2006/04/04/a0147.

Bräutigam, Hansgeorg. "Die Toten an der Berliner Mauer und an der innerdeutschen Grenze und die bundesdeutsches Justiz. Versuch einer Bilanz." *Deutschland Archive* 6 (2004): 969–976.

Buchner, Kathrin. "Schneewittchen und die Stasi-Schergen." *Stern*, May 31, 2010, www.stern.de/kultur/tv/tatort-kritik-schneewittchen-und-die-stasi-schergen-1570291.html.

Burger, Reiner. "Vorbei, vergangen, vergessen?" *Frankfurter Allgemeine Zeitung*. December 23, 2008, www.faz.net/aktuell/politik/inland/ddr-unrecht-vorbei-vergangen-vergessen-1741834.html.

Fischer-Solms, Herbert. "IM Torsten: Der Stasi-Fall des Eislauf-Trainers Ingo Steuer." *Deutschland Archiv* 2 (2006): 197–200.

Föller, Hans-Joachim. "Gestern IM, heute Redakteur beim MDR." *Horch und Guck* 3 (2000): 45–46.

Frasch, Timo. "Ingo Steuer: 'Schandfleck' in meinem Leben." *Frankfurter Allgemeine Zeitung*, March 20, 2006, www.faz.net/aktuell/sport/wintersport/stasi-vergangenheit-ingo-steuer-schandfleck-in-meinem-leben-1302876.html.

Gauck, Joachim. *Die Stasi-Akten. Das unheimliche Erbe der DDR*. Hamburg: Rowohlt, 1991.

Gauck, Joachim. "Dealing with a Stasi Past." *Daedalus* 123, no. 1 (1994): 277–284.

Gauck, Joachim. "Opening of Files and Public Access to them: An Important Contribution to Dealing with the Communist Dictatorship." In *Totalitarian and Authoritarian Regimes in Europe: Legacies and Lessons from the Twentieth Century*, edited by Jerzy W. Borejsza, Klaus Ziemer, and Magdalena Hułas, 431–439. New York: Berghahn, 2006.

Gauck, Joachim. "Unser Land." in *Frankfurter Allgemeine Zeitung*, March 24, 2012.

Geipel, Ines. "Kontaminierte Gesellschaft." *Die Welt*, April 31, 2007.

Grasemann, Hans-Jürgen. "Täter haben ein Gesicht. Die Notwendigkeit zur Benennung von Täternamen bei der Aufarbeitung des SED-Unrechts." *Freiheit und Recht* 2 (2009), www.bwv-bayern.org/component/content/article/3-suchergebnis/69-taeter-haben-ein-gesicht.html.

Grasemann, Hans-Jürgen. "Gerichte geben Tätern ein Gesicht. Wegweisende Urteile gegen Stasi-Spitzel." *Freiheit und Recht* 3/4 (2010), www.bwv-bayern.org/component/content/article/3-suchergebnis/104-gerichte-geben-taetern-ein-gesicht.html.

Grassmann, Philip. "Die PDS wird sich für Mauerbau nicht entschuldigen." *Süddeutsche Zeitung*, June 15, 2001.

Hecht, Marco and Gerald Praschl, eds. *Ich habe 'Nein!' gesagt: über Zivilcourage in der DDR*. Berlin: Homilius, 2002.

Herzog, Roman. "Rede von Bundespräsident Roman Herzog vor der Enquete-Kommission "SED-Diktatur." March 26, 1996. Available at: www.bundespraesident.de/SharedDocs/Reden/DE/Roman-Herzog/Reden/1996/03/19960326_Rede.html.

Hildebrandt, Tina. "Die Grenzen der Schuld." *Die Zeit*, November 12, 2009, www.zeit.de/2009/47/Linke-Brandenburg-Kaiser.

Jaeger, Manfred. "Fritz Rudolf Fries – IM 'Pedro Hagen.' " *Deutschland Archiv* 4 (1996): 346–348.

Kaiser, Kerstin. "Zu meiner politischen Vergangenheit. Erklärung zur Zusammenarbeit mit dem MfS." Accessible at: www.kerstin-kaiser.eu/persoenlich/meine_vergangenheit/.

Kaufmann, Hans Bernhard. "Verstörte Gewissen – beschädigte Seelen. Junge Menschen wurden als IM missbraucht." *Horch und Guck* 6 (1997): 1–11.

Kellerhoff, Sven Felix and Uwe Müller. "Indiskreter Hotelier. Wenn Rechtsstaat und Stasi-Aufarbeitung kollidieren: Der Fall Thomas Klippstein." *Deutschland Archiv* 6 (2006): 983–990.

Kleine-Cosack, Michael. "Geschichtsblind und inhuman – eine deutsche Reinigung." *Frankfurter Allgemeine Zeitung*, November 21, 2011, www.faz.net/aktuell/politik/staat-und-recht/stasi-unterlagen-gesetz-geschichtsblind-und-inhuman-eine-deutsche-reinigung-11530926.html.

Knabe, Hubertus. *Die Täter sind unter uns: Über das Schönreden der SED-Diktatur*. Berlin: List, 2008.

Kopietz, Andreas. "Der Gentleman IM." *Berliner Zeitung*, February 2, 2008, www.berliner-zeitung.de/archiv/karlheinz-schaedlich-liebte-tweedjackets-schmuggelte-kameras-und-spitzelte-guenter-grass-aus-im-dezember-hat-er-sich-in-berlin-erschossen-der-gentleman-im,10810590,10536190.html.

Langguth, Gerd. "Plädoyer für eine Entzauberung der Linkspartei." *Der Spiegel*, September 25, 2009, www.spiegel.de/politik/deutschland/verdraengte-parteigeschichte-plaedoyer-fuer-eine-entzauberung-der-linkspartei-a-650626.html.

Lier, Axel, Dirk Banse and Steffen Pletl. "Grass' Stasi-Spitzel erschießt sich auf Parkbank." *Berliner Morgenpost*, December 18, 2007, www.morgenpost.de/kultur/wie-es-war/article554032/Grass-Stasi-Spitzel-erschiesst-sich-auf-Parkbank.html.

Lötzsch, Gesin. "Unrechtsstaat." *Neues Deutschland*, December 6, 2008. The text is available at http://linksfraktion.de/im-wortlaut/unrechtsstaat/.

Lutz, Martin and Uwe Müller. "Stasi-Spitzel drängen für Linke in die Parlamente." *Die Welt*, September 24, 2009, www.welt.de/politik/deutschland/article4611336/Stasi-Spitzel-draengen-fuer-Linke-in-die-Parlamente.html.

Machado, Lola Huete. "Un archivo guarda el horror y el coraje de muchos." *El País*, May 23, 2010, http://elpais.com/diario/2010/05/23/eps/1274596014_850215.html.

Marx, Iris and Benedict Maria Mülder. "Pro und Contra: Dürfen ehemalige Stasi-IM Minister werden?" News broadcast *Klartext*. Available at: www.rbb-online.de/klartext/ueber_den_tag_hinaus/diktaturen/pro_und_contra__duerfen.html.

Müller, Uwe and Hartmann, Grit. *Vorwärts und Vergessen! Kader, Spitzel und Komplizen: Das gefährliche Erbe der SED-Diktatur*. Berlin: Rowohlt, 2009.

Müller, Uwe. "Haben Ex-Stasi-Spitzel ein Recht auf Vergessen?" *Die Welt*, March 18, 2009, www.welt.de/politik/article3394268/Haben-Ex-Stasi-Spitzel-ein-Recht-auf-Vergessen.html.

Oschiles, Renate. "Der Denunziant." *Berliner Zeitung*, June 16, 2005, www.berliner-zeitung.de/archiv/die-birthler-behoerde-hat-die-spitzelakte-von-heinrich-fink-vorgelegt-der-theologe-bestreitet-aber-weiterhin-seine-zusammenarbeit-mit-der-stasi-der-denunziant,10810590,10293860.html.

Pfeil, Gerhard. "Vergangenheit on Ice." *Der Spiegel*, April 3, 2008, www.spiegel.de/spiegel/print/d-56047445.html.

Platzeck, Matthias. "Versöhnung ernst nehmen." *Der Spiegel*, November 2, 2009, www.spiegel.de/spiegel/print/d-67596369.html.

Ploenus, Michael. "Der Fall des 'roten Franz' von Kapellendorf." *Gerbergasse* 18, no. 4 (2006): 15–19.

Purschke, Thomas. "Bemerkenswerte Stasi-Personalie." *Gerbergasse* 18, no. 4 (2003): 2–5.

Purschke, Thomas. "Nur die üblichen Berichte: wieder ein Stasi-Fall im Thüringer Wintersport." *Gerbergasse* 18, no. 1 (2003): 7–9.

Purschke, Thomas. "Gauck setzt sich für Stasi-Spitzel ein." *Die Welt*, May 4, 2007, www.welt.de/welt_print/article849780/Gauck-setzt-sich-fuer-Stasi-Spitzel-ein.html.

Reichert, Steffen. "Verraten und Verhaftet." *Horch und Guck* 2 (2008): 48–50.

Schädlich, Susanne. *Immer wieder Dezember*. Droemer: München, 2009.

Schlegel, Matthias. "Streit um IM-Klarnamen bald wieder vor Gericht." *Der Tagesspiel*, May 31, 2008, www.tagesspiegel.de/politik/streit-um-im-klarnamen-bald-wieder-vor-gericht/1245674.html.

Schmidt, Wolf. "Fragen Sie Ihren Arzt und Spitzel." *die tageszeitung*, November 21, 2007, www.taz.de/!7896/.

Schneider, Rolf. "Vielleicht war es Scham." *Die Welt*, December 19, 2007, www.welt.de/welt_print/article1475666/Vielleicht-war-es-Scham.html.

Schönhofer, Albrecht, ed. *Ein Volk am Pranger? Die Deutschen auf der Suche nach einer neuen politischen Kultur.* Halle: Aufbau, 1991.

Schorlemmer, Friedrich. *Versöhnung in der Wahrheit. Nachschläge und Vorschläge eines Ostdeutschen.* Berlin: Knaur, 1992.

Schröder, Richard. "Versöhnung – mit wem?" *Der Spiegel*, November 9, 2009, www.spiegel.de/spiegel/print/d-67682689.html.

Schwan, Gesine. "In der Falle des Totalitarismus." *Die Zeit*, June 25, 2009, www.zeit.de/2009/27/Oped-Schwan.

Schwarz, Ulrich and Gerhard Spörl. "Es geht nicht um Siegerjustiz." *Der Spiegel* 39, 23.09.1991, www.spiegel.de/spiegel/print/d-13492151.html.

Starke, Thomas. "'Ach wie gut, das niemand weiß…' Darf man die Namen von Stasi-Mitarbeitern nennen?" *Deutschland Archive* 2 (2009): 197–206.

Stolpe, Manfred. *Schwierige Aufbruch.* Berlin: Goldmann Verlag, 1992.

von Altenbockum, Jasper. "Deutsche Eisberge." *Frankfurter Allgemeine Zeitung*, September 30, 2011, www.faz.net/aktuell/politik/stasi-unterlagen-gesetz-deutsche-eisberge-11410855.html.

Von Banse, D., R. Herzinger, and T. Schmid. "Viele Stasi-Spitzel im Westen noch nicht enttarnt." *Die Welt*, May 24, 2009, www.welt.de/politik/article3793176/Viele-Stasi-Spitzel-im-Westen-noch-nicht-enttarnt.html.

Von Bullion, Constanze. "Platzeck kennt keine 'Jammer-Ossis.'" *Süddeutsche*, May 17, 2010. Available at www.sueddeutsche.de/politik/33/488429/text/.

Von Wensierski, Peter. "Recht Auf Vergessen?" *Der Spiegel*, November 17, www.spiegel.de/spiegel/print/d-62127251.html.

Wilhelm, Cathrin. "Was macht eigentlich Pfarrer Käbisch?" *Cicero*, June 2008, www.cicero.de/berliner-republik/was-macht-eigentlich-pfarrer-k%E4bisch/38719.

"Der Mann bei dem Honi wohnte: 'Ich habe ihm damals schon verziehen.'" *SuperIllu* December 4, 2009.

"Der Schmutz bleibt." *Der Spiegel*, March 9, 2009, www.spiegel.de/spiegel/print/d-64497256.html.

"Die ängstliche Margarete." *Der Spiegel*, January 25, 1993, www.spiegel.de/spiegel/print/d-13680284.html.

"Die Schuld des Ingo Steuer hilft Offenheit, dem Eislauftrainer zu verzeihen?" 3 Sat, June 5, 2008.

"Die Stasi macht wieder mobil – wehret den Anfängen!" *Pamphlet.* [n.d.]. www.moak.de/forum/forum_entry.php?id=1536.

"Erinnern kann nicht gerichtlich verboten werden. Zur Ausstellung 'Christliches Handeln in der DDR' im Rathaus Reichenbach." In www.spiegel.de/politik/deutschland/brief-im-wortlaut-stelle-dich-der-vergangenheit-genau-wie-wir-es-tun-mussten-a-546173.html.

"Ex-Stasi-Spitzel muss Identifizierung hinnehmen." *Die Welt*, 15 April 2009.

"Halten Sie die Enttarnung von ehemaligen inoffiziellen Stasi-Mitarbeitern weiterhin fuer gerechtfertigt oder sollte ein Schlussstrich gezogen werden?" In http://de.statista.com/statistik/daten/studie/173483/umfrage/nicht-mehr-nach-stasi-vergangenheit-fragen/.

"Homepage von Dr. Käbisch. NS-DDR-Kirche Aufarbeitung." www.dr-kaebisch.de/index.php?site=im_schubert.

"Im Zweifel für die Ehre." *die tageszeitung*, November 17, 2005.

"In Zukunft mit Schere im Kopf." *die tageszeitung*, November 18, 2005.

"Inhaltliche Entscheidung zu Klarnamen wäre besser." *Mitteldeutsche Zeitung*, April 22, 2008, www.mz-web.de/politik/ddr-geschichte-inhaltliche-entscheidung-zu-klarnamen-waere-besser,20642162,18323148.html.

"Japan PM Shinzo Abe visits Yasukuni WW2 shrine." *BBC News Asia*, December 26, 2013, available at www.bbc.com/news/world-asia-25517205.

"Kabarettistin Gisela Oechelhaeuser schämt sich für Stasi-Vergangenheit." *Die Welt*, July 30, 2002.

"Kanzlerin Merkel rechnet mit DDR als 'Unrechtsstaat' ab." *Die Welt*, May 9, 2009, www.welt.de/welt_print/article3705724/Kanzlerin-Merkel-rechnet-mit-DDR-als-Unrechtsstaat-ab.html.

"Kein Opfer. Über die Unfähigkeit von IM über ihre Vergangenheit zu sprechen." *Berliner Zeitung*, September 30, 2006.

"Kein Schlussstrich." *Focus*, April 30, 2007.

"Menschen brechen." *die tageszeitung*, February 12, 2007.

"Muntere Stasi-Aktivisten. Eine Abrechnung mit allen DDR-Nostalgikern." *Süddeutsche*, April 16, 2006.

"Nicht auf dem Boden der Verfassung! Eine Analyse und Dokumentation zur Partei Die Linke." 2008, 29. Available at www.epenportal.de/core/files/spezial/cdu-fraktion-hessen/analyse_partei_die_linke.pdf.

"PDS-Politiker lobt Mauerbau." *Bild-Zeitung*, January 24, 1999.

"Platzeck fordert Versöhnung mit Erben der SED." *Die Welt*, October 31, 2009, www.welt.de/politik/article5036631/Platzeck-fordert-Versoehnung-mit-Erben-der-SED.html.

"Reue vor Versöhnung." *die tageszeitung*, November 24, 2009, www.taz.de/1/archiv/digitaz/artikel/?ressort=a2&dig=2009/11/24/a0133&cHash=81e845f3d7.

"Sollte man endlich aufhoeren danach zu fragen, ob jemand in der DDR fuer die Stasi gearbeitet hat?" In http://de.statista.com/statistik/daten/studie/195/umfrage/enttarnung-von-stasi-mitarbeitern/.

"Stasi wollte Angela Merkel anwerben." *Der Spiegel*, May 19, 2009, www.spiegel.de/politik/deutschland/ddr-vergangenheit-stasi-wollte-angela-merkel-anwerben-a-625764.html.

"Stasi-Verstrickungen: Platzeck fühlt sich getäuscht und geprellt." *Berliner Morgenpost*, December 4, 2009, www.morgenpost.de/brandenburg/article1218166/Platzeck-fuehlt-sich-getaeuscht-und-geprellt.html.

Ulrike Poppe. "'Es gab ein richtiges Leben im falschen,' Künftige Stasiunterlagen-Beauftragte." *Der Tagesspiegel*, December 9, 2009, www.tagesspiegel.de/berlin/brandenburg/kuenftige-stasiunterlagen-beauftragte-ulrike-poppe-es-gab-ein-richtiges-leben-im-falschen/1646008.html.

"Sympathien für Stolpe ungebrochen." *Tagesspiegel*, December 4, 1993.

"Tod eines Spitzels." *Bild-Zeitung*, December 19, 2007.

"Unterm Strich." *die tageszeitung*, April 14, 2006.

"Verdrängen, verklären, bereuen." Interview available at http://daserste.ndr.de/panorama/media/stasi104.html.

"Vergeben ja, vergessen nein." www.freiepresse.de/NACHRICHTEN/HINTERGRUND/HINTERGRUND18/1432299.php.

"Viele wollen nicht daran erinnert werden." *Frankfurt Allgemeine Zeitung*, May 18, 2009.

"Was würde Jesus dazu sagen?" *Bild-Zeitung*, November 26, 2009, 17.

"Wie sollen wir es mit der Stasi halten, Frau Poppe?" *SuperIllu*, December 16, 2009.

LEGAL DOCUMENTS

Bericht der Enquete-Kommission. "Aufarbeitung von Geschichte und Folgen der SED-Diktatur," ed. Deutscher Bundestag, May 31, 1994, http://dipbt.bundestag.de/dip21/btd/12/078/1207820.pdf.

Bericht der Enquete-Kommission. "Überwindung der Folgen der SED-Diktatur im Prozess der deutschen Einheit," ed. Deutscher Bundestag, June 10, 1998. http://dip21.bundestag.de/dip21/btd/13/110/1311000.pdf.

Cox Broadcasting Corp. v. Cohn, 420 U.S. 469 (1975).
Decision of the Federal Constitutional Court (Lebach Case), BVerfGE 35, 202, 235 (1973).
Decision of the Federal Constitutional Court, BVerfG, 1 BvR 1582/94 of February 23, 2000, Absatz-Nr. (1 – 39), www.bverfg.de/entscheidungen/rk20000223_1bvr158294.html.
Decision of the Federal Court of Justice of July 12, 1994, VI ZR 1/94.
Gesetz über die Unterlagen des Staatssicherheitsdienstes der ehemaligen Deutschen Demokratischen Republik," available at www.gesetze-im-internet.de/bundesrecht/stug/gesamt.pdf.
Haynes v. Alfred A. Knopf, Inc. 8.3d 1222 (7th Cir. 1993).
Melvin v. Reid, 112 Cal. App. 285, 297.
Neubert, Ehrhart, ed. *Abschlussbericht des Stolpe-Untersuchungsausschusses*. Köln: Heinrich-Böll-Stiftung, 1994.
Restatement (Second) of Torts
Whitney v. California, 274 U.S. 357 (1927).

ACADEMIC REFERENCES

On Germany and Comparative Cases

Augustine, Dolores. "The Impact of Two Reunification-Era Debates on the East German Sense of Identity." *German Studies Review* 27, no. 3 (2004): 563–578.
Beattie, Andrew. *Playing Politics with History: The Bundestag Inquiries into East Germany*. New York: Berghahn Books, 2008.
Borneman, John. *Settling Accounts. Violence, Justice, and Accountability in Postsocialist Europe*. Princeton, NJ: Princeton University Press, 1997.
Borneman, John. "Public Apologies as Performative Redress." *SAIS Review of International Affairs* 25, no. 2 (2005): 53–66.
Broer, Bärbel. *Die Innere Struktur der Behörde für die Unterlagen des Staatssicherheitsdienstes der ehemaligen DDR*. Master's Thesis, University of Hannover, 1995.
Bruce, Gary. "Access to Secret Police Files, Justice and Vetting in East Germany since 1989." *German Politics and Society* 25, no. (2008): 82–111.
Bruce, Gary. *The Firm. The Inside Story of the Stasi*. New York: Oxford University Press, 2010.

Clarke, David. "Compensating the Victims of Human Rights Abuses in the German Democratic Republic: The Struggle for Recognition." *German Politics* 21, no. 1 (2012): 17–33.

Cooke, Paul. *Representing East Germany since Unification. From Colonization to Nostalgia*. Oxford: Berg, 2005.

Craig, John and Nolte, Nico. "Privacy and Free Speech in Germany and Canada: Lessons for an English Privacy Tort." European Human Rights Law Review *2 (*1998): 162–180.

Dümcke, Wolfgang and Vilmar, Fritz (eds.). *Kolonialisierung der DDR: Kritische Analysen und Alternativen des Einigungsprozesses*. Münster: Agenda Verlag, 1996.

Dümmel, Karsten. "Motive, Motivketten und Kriterien für die Mirarbeit bei der Stasi." In *Was war die Stasi? Einblicke in das Ministerium für Staatssicherheit der DDR (MfS)*, edited by Karsten Dümmel and Christian Schmitz, 92–94. Konrad Adenauer Stiftung: Sankt August, 2002.

Dümmel, Karsten. "Verweigerung der Mitarbeit." In *Was war die Stasi? Einblicke in das Ministerium für Staatssicherheit der DDR (MfS)*, edited by Karsten Dümmel and Christian Schmitz, 95. Konrad Adenauer Stiftung: Sankt August, 2002.

Eckert, Rainer. "'Entnazifizierung' und 'Entstasifizierung.'" In *Prägekräfte des 20. Jahrhundertes. Demokratie, Extremismus, Totalitarismus*, edited by Eckhard Jesse and Steffan Kailitz, 305–325. Baden-Baden: Nomos, 1997.

Eckhard Jesse. "'Entnazifizierung' und 'Entstasifizierung' als politisches Problem. Die doppelte Vergangenheitsbewältigung." In *Diktaturen in Deutschland. Diagnosen und Analysen*, edited by Eckhard Jesse, 297–311. Baden-Baden: Nomos, 2008.

Faulenbach, Bernd. "Die Enquete-Kommissionen und die Geschichtsdebatte in Deutschland seit 1989." In *The GDR and Its History: Rückblick und Revision. Die DDR im Spiegel der Enquete-Kommissionen*. Amsterdam: Rodopi, 2000.

Faust, Siegmar. "Die Folgen für die Betroffenen – bis heute." In *Was war die Stasi? Einblicke in das Ministerium für Staatssicherheit der DDR (MfS)*, edited by Karsten Dümmel and Christian Schmitz, 57–58. Konrad Adenauer Stiftung: Sankt August, 2002.

Frei, Norbert. *Adenauer's Germany and the Nazi Past: The Politics of Amnesty and Integration*, trans. Joel Golb. New York: Columbia University Press, 2002.

Frei, Norbert. *Vergangenheitspolitik. Die Anfänge der Bundesrepublik und die NS-Vergangenheit.* Beck: München, 1996.

Fritze, Lothar. *Täter mit gutem Gewissen: Über menschliches Versagen im diktatorischen Sozialismus.* Cologne: Böhlau Verlag, 1998.

Fulbrook, Mary. *Anatomy of a Dictatorship. Inside the GDR 1949–1989.* New York: Oxford University Press, 1995.

Gellately, Robert. "Denunciations in Twentieth-Century Germany: Aspects of Self-Policing in the Third Reich and the German Democratic Republic." *The Journal of Modern History* 68, no. 4 (1996): 931–967.

Gieseke, Jens. *Mielke –Konzern, Die Geschichte der Stasi 1945–1990.* München: Deutsche Verlags-Anstalt, 2001.

Gieseke, Jens. *The History of the Stasi: East Germany's Secret Police, 1945–1990.* New York: Berghahn, 2014.

Glaeser, Andreas. "Power/Knowledge Failure: Epistemic Practices and Ideologies in the Secret Police of Former East Germany," *Social Analysis* 47, no. 1 (2003): 10–26.

Glaeser, Andreas. *Political Epistemics: The Secret Police, the Opposition and the End of East German Socialism.* Chicago: University of Chicago Press, 2011.

Gordley, James. *An Introduction to the Comparative Study of Private Law; Readings, Cases, Materials.* New York: Cambridge University Press, 2006.

Gosche, Ann. *Das Spannungsverhältnis zwischen Meinungsfreiheit und Ehrenschutz in der fragmentierten Öffentlichkeit.* Baden-Baden: Nomos, 2007.

Hackeling, Joan. "To whom, and for whom, must I respond? Negotiating responsibility during the last years of East German state socialism." *Geografiska Annaler* 84, no. 1 (2002): 27–32.

Hasso, Philipp and Andreas Rein. *Zugang zu Stasi-Unterlagen und Persönlichkeitsrecht*, PhD. Diss, University of Bonn, 2008.

Hauch, Jeanne M. "Protecting Private Facts in France: The Warren & Brandeis Tort is Alive and Well and Flourishing in Paris." *Tulane Law Review* 68 (1994): 1219–1301.

Herf, Jeffrey. "The Emergence and Legacies of Divided Memory: Germany and the Holocaust after 1945." In *Memory and Power in Postwar in Europe. Studies in the Presence of the Past*, edited by Jan-Werner Müller, 184–205. Cambridge: Cambridge University Press, 2002.

Hochhuth, Martin. "Kein Grundrecht auf üble Nachrede –Der Stolpe-Beschluss des BVerfG schütz das Personal der Demokratie." *Neue Juristische Wochenschrift* 59, no. 4 (2006): 189–191.

Kaminski, Marek M. and Monika Nalepa. "Judging Transitional Justice: A New Criterion For Evaluating Truth Revelation Procedures." *Journal of Conflict Resolution* 50:3 (2006), 383–408.

Kapczynski, Jennifer M. *The German Patient. Crisis and Recovery in Postwar Culture*. Ann Arbor: University of Michigan Press, 2008.

Kerz-Rühling, Ingrid and Thomas Plänkers. *Verräter oder Verführte. Eine psychoanalytische Untersuchung Inoffizieller Mitarbeiter der Stasi*. Berlin: Links, 2004.

Knabe, Hubertus. "Zersetzungmaßnahmen." In *Was war die Stasi? Einblicke in das Ministerium für Staatssicherheit der DDR (MfS)*, edited by Karsten Dümmel and Christian Schmitz, 26–31. Konrad Adenauer Stiftung: Sankt August, 2002.

Koehler, John, *Stasi: The Untold Story of the East German Secret Police*. New York: Basic Books, 1999.

Kommers, Donald. *The Constitutional Jurisprudence of the Federal Republic of Germany*. Durham, NC: Duke University Press, 1997.

Lutomski, Pavel. "Private Citizens and Public Discourse: Defamation Law as a Limit to the Right of Free Expression in the U.S. and Germany." *German Studies Review* 24, no. 3 (2001): 571–592.

Malia, Martin. "To the Stalin Mausoleum." *Daedalus* 119 (Winter 1990): 295–344.

Markovits, Andrei and Beth Simone Noveck. "West Germany." In *The World Reacts to the Holocaust 1945–1990*, edited by David Wyman, 391–446. Baltimore: Johns Hopkins University Press, 1996.

Markovits, Inga. "Selective Memory: How the Law Affects What We Remember and Forget About the Past. The Case of East Germany." *Law & Society Review* 35, no. 3 (2001), 513–563.

Metodiev, Momchil. "Bulgaria." In *Transitional Justice in Eastern Europe and the Former Soviet Union: Reckoning with the Communist Past*, edited by Lavinia Stan, 152–175. London: Routledge, 2008.

Miller, Barbara. *Narratives of Guilt and Compliance in Unified Germany. Stasi Informers and their Impact on Society*. London: Routledge, 1999.

Miller, John. "Settling Accounts with a Secret Police. The German Law on the Stasi Records." *Europe-Asia Studies* 50, no. 2 (1998): 305–330.

Müller-Enbergs, Helmut. "Der 'inoffizielle Mitarbeiter': Anatomie eines Spitzels." *Damals: das aktuelle Geschichtsmagazin* 25, no. 6 (1993), 17–23.

Müller-Enbergs, Helmut, ed., *Inoffizielle Mitarbeiter des Ministeriums für Staatssicherheit: Richtlinien und Durchführungsbestimmungen*. Berlin: Links, 1996.

Müller-Enbergs, Helmut. "Brandenburgs Bürgerbewegung und das Erbe der Staatssicherheit." *Horch und Guck* 4 (2000), 1–9.

Müller-Enbergs, Helmut. "Über Ja-Sager und Nein-Sager – Inoffizielle Mitarbeiter und stille Verweigerer." In *"Ich habe 'Nein!' gesagt: über Zivilcourage in der DDR."* edited by Marco Hecht and Gerald Praschl, 147–166. Berlin: Homilius, 2002.

Müller-Enbergs, Helmut. "Die inoffiziellen Mitarbeiter." In *MfS-Handbuch: Anatomie der Staatssicherheit – Geschichte, Struktur, Methoden*, edited by BStU, 1–53. Berlin: 2008.

Neethling, Johann. "Personality Rights: a Comparative Overview." *Comparative and International Law Journal of Southern Africa* 38, no. 2 (2005): 210–245.

Nolte, Georg. "Falwell v. Strauss: Die rechtlichen Grenzen politischer Satire in den USA und der Bundesrepublik." *Europäische Grundrechtezeitschrift* 14 (1988): 253–259.

Peck, Jeffrey. "East Germany." In *The World Reacts to the Holocaust 1945–1990*, edited by David Wyman, 447–472. Baltimore: Johns Hopkins University Press, 1996.

Pollaczek, Annina. *Pressefreiheit und Persönlichkeitsrecht: am Beispiel des Stasi-Unterlagen-Gesetzes*. Saarbrücken: VDM Verlag, 2007.

Reinke, Herbert. "Policing Politics in Germany from Weimar to the Stasi." In *The Politics of Policing in the Twentieth Century*, edited by Mark Mozower. Oxford: Berghahn, 1997.

Robers, Norbert. *Joachim Gauck. Die Biografie einer Institution*. Berlin: Henschel, 2000.

Sa'adah, Anne. *Germany's Second Chance: Trust, Justice, and Democratization*. Cambridge: Cambridge University Press, 1998.

Saunders, Rebecca. "Questionable Associations: The Role of Forgiveness in Transitional Justice," *The International Journal of Transitional Justice* 5, no. 1 (2011): 119–141.

Schlink, Bernhard. *Vergangenheitsschuld*. Frankfurt am Main: Suhrkamp, 2002.

Weberling, Johannes. "Zur Veröffentlichung der Namen ehemaliger Stasi-Mitarbeiter in einem wissenschaftlichen Bericht." *AfP – Zeitschrift für Medien –und Kommunikationsrecht* 3 (2006): 272–273.

Whitman, James. "Enforcing Civility and Respect: Three Societies." *Yale Law Journal* 109 (2000): 1279–1398.

Whitman, James. "The Two Western Cultures of Privacy: Dignity versus Liberty," *Yale Law Journal* 113 (2004): 1151–1221.

Wilke, Christiane. "The Shield, the Sword, and the Party: Vetting in post-1989 Germany." In *Justice as Prevention: Vetting Public Employees in Transitional Societies*, edited by Alexander Mayer-Rieckh and Pablo de Greiff. New York: SSRC, 2007.

Yode, Jennifer A. *From East Germans to Germans?: The New Postcommunist Elites*. Durham, NC: Duke University Press, 1999.

Zimmerli, Walter Ch. and Joachim Landkammer, "Erinnerungsmanagement und politische Systemwechsel: Kleine Versuche zur Erklärung eines grossen Problems." In *Erinnerungsmanagement. Systemtransformation und Vergangenheitspolitik im internationalen Vergleich*, edited by Joachim Landkammer, Thomas Noetzel, and Walter Ch. Zimmerli. München: Wilhelm Fink Verlag, 2006.

Political and Legal Theory/Philosophy

Allais, Lucy. "Wiping the Slate Clean. The Heart of Forgiveness." *Philosophy and Public Affairs* 36, no. 1 (2008): 33–68.

Anderson, Elizabeth. "Is Women's Labor a Commodity?" *Philosophy and Public Affairs* 19, no. 1. (1990): 71–92.

Anderson, Elizabeth. "Emotions in Kant's Later Moral Philosophy: Honour and the Phenomenology of Moral Value." In *Kant's Ethics of Virtues*, edited by Monika Betzler, 123–146. Berlin: Walter De Gruyter, 2008.

Andrieu, Kora. *La justice transitionnelle. De l'Afrique du Sud au Rwanda*. Paris: Gallimard, 2012.

Arendt, Hannah. "The Aftermath of Nazi Rule. Report from Germany," *Commentary* 10, no. 4 (1950): 342–353.

Arendt, Hannah. *The Human Condition*. Chicago: University of Chicago Press, 1958.

Arendt, Hannah. *Eichmann in Jerusalem. A Report on the Banality of Evil*. New York: Penguin, 1963.

Arendt, Hannah. "Collective Responsibility." In *Amor Mundi: Explorations in the Faith and Thought of Hannah Arendt*, edited by James Bernauer, 43–50. Boston: Martin Nijhoff, 1987.

Arendt, Hannah. "Organized Guilt and Universal Responsibility." In *The Portable Arendt*, edited by Peter Baehr, 146–156. New York: Penguin, 2003.

Augustine-Adams, Kif. "What is Just?: The Rule of Law and Natural Law in the Trials of Former East German Border Guards." In *Transitional Justice: How Emerging Democracies Reckon with Former Regimes*, edited by Neil J. Kritz, 625–640, Washington, DC: United States Institute of Peace, 1995.

Baker, Edwin C. "Autonomy and Informational Privacy or Gossip: The Central Meaning of the First Amendment." *Social Philosophy and Policy* 21, no. 2 (2004): 215–268.

Barkan, Elazar and Alexander Karn. "Group Apology as an Ethical Imperative." In *Taking Wrongs Seriously: Apologies and Reconciliation*, edited by Elazar Barkan and Alexander Karn, 3–32. Stanford, CA: Stanford University Press, 2006.

Bennet, Christopher. "Is Amnesty an Act of Political Forgiveness?" *Contemporary Political Theory* 2, no. 1 (2003): 67–76.

Boxill, Bernard. "Self-Respect and Protest." In *Dignity, Character, and Self-Respect*, edited by Robin Dillon, 93–104. New York: Routledge, 1995.

Bird, Colin. "Status, Identity, and Respect," *Political Theory* 32, no. 2 (2004): 207–232.

Bird, Colin. "Self-Respect and Respect for Others." *European Journal of Philosophy* 18, no. 1 (2010): 17–40.

Blustein, Jeffrey. *The Moral Demands of Memory*. Cambridge: Cambridge University Press, 2008.

Buchanan, Allen. "Judging the Past: The Case of the Human Radiation Experiments." *The Hastings Center Report* 26, no. 3 (1996): 25–30.

Buchanan, Allen. "Social Moral Epistemology." *Social Philosophy and Policy* 19, no. 2 (2002): 126–152.

Buchanan, Allen. "Political Liberalism and Social Epistemology." *Philosophy and Public Affairs* 32, no. 2 (2004): 95–130.

Buchanan, Allen. "Social Moral Epistemology and the Tasks of Ethics." In *Ethics and Humanity: Themes from the Philosophy of Jonathan Glover*, edited by N. Ann Davis, Richard Keshen, and Jeff McMahan, 105–125. New York: Oxford University Press, 2010.

Carter, Ian. "Respect and the Basis of Equality." *Ethics* 121, no. 3 (2011): 538–571.

Chekola, Mark. "Outing, Truth-telling, and the Shame of the Closet." In *Gay Ethics: Controversies in Outing, Civil Rights, and Sexual Science*, edited by Timothy F. Murphy, 67–90. Binghamton, NY: Haworth Press, 1994.

Chen, Joseph and David Miller. "Elster on Self-Realization in Politics: A Critical Note." *Ethics* 102, no. 1(1991): 96–102.

Chiba, Shin. "Hannah Arendt on Love and the Political: Love, Friendship, and Citizenship." *The Review of Politics* 57, no. 3 (1995): 505–535.

Celermajer, Danielle. *The Sins of the Nation and the Ritual of Apologies*. Cambridge: Cambridge University Press, 2009.

Coetzee, J. M. *Disgrace*. New York: Penguin, 2000.

Chiu, Yvone. "Liberal Lustration." *Journal of Political Philosophy* 19, no. 4 (2011): 440–464.

Crocker, David. "Truth Commissions, Transitional Justice, and Civil Society." In *Truth v. Justice: The Morality of Truth Commissions*, edited by Robert I. Rotberg and Dennis Thompson, 99–121. Princeton, NJ: Princeton University Press, 2000.

Darwall, Stephen. "Two Kinds of Respect." *Ethics* 88, no. 1 (1977): 36–49.

Darwall, Stephen. *The Second-Person Standpoint: Morality, Respect, and Accountability*. Cambridge, MA: Harvard University Press, 2006.

Derrida, Jacques. *On Cosmopolitanism and Forgiveness*. London: Routledge, 2001.

Digeser, P. E. "Forgiveness and Politics: Dirty Hands and Imperfect Procedures." *Political Theory* 26, no. 5 (1998): 700–724.

Digeser, P. E. *Political Forgiveness*. Ithaca, NY: Cornell University Press, 2001.

Dillon, Robin (ed.). *Dignity, Character, and Self-Respect*. New York: Routledge, 1995.

Dillon, Robin. "Respect." *The Stanford Encyclopedia of Philosophy* (Spring 2014 Edition), Edward N. Zalta (ed.), at http://plato.stanford.edu/archives/spr2014/entries/respect/.

Eisikovits, Nir. "Transitional Justice." *The Stanford Encyclopedia of Philosophy* (Summer 2014 Edition), Edward N. Zalta (ed.), at http://plato.stanford.edu/archives/sum2014/entries/justice-transitional/.

Elster, Jon. *Sour Grapes: Studies in the Subversion of Rationality*. Cambridge: Cambridge University Press, 1983.

Elster, Jon. *Alchemies of the Mind: Rationality and the Emotions*. Cambridge: Cambridge University Press, 1998.

Elster, Jon. *Closing the Books. Transitional Justice in Historical Perspective*. New York: Cambridge University Press, 2004.

Elshtain, Jean Bethke. *Democracy on Trial*. New York: Basic Books, 1995.

Espindola, Juan. "The Case for the Moral Permissibility of Amnesties: An Argument from Social Moral Epistemology." Ethical Theory and Moral Practice (issue not assigned), 2014.

Fischer, John Martin. "Recent Work on Moral Responsibility," *Ethics* 110, no. 1 (1999): 93–139.

Forst, Rainer. *The Right to Justification: Elements of a Constructivist Theory of Justice*. New York: Columbia University Press, 2012.

Frankfurt, Harry. "The Principle of Alternate Possibilities." *Journal of Philosophy* 66, no. 3 (1969): 828–39.

Gamlund, Espen. "Supererogatory Forgiveness." *Inquiry* 53, no. 6 (2010): 540–564.

Gilabert, Pablo. "Human Rights, Human Dignity, and Power." In *The Philosophical Foundations of Human Rights*, edited by Rowan Cruft, Matthew Liao, and Massimo Renzo. Oxford: Oxford University Press, 2015.

Goffman, Erving. *The Presentation of the Self in Everyday Life*. New York: Doubleday, 1959.

Goffman, Erving. *Stigma: Notes on the Management of Spoiled Identity*. New York: Simon & Schuster, 1963.

Govier, Trudy. *Forgiveness and Revenge*. London: Routledge, 2002.

Green, Leslie. "Two Worries About Respect for Persons." *Ethics* 120, no. 2 (2010): 212–231.

Griswold, Charles. *Forgiveness: A Philosophical Exploration*. Cambridge: Cambridge University Press, 2007.

Gross, Larry. *Contested Closets. The Politics and Ethics of Outing*. Minneapolis: University of Minnesota Press, 1993.

Gutmann, Amy and Dennis Thompson. "The Moral Foundations of Truth Commissions." In *Truth v. Justice: The Morality of Truth Commissions*, edited by Robert I. Rotberg and Dennis Thompson, 22–44. Princeton, NJ: Princeton University Press, 2000.

Habermas, Jürgen. "Bemerkungen zu einer verworrenen Diskussion. Was bedeutet '*Aufarbeitung* der Vergangenheit' heute?" *Die Zeit*, April 3, 1992.

Habermas, Jürgen. "Burdens of the Double Past." *Dissent* 41, no. 4 (1994): 514–515.

Habermas, Jürgen. "On the Public Use of History." *The Postnational Constellation: Political Essays*. Cambridge, MA: MIT Press, 2001.

Habermas, Jürgen. "Hat die Demokratie noch eine epistemische Dimension? Empirische Forschung und normative Theorie." in *Ach, Europa*. Frankfurt am Main: Suhrkamp, 2008.

Herman, Barbara. *The Practice of Moral Judgment*. Cambridge, MA: Harvard University Press, 1993.

Herzog, Don. *Cunning*. Princeton, NJ: Princeton University Press, 2007.

Hill Jr., Thomas. "Servility and Self-Respect." In *Dignity, Character, and Self-Respect*, edited by Robin Dillon, 76–92. New York: Routledge, 1995.

Hill Jr., Thomas. "Respect for Persons," *Encyclopedia of Philosophy*, vol. 8, edited by Edward Craig. New York and London: Routledge, 1998.

Hill Jr., Thomas. "Moral Responsibilities of Bystanders." *Journal of Social Philosophy* 41, no. 1 (2010): 28–39.

Honneth, Axel. *The Struggle for Recognition. The Moral Grammar of Social Conflict*. Cambridge: Polity, 1995.

Jaspers, Karl. *Die Schuldfrage*. München: Piper, 1965.

Jones, William. *Insult to Injury: Libel, Slander, and Invasions of Privacy*. Boulder: University Press of Colorado, 2003.

Kant, Immanuel. "An Answer to the Question: What is Enlightenment? (1784)." In *Practical Philosophy*, edited by Mary J. Gregor, 11–22. Cambridge: Cambridge University Press, 1999.

Kant, Immanuel. "Towards Perpetual Peace (1795)." In *Practical Philosophy* edited by Mary J. Gregor, 311–352. Cambridge: Cambridge University Press, 1999.

Kant, Immanuel. "The Metaphysics of Morals (1797)." In *Practical Philosophy*, edited by Mary J. Gregor, 353–604. Cambridge: Cambridge University Press, 1999.

Kant, Immanuel. "On a Supposed Right to Lie From Philanthropy (1797)." In *Practical Philosophy*, edited by Mary J. Gregor, 605–616. Cambridge: Cambridge University Press, 1999.

Kiss, Elizabeth. "Moral Ambition Within and Beyond Political Constraints: Reflections on Restorative Justice." In *Truth v. Justice: The Morality of Truth Commissions*, edited by Robert I. Rotberg and Dennis Thompson, 68–98. Princeton, NJ: Princeton University Press, 2000.

Kirshner, Alexander. *A Theory of Militant Democracy. The Ethics of Combating Political Extremism*. New Haven, CT: Yale University Press, 2014.

Kohler, Lotte and Hans Saner (eds.). *Hannah Arendt-Karl Jaspers Correspondence 1926–1969*. New York: Harvest Edition, 1993.

Korsgaard, Christine M. *Creating the Kingdom of Ends*. Cambridge: Cambridge University Press, 1996.

Kutz, Christopher. *Complicity, Ethics and Law for a Collective Age*. New York: Cambridge University Press, 2000.

LaVaque-Manty, Mika. *Arguments and Fists. Political Agency and Justification in Liberal Theory*. New York: Routledge, 2002.

LaVaque-Manty, Mika. "Dueling for Equality: Masculine Honor and the Modern Politics of Dignity." *Political Theory* 34, no. 6 (2006): 715–740.

LaVaque-Manty, Mika. "Kant's Children." *Social Theory and Practice* 32, no. 3 (2006): 365–388.

LaVaque-Manty, Mika. *The Playing Fields of Eton. Equality and Excellence in Modern Meritocracy*. Ann Arbor: University of Michigan Press, 2009.

Le Caze, Marguerite. "The Asymmetry between Apology and Forgiveness." *Contemporary Political Theory* 5, no. 4 (2006): 447–468.

Lepora, Chiara and Robert Goodin. *On Complicity and Compromise.* Oxford: Oxford University Press, 2013.

Levy, Neil. "The Good, the Bad, and the Blameworthy." *Journal of Ethics and Social Philosophy* 1, no. 2 (2005): 2–16.

Levy, Neil. "Culpable Ignorance and Moral Responsibility: A Reply to FitzPatrick." *Ethics* 119, no. 4 (2009): 729–741.

Levy, Neil and Michael McKenna. "Recent Work on Free Will and Moral Responsibility." *Philosophy Compass* 4, no. 1 (2009): 96–133.

Lewis, Alison. "En-Gendering Remembrance: Memory, Gender and Informers for the Stasi." *New German Critique* 86 (2002): 103–134.

List, Christian and Philip Pettit. *Group Agency. The Possibility, Design, and Status of Corporate Agents.* Princeton, NJ: Princeton University Press, 2011.

Locke, Jill. "Work, Shame, and the Chain Gang: The New Civic Education." In *Vocations of Political Theory: Political Imagination in an Age of Uncertainty*, edited by Jason Frank and John Tambornino, 284–304. Minneapolis: University of Minnesota Press, 2000.

Mayo, David and Martin Gunderson. "Privacy and the Ethics of Outing." In *Gay Ethics: Controversies in Outing, Civil Rights, and Sexual Science*, edited by Timothy Murphy, 47–66. Binghamton, NY: Haworth Press, 1994.

McAdams, A. James. *Judging the Past in Unified Germany.* Cambridge: Cambridge University Press, 2001.

Meier, Charles S. "Doing History, Doing Justice: The Narrative of the Historian and of the Truth Commission." In *Truth v. Justice: The Morality of Truth Commissions*, edited by Robert I. Rotberg and Dennis Thompson, 281–278. Princeton, NJ: Princeton University Press, 2000.

Middleton, David. "Three Kinds of Self-respect." *Res Publica* 12, no. 1 (2006): 59–76.

Miller, William. *The Anatomy of Disgust.* Cambridge, MA: Harvard University Press, 1997.

Mohr, Richard. *Gay Ideas: Outings and Other Controversies.* Boston: Beacon Press, 1992.

Moody-Adams, Michele. "Race, Class, and the Social Construction of Self-Respect." In *Dignity, Character, and Self-Respect*, edited by Robin Dillon, 271–289. New York: Routledge, 1995.

Murphy, Colleen. *A Moral Theory of Reconciliation.* Cambridge: Cambridge University Press, 2010.

Murphy, Jeffrey G. *Getting Even: Forgiveness and Its Limits*. Oxford: Oxford University Press, 2003.

Nagel, Thomas, *Mortal Questions*. New York: Cambridge University Press, 1979.

Neumann, Michael. "Did Kant Respect Persons?" *Res Publica* 6, no. 1 (2000): 1–15.

Neumann, Michael. "Can't We All Just Respect One Another a Little Less?" *Canadian Journal of Philosophy* 34, no. 4 (2005): 463–484.

Noelle-Neumann, Elisabeth. *The Spiral of Silence: Public Opinion–Our Social Skin*. Chicago: University of Chicago Press, 1993.

Offe, Claus. "Disqualification, Retribution, Restitution: Dilemmas of Justice in Post-communist Countries." *Journal of Political Philosophy* 1, no. 1 (1993): 17–44.

Osiel, Mark. *Mass Atrocity, Ordinary Evil, and Hannah Arendt*. New Haven, CT: Yale University Press, 2001.

Osiel, Mark. *Obeying Orders*. New Brunswick, NJ: Transaction Publishers, 2009.

Pettigrove, Glen. "Hannah Arendt and Collective Forgiveness." *Journal of Social Philosophy* 37, no. 4 (2006): 483–500.

Posner, Richard. *Overcoming Law*. Cambridge, MA: Harvard University Press, 1995.

Post, Robert. "The Social Foundations of Defamation Law: Reputation and the Constitution." *California Law Review* 74 (1986): 691–742.

Post, Robert. *Constitutional Domains. Democracy, Community, Management*. Cambridge, MA: Harvard University Press, 1995.

Post, Robert. "Three Concepts of Privacy." *Georgetown Law Journal* 89, no. 6 (2001).

Preus, Anthony. "Aristotle and Respect for Persons." In *Essays in Ancient Greek Philosophy IV*, edited by John P. Anton, 97–106. Albany: State University of New York Press, 1991.

Radzik, Linda. *Making Amends: Atonement in Morality, Law, and Politics*. Oxford: Oxford University Press, 2009.

Rawls, John. *Justice as Fairness: A Restatement*. Cambridge, MA: Harvard University Press, 2001.

Reiff, Mark. "Terrorism, Retribution, and Collective Responsibility." *Social Theory and Practice* 34, no. 2 (2008): 209–242.

Rousseau, Jean-Jacques. *The Basic Political Writings*. Indianapolis, IN: Hackett, 1987.

Rosen, Gideon. "Culpability and Moral Ignorance." *Proceedings of the Aristotelian Society* 103, no. 1 (2003): 61–84.

Schauer, Frederick. "Categories and the First Amendment: A Play in Three Acts." *Vanderbilt Law Review* 34 (1981): 265–307.

Schauer, Frederick. "The Exceptional First Amendment." In *American Exceptionalism and Human Rights*, edited by Michael Ignatieff, 29–56. Princeton, NJ: Princeton University Press, 2005.

Schauer, Frederick. "Freedom of Expression Adjudication in Europe and America: A Case Study in Comparative Constitutional Architecture." In *European and US Constitutionalism*, edited by Georg Nolte, 49–69. Cambridge: Cambridge University Press, 2005.

Schaap, Andrew. "Political Grounds for Forgiveness." *Contemporary Political Theory* 2, no. 1 (2003): 77–87.

Scheff, Thomas. "Shame and the Social Bond: A Sociological Theory." *Sociological Theory* 18, no. 1 (2000): 84–99.

Schmeidel, John. *Stasi: Shield and Sword of the Party*. New York: Routledge, 2008.

Sher, George. *Desert*. Princeton, NJ: Princeton University Press, 1985.

Smith, Angela M. "Control, Responsibility, and Moral Assessment." *Philosophical Studies* 138, no. 3 (2008): 367–392.

Smith, Nick. *I Was Wrong: The Meanings of Apologies*. Cambridge: Cambridge University Press, 2008.

Stan, Lavinia. "Introduction: Post-communist Transition, Justice, and Transitional Justice." In *Transitional Justice in Eastern Europe and the Former Soviet Union: Reckoning with the Communist Past*, edited by Lavinia Stan, 1–14. London: Routledge, 2008.

Subotic, Jelena. "Expanding the Scope of Post-Conflict Justice: Individual, State and Societal Responsibility for Mass Atrocity." *Journal of Peace Research* 48, no. 2 (2011): 157–169.

Sussman, David. "Kantian Forgiveness." *Kant-Studien* 96, no. 1 (2005): 85–107.

Tarnopolsky, Christina. "Prudes, Perverts, and Tyrants. Plato and the Contemporary Politics of Shame." *Political Theory* 32 no. 4 (2004): 468–494.

Tavuchis, Nicholas. *Mea Culpa: A Sociology of Apology and Reconciliation*. Stanford, CA: Stanford University Press, 1991.

Teubel, Kirsten. "Unterlassungsanspruch bei mehrdeutigen Äusserungen und zweifelhaftem Wahrheitsgehalt." *Archiv für Presserecht-Zeitschrift für Medien-und Kommunikationsrecht* 1 (2006): 20–24.

Thaler, Mathias. "Just Pretending: Political Apologies for Historical Injustice and Vice's Tribute to Virtue." *Critical Review of International Social and Political Philosophy* 15, no. 3 (2012): 259–278.

Thomas, Laurence. "Self-Respect: Theory and Practice." In *Dignity, Character, and Self-Respect*, edited by Robin Dillon, 251–270. New York: Routledge, 1995.

Thompson, Janna. "Is Apology a Sorry Affair? Derrida and the Moral Force of the Impossible." *The Philosophical Forum* 41, no. 3 (2010): 259–274.

Tucker, Aviezer. "Scarce Justice: The Accuracy, Scope, and Depth of Justice." *Politics, Philosophy, and Economics* 11, no. 1 (2012): 76–96.

Velleman, David J. "The Genesis of Shame." *Philosophy and Public Affairs* 30, no. 1 (2001): 27–52.

Velleman, David J. "Distortions of Normativity." *Ethical Theory and Moral Practice* 14, no. 3 (2011): 329–356.

Verdeja, Ernesto. *Unchopping a Tree*. Philadelphia: Temple University Press, 2009.

Verdeja, Ernesto. "Official Apologies in the Aftermath of Political Violence." *Metaphilosophy* 41, no. 4 (2010): 563–581.

Walker, Margaret Urban. *Moral Repair: Reconstructing Moral Relations after Wrongdoing*. Cambridge: Cambridge University Press, 2006.

Walzer, Michael. "Political Action: The Problem of Dirty Hands," *Philosophy and Public Affairs* 2, no. 2 (1973): 160–180

Walzer, Michael. *Spheres of Justice. A Defense of Pluralism and Equality*. New York: Basic Books, 1983.

Warner, Michael. *The Trouble with Normal: Sex, Politics and the Ethics of Queer Life*. Cambridge, MA: Harvard University Press, 1999.

Warner, Michael. "Publics and Counterpublics." *Public Culture* 14, no. 1 (2002): 49–90.

Watson, Gary. "Two Faces of Responsibility." *Philosophical Topics* 24, no. 2 (1996): 227–248.

Wedeen, Lisa. "Conceptualizing Culture: Possibilities for Political Science." *American Political Science Review* 96, no. 4 (2002): 713–728.

Williams, Bernard. *Moral Luck. Philosophical Papers 1973–1980*. Cambridge, MA: Cambridge University Press, 1981.

Williams, Melissa S. "Citizenship as Agency within Communities of Shared Fate." In *Unsettled Legitimacy. Political Community, Power, and Authority in a Global Era*, edited by Steven Bernstein and William D. Coleman, 33–52. Vancouver: University of British Columbia Press, 2009.

Young-Bruehl, Elisabeth. *Why Arendt Matters*. New Haven, CT: Yale, 2006.

Young, Iris. *Responsibility for Justice*. New York: Oxford University Press, 2010.

INDEX

CPSIA information can be obtained at www.ICGtesting.com
Printed in the USA
LVOW08*0615310315

432704LV00009B/21/P

9 781107 083127